HISTORY CAPE NEGRO AND BLANCHE

[Nova Scotia, Canada]

Third Edition with Corrections

Joseph R. Ross

HERITAGE BOOKS
2019

HERITAGE BOOKS
AN IMPRINT OF HERITAGE BOOKS, INC.

Books, CDs, and more—Worldwide

For our listing of thousands of titles see our website
at
www.HeritageBooks.com

Published 2019 by
HERITAGE BOOKS, INC.
Publishing Division
5810 Ruatan Street
Berwyn Heights, Md. 20740

Copyright © 2007 Joseph R. Ross

Heritage Books by the author:
Clan Ross: The Clanna Siol Aindrea
History Cape Negro and Blanche: Third Edition with Corrections

All rights reserved. No part of this book may be reproduced or transmitted in any form or by any means, electronic or mechanical, including photocopying, recording or by any information storage and retrieval system without written permission from the author, except for the inclusion of brief quotations in a review.

International Standard Book Number
Paperbound: 978-0-7884-4455-5

Contents

Dedication, Anna Jane Smith Ross
Indians and First Settlers
15. Where They Lived
43. Good Days and Old Ways
61. Pictures
63. Pictures
69. Pictures
73. Blanche School and Chapel
81. Blanche Hall
98. Cape Negro Church
102. Cape Negro Cemetery
120. Cape Negro School
122. Cape Negro Hall
126. Cape Negro Hawlover
130. Picture, Reuben Smith Wharf
132. Blanche Life Boat
137. Blanche Sheep Shearing
141. The Goose Shooting War
145. Bits and Pieces
150. Local Place Names
152. Stores
154. The Old Road
157. Lobster Factory
158. Railway at Port Clyde
159. Telephones
160. What I Remember
170. The Run Away Horse
172. How I Remember Slateville
177. How I Remember Blanche
181. Geneology - SMITH
        SWAINE
        REYNOLDS
        KING
        LYLE
        OBED
233. The Author
234. Acknowledgements

This book was written in memory of my Mother, Anna Jane (Jenny) Smith Ross, who encouraged me to study my lessons on the kitchen table by light of the kerosene lamp. And also my dedicated school teachers, Mildred MacKay, Mildred Sholds and Mrs. Roy Matherson, who instilled in me the thirst for knowledge and nurtured my interest in books.

Champlain names Cap Negre' 1604

Indians and the Early Settlers

Archaeologists have uncovered artifacts that clearly indicate that five to six thousand years ago the Indians lived and travelled in this part of Nova Scotia.

The Indians were Magumaagee which the European settlers translated as Micmac. They did not cultivate land to any degree, as they were nomads to the extent of having winter camping grounds in the far inland and migrating to the coast in the summer. They provided for their needs by hunting, fishing and various means of trapping. In spring they migrated from their winter inland homes by coming down the Clyde River, in their large birch bark canoes. They stopped at Lyles Falls (Oo-ne-gun-sook) to catch kiaks, smelts and possibly salmon, then continuing south to Kes-poog-witk (Lands End) or the Haul Over. The Indians camped here each migration, put up their wigwams, caught fish and dug clams. They were known to camp here until late 1800. In later years they traded or sold baskets to the local settlers. (My mother recalls Indians camped at the Haul Over in the 1890s).

They would portage their canoes and belongings across the salt meadow and enter Eel Bay, proceed to the Crick at Port LaTour, and would portage across to The Ponds and Barrington Bay. Some Homes to this day still have solid birch bark baskets or split ash woven baskets traded from the Indians at the Haul Over. However their large piles of clam shells have long disappeared as they proved to provide excellent material for making plaster once the Europeans started building homes.

The Indians of this area were not war like. They were kind to the first settlers. Except for a few minor incidents, mainly spearheaded by a European leader, they did not have serious conflict with the various colonists that came.

The Indians were not a large group. Although no accurate census exists, it is estimated that less than 200 lived in this south-west area. They travelled in family groups which would be about 15 to 20 in all. This nomadic group of people did not survive well with the introduction of the white man's diseases, such as small pox, diphtheria and etc.. Over the years their numbers have decreased until within living memory only a few Indian families lived at Clyde River. The ones remaining to this day are well assimilated into the white man's culture, speaking English, singing cow boy songs and no longer forge the mighty Clyde River for the summer migration.

It is not definitely known when the first European fishermen, Portuguese, Basque and French came along this part of our coast. Some French maps of the 1558 era show an outline of our coast, but place names are few. However in 1563 a map by Lazaro Luis indicates Bacalhaos (Baccaro), which is the Portuguese name for dried cod fish.

Maps of the 1500s indicate that these fishermen were resonably familiar with the harbours, bays and inlets along our coast. As their ships were not that large, they would land at some of these harbours for fresh water and possibly even to have temporary fishing stages. Therefore it is within reason to assume the Indians would have seen and possibly contacted some of the foreign fishermen.

In 1604 DeMonts under a charter of the King of France, was in charge of an expedition to explore the southern coast for the purpose of locating suitable sites for settlement and trade. DeMonts' expedition spent a month in Port Mouton, and while he waited for one of his ships to join him, Champlain in a small shallop came south along the coast to explore and locate a site for a settlement. Champlain recorded the following, "There is a harbour very good for vessels, and the head of it has a little river, which runs from a distance inland, which I named the port Cape Negrè, on account of a rock which at a distance resembles one, four leagues from it, and ten to Port du Mouton. The Cape is very dangerous on account of the rocks." Champlain after exploring Cape Negro Harbour continued on across Bay Sable as far as Isle Cormorants. This was the first accurate recording of the coast and place names. Therefore in 1604 Cape Negrè had the distinction of being named by the explorer Champlain, who in later years became Governor of Port Royal and introduced the Order of The Good Time, and many other accomplishments which our history books will confirm. And proud we should be of this event.

DeMonts' expedition continued along the coast and round the Bay of Fundy to the St. John River. At Ste. Croix they built a fort where they passed the winter. The following spring they explored down the coast of New England, and later that summer, 1605, they returned and established Port Royal.

French history and tradition maintain that the first Catholic Mass in Nova Scotia was said on a flat rock at the shore of Port La Tour, possibly where the La Tour Fort was later built. Could this be the reason for the cross on the shore at this site?

The French fort at Port Royal expanded and flourished for about 8 years. In 1613 it was attacked and completely destroyed by Samuel Argall of the English colony of Virginia. During the attack on the fort a number of the French escaped and took refuge with the Indians in the woods. One of these was Charles de la Tour, who had come from Champagne, France, with his father, Claude de la Tour, who it is maintained was of noble birth. Charles was 14 when they first arrived at Port Royal in 1609.

Poutrincourt the Governor of Port Royal had a son, Biencourt. He and Charles formed a partnership and built a trading fort called Lameron, which was near Cape Sable. (Most historians agree that Lameron was Fort St. Louis at Port La Tour but some others maintain it was at Shag Harbour). In 1602 Biencourt returned to France and assigned his interests in the venture at Lameron to Charles de la Tour. In 1627 the King of France made Charles commandant of the coast of Acadie. It is recorded that "he finished and fortified the fort at Port La Tour".

In 1628 Claude de la Tour was captured by Kirk in the Gulf of St. Lawrence and was transported to England. Claude was a Huguenot (Protestant) and during this time the English were engaged with the Huguenots in fighting the French. Claude joined in this fight with the English. He eventually married a genteel English woman and also at this time became associated with Sir William Alexander, who was attempting to organize English colonies in Nova Scotia. Claude thought he could induce his son, Charles at Fort St. Louis, Port LaTour, to join the English, and accepted from Alexander, for himself and his son the titles Baronets of Nova Scotia. This also entailed a land grant of Acadie, from Cape Fourchu to Mirlegash (Lunenburg). In 1630 in two ships carrying Scotch settlers for Port Royal, Claude stopped at the fort at Port LaTour but his son would not accept the terms his father, had made with the English. This resulted in Claude and the ships company attacking the fort, but Charles' defences were well organized and effective, resulting in a number of the English being killed and wounded. After two days of attacking the Fort, the captain of the ship decided to withdraw and Claude went with them to Port Royal. Claude, having rather poor prospects with the English at Port Royal, obtained permission from his son, Charles, for him and his wife to return to Port La Tour. Charles imposed the condition that Claude and his wife were never to enter the fort but would be provided with a house nearby. Claude and his English wife came to Port La Tour and lived in the house provided by his son. They had 2 male and 2 female servants and Charles kept them supplied with provisions. Denys' history of Acadia relates following "In 1635 I went to see Charles de la Tour, who received me very well, and permitted me to see his father in his dwelling. He received me very well and insisted that I dine with him and his wife. They were amply provided. During the time I was there a Rocollet Father arrived, to whom the wife confided the pleasure that she had in seeing me. Then I discoursed with the Recollet who gave me an account of his garden; he invited me to go see it, and I accepted. I was curious to see everything and to observe also anything that turned up worthy of note. He had me embark with him in his canoe without making any comment upon the danger to which I exposed myself, having never as yet tried this kind of navigation. The Father adjusted the sails, and spread it to the wind, and we crossed the bay which was a league and a half broad. In approaching the land my conductor wished to lower his sail, in fear of grounding to roughly and breaking his canoe. From the front where he had placed me, I took a notion to look behind, and although I did little more than turn my head, never the less by this slight movement the canoe was thrown out of the balance in which it was, and it overturned in an instant. Happily we were close to shore. This kind of navigation is unnatural, difficult and dangerous, especially when one makes his first attempts at it. We arrived at the garden and he told me he had cleared it all alone. He might have had about a half arpent of ground, and he had there a quantity of very fine well-headed cabbages, and of all other sorts of pot herbs and vegetables. He had also some apple and pear trees, which were well started and very fine, but not yet in condition to bear, since they were brought small from France, and had been planted only in the preceding year. I was much pleased to see all this, but much more when he showed me his peas and his wheat which he had sowed. It charmed me to see the height of the peas, they were staked but so covered with pods that it could only be believed by seeing it, and the wheat was the same.... The young La Tour also had a garden near his fort, with wheat and peas which were not so carefully cared for as those of the Rocellet. The land is flat in the bottom of this bay, in which fish are caught, small cod, mackerel and flounder and other kinds, at the mouth of the streams a great quantity of smelts in spring. There is also here a river in which are caught salmon and trout, and toward Cap-de-Sable there are found plenty of shell fish, as clams, whelks, mussels, razor clams and other molluscs, and lobster. There are some which the shell of the front claws holds a pint or more. Plenty of fine meadows are found in ascending this river and along the streams which empty into it."

The translator of Denys' writings, William F. Gagnong, has put as an author's note the following: "While our author does not locate the priest's garden for us, we can yet place it with some probability. That it was on Port La Tour and not at some of the known French sites round Sable (Barrington) Bay, is proven by Champlain's statements, that the Recollet Fathers were living at Port La Tour in 1630. Our author's own account shows it was across the harbour or bay (as Champlain also called it). While most of the east coast of the harbour is rocky and unsuited for good gardens, the narrow neck connecting Cape Negro peninsula with the mainland is of excellent fertile land, and, further at this place there is a flat, formerly a marsh or meadow, still called French

Meadows. That the distance from the fort is not so great as Denys states is of no consequences, since nearly all of his distances are exaggerated. There is now a boat canal cut across the neck, where no doubt the Indians had once a short portage into Cape Negro Harbour. Here on the good land of the neck, I believe the priest had his garden and he lived, selecting this situation, presumably, because it was central for labour (converting) the Indians who resorted to these harbours."

When considering the writings in these historical documents one has to conclude that in 1635, and possibly a number of years before ? the priest was living and had his garden near the French Meadows at Cape Negro which is where we today call the Haul Over.

Later in 1635, Charles de la Tour was given a grant and commission and moved to the mouth of the St. John River where he maintained his new fort. The history of him and his wife at this fort is well documented in history books. Claude de la Tour and his wife remained at Port La Tour. How long he continued to live there is not known. The only other information available is he died about 1650.

In 1656 Charles de la Tour held a joint commission with two Englishmen, Thomas Temple and William Crowne. They held the fur monopoly for Nova Scotia (Acadie). Temple repaired and rebuilt the fort at Port La Tour. Charles de la Tour died at Port La Tour in 1663.

In the French census of 1671 which was recorded by Laurent Molin, there were at Cap Negrè the following, Amand Lalloue and his wife, Elizabeth, with a grown son and four smaller children. They had considerable land under cultivation with gardens of grain, peas and other vegetables, also a sizeable herd of goats for milk and meat and a large number of pigs. Nearby were a number of Indian families with children living in wigwams. Unfortunately the full contents of French census are not now available.

From 1604 the time of Champlain naming Cap Negrè to 1713 the area in Nova Scotia which the French called Acadie went from French rule to British and back again several times. It is therefore necessary to consult other history books for fuller details, however in 1713 Nova Scotia again come under the British Crown. Little detail is available about the French in the Port La Tour area, but it is known that they increased in numbers and were prosperous. They traded furs at the fort at Port La Tour, they fished and also had good gardens, with grain and vegetables and cultivated apple and other fruit trees, as well as keeping live stock of horned cattle, sheep, pigs, goats, geese and hens, with the French Meadows at Cap Negrè producing ample salt hay for over wintering of livestock.

In 1755 the French were expelled from Grand Pre and the Annapolis Valley. In 1756 a battalion of New England soldiers returning from duty in Nova Scotia under the command of Major Probbles on board a collection of ships and schooners, was instructed by Governor Lawrence in Halifax to stop at Port La Tour and land and seize as many of the Acadians as possible and carry them to Boston. "You are to burn and destroy the houses of said inhabitants, and carry their utensils and cattle of all kinds, and make a distribution of them to the troops under your command as a reward for the performance of this service, and to destroy such things as cannot conveniently be carried off." The contents of a letter written on board the ship, "Vulture" in Baccaro Passage, April 24th, 1756.

Sir -
I have the pleasure to inform Your Excellency that after a tedious passage we arrived in Port La Tour the 21st. inst. landed 167 men, officers included, marched overland in the night, surprised the French people in their beds, and have since embarked them on one of the transports you were pleased to appoint for that purpose, the number and names of which I herewith send you enclosed.

. . . I have the troops now all embarked and design to sail this night for New England.

                              Jeddidiah Prebble

The French settlers' houses, barns and other buildings were all burned, their valuables confiscated by the New England troops, the cattle and livestock that could not be carried away were put in barns and burned. As much as possible, everything was destroyed. Not all of the French were captured as some escaped and joined the Indians in the woods. This last group of French either surrendered or was rounded up and expelled in 1658, being taken by ship to Halifax and held on St. Georges Island before being sent to England, thence to France. The larger group expelled by Prebbles was taken to Boston where they remained and refused being transferred to Virginia, and some a few years later, returned and was given grants of land in the Pubnico area.

Three years after the final expulsion of the French the New Englanders came to Barrington. Their detailed history is well documented in Crowell's History of Barrington. At first these settlers were given grants of land at Barrington but over a period of time many did not remain there but took up land at Port la Tour and Cape Negro. One of the reasons the New Englanders in Barrington did not form themselves into a close community was due to the fact they took possession and occupied the cleared lands, orchards and meadow lands, so recently evacuated by the French.

Author's note: I have found no record of French having lived at Blanche. The name however is recorded as Blanc derived from the reflection of the ridges of white beach rocks. In English spelling Blanc became Blanch but the 'E' was not added until more recent times.

There are no accurate written records which clearly designate exactly where the French lived in Cape Negro, but by word of mouth from elderly people many years ago, to reference of "French Cellars at various places" as well as French apple trees, we would have to assume by tradition the French occupied cleared land and gardens at the French Meadows at the Haul Over, which would be lands later occupied by Capt. Joseph Freeman Swaine, the Smiths and Daniel Matherson, also the lands by the meadows at Mac-Dougals Bridge, the lands of Joshua Pierce, Jonathan Smith, Capt. Matthew Swaine.

The first New England settlers at Cape Negro were: Peleg Coffin, Sacco Barnes, Timothy Bryant, Samuel Knowles. Crowell's history states that they all had houses close to Purgatory Point. It would be more accurate to state they had houses close to the French Meadows at the Haul Over and occupied lands later held by Captain John Smith, Samuel Smith, Daniel Matherson.

MacKillop bought out Peleg Coffin. Samuel Knowles was drowned taking cattle across the Clyde River before 1769.

John MacKillop kept 40 head of cattle on his property. His son-in-law, Capt. Longhurst, lived with him and they were first to be buried in the Chapel Cemetery at Cape Negro (which is next to present church). After MacKillop's death, his son kept a tavern.

Benjamin Barss lived at Barss Cove; his wife, Mary, was a daughter of David Smith of Sherose Island. Barss gave the land for the first burial ground, Chapel Cemetery. He sold his land to Joseph Swain and moved to Sambro. He returned when very old and is buried in Chapel Cemetery.

There are no known descendants of these first early settlers residing in this area.

The first settler at Blanch was Samuel Bootman who lived at shore east of the Myrick house. His daughter, Elizabeth, married John Coffin, Jr. and lived near them.

Nathan Nickerson and his wife, Susan, lived first at Eel Bay but sold their property to John Reynolds which later became Reynoldscroft. They moved to Blanche and lived at what is now called "Chaps Old Place". Their daughter, Susan, married Chapman Swaine, Jr. and lived with them. Both Nathan and his wife are buried near where their house stood at Chaps Old Place. Frederick Slate came from La Have, Lunenburg County, and lived at what was later called Slateville or Slatetown. His son, Martin, was married when they came; a daughter, Barbara, was the first wife of Elam Thomas; Catherine, the daughter of Martin Slate was Elam's second wife.

James Obed, a ship wrecked sailor, married Elizabeth, a daughter of Robert Barry Crowell and lived at west side of Blanch, toward the shore below where his grandson, Archeleus Obed lived. He was drowned in 1883. A number of descendants of James Obed reside in this area.

Peter Conk married a daughter of Frederick Slate and first lived on west side of Blanche, which today is called Lyles Old Place. The house was nearly down to the Peg-A-Knowls. They later returned and lived at Slateville, possibly with her father, Frederick. When Peter Conk died he was buried at Chapel Cemetery and his family moved east, possibly back to LaHave.

Elam Thomas, son of John Thomas, bought the house of John Coffin, Jr. (see above Bootman). He was married twice (see above Frederick Slate) and had eight children. The full Thomas history can be found in Crowell's History of Barrington and the History of Port Clyde, which also includes Thomasville. Many descendants of both John, Sr. and Elam Thomas reside in this area.

Steven Smith, son of Theodore and grandson of Solomon Smith of Indian Brook (Port Saxon) married Barbara, daughter of Elam Thomas and built a house on the first ridge just inside Blanche Beach. A number of descendants reside in this area.

Later came the Lyles who were descendants of John Lyle of Port Clyde lived at what is called "Lyles Old Place". Also there lived the Chatwynds who were descendants of

Thomas Chetwynd a Loyalist grantee of Shelburne. The Perrys were descendants of Samuel Perry who was a Loyalist Grantee of Shelburne and lived at Black Point. His son, James, married Sophia, daughter of Isaac King and lived near Purgatory Point. Silas married Susanna, daughter of Abram Smith and their son, Abram Perry, settled near Purgatory Point also.

Isaac King, Jr. married Lydia, a daughter of Samuel Smith and grand-daughter of Jonathan Smith, Sr. They lived between Purgatory Point and Leighton Perry's, close to the shore; they had a large family. Several descendants still live in this area.

Author's note: In the French writings they refer to Port La Tour which embraced all Port La Tour Harbour and the Eel Bay. In refering to Cape Negro they also embraced all Cape Negro Harbour, as Port Clyde, Port Saxon, Thomasville were not defined until the mid-1800's did each community have boundaries. To locate where the first inhabitants lived I had to reconcile the old cellars. This was an impossible task because the French cellars were not recorded and the later settlers built near these their first homes. But as they became more prosperous they built better homes, thus making many cellars which I have no way of establishing their makers.

Isaac and Margaret Lyle before moving from Lyles Old Place, West Blanche

Bill Smith & wife, Sarah Ann, Stewart Swaine and Wife, Sarah

Alexander & Annie Lyle

Where They Lived

To list the houses, their occupiers, and some of their children, we shall start at the end of Blanche, on East Side, just above and north west of the old sheep pens, is Chaps' Old Place.

Nathan Nickerson and his wife, Susan, had lived on west side of the Eel Bay. They sold this property to John Reynolds and moved to what is called Chaps' Old Place. Their daughter, Susan, married Chapman, Jr., son of Chapman Swaine, Sr. of Port La Tour, and lived with her parents, having their property when they died. Both Nathan and Susan Nickerson are buried not far from their old house at Chaps' Old Place. After the Nickersons' death, Chapman and Susan moved further up the Cape Negro Harbour, to what is now called Jimmy's Old Place, which is some distance south of Goose Berry Pond.

The next house north was built on a ridge inside Blanche Beach by Steven Smith and his wife, Barbara, who was a daughter of Elam Thomas. Their children were, William, Elizabeth, Sarah, Martha, Henry and Mary Ann. The cellar of this house is still discernible

The next house west of Steven Smith, was built by his son, William, and his wife, Sarah Ann, who was a sister of Stewart Swaine of Cape Negro. Their children were John, who married Izola Brown of Bear Point and later moved to Cape Negro and Reuben who married Leah, daughter of Captain William L. Ross, and widow of Samuel Swaine, who had a daughter, Lottie. On William's death the house was sold to Arthur and Nell Moors and recently sold to Lawrence and Dorothy Ross. Lawrence is the son of Albert Ross and grandson of Edgar Swaine.

The next house north, was built by Reuben and his wife, Leah Smith, from a house taken down and moved from Cape Negro. Their children were Lottie, daughter of Leah, by her first marriage; Francis who married John Drew and moved to Montreal; Ruby who married Olsen Perry and occupies the home today. Francis had two daughters, Caroline and Judy. Ruby had no issue. Lottie married Emerson Thomas and moved to Cape Negro, Having a son Llewellyn.

The next house north, which is west of the beach, now called Sal's Old Place, a house built by Seth and Sarah Lyle. Their children were, Alexander, Fred, William and Charlie. Seth was a brother of Alexander Lyle, sons of John of Port Clyde. Seth died and Sarah (Sal) lived there as a widow. On her death the house was taken down.

Alexander, son of Seth, married Annie Goodick. Their children were Idella who remained unmarried; Stella married Clifford Perry of Cape Negro Island, their only child, Mervin married Lillian, a daughter of Thomas Scott of Barrington. Clifford Perry died recently and the house is now owned by his widow, Stella.

The next house east, which is presently referred to as Melissa's Place, was a double house occupied by the two sons of Elam Thomas, Jr. James Thomas married Effie Smith and they had two children, Mary, who married Enzor and moved to the U.S.A., and Emerson who married Lottie Swaine and moved to Cape Negro. Howard married Melissa of Lockeport, and their children were, Jenny, Myrtle, Hilda, Kathleen, Trueman. As a widow, Melissa lived here for a number of years and on her death the house was taken down.

The next house east, which is now called Sophie's Hill was built by Thomas Thomas and his wife, Sophie Swaine. This house on the little hill was nearest the road. Thomas died and Sophie lived here a widow for many years. On her death the house was taken down.

On this ridge from Sophie's Hill to Melissa's Place are several old cellars. There is also one immediately across the road. These old cellars all had houses once occupied by Elam, Thomas, John Thomas. I have been unable to establish the various owners other than they were all occupied by various members of the Thomas family.

Next to the beach is a foundation which is all that remains of the fishing shanty, which was a temporary dwelling for the Thomas men who came from Thomasville and Cape Negro and lived there while engaged in summer fishing or lobstering. The building was eventually taken down some time around the second war.

The next house north, near the road, was built by an Elam Thomas around 1827. Later his son, John, occupied the house, and it was eventually sold to Walter Myrick, Sr. and his wife, Reine, a daughter of James Obed, Jr. Their children were, Evelyn and Thomas, who were unmarried; Ada married Surette and moved to Yarmouth; Frank married Jenny, daughter of Howard Thomas and widow of Joshua Selig. They moved to Cape Negro. Sadie's first husband was Franklin Perry of Cape Negro Island and on his death she married Sears and lived in Halifax. Amos married and moved to Birchtown; Ina married Henry Hogg and moved to Barrington Passage; Walter married Ida Perry, a daughter of Paul Swaine and widow of Ernest Perry; Lena never married and moved to Shelburne; Mildred married Raymond Swaine and moved to North West Harbour. Bessie married Milford King and moved to Port laTour. On the death of Walter, Sr. the house was owned by Walter, Jr. who later sold it to Joseph and Susan Ross, who now live there.

The next house east, near the shore, was a log house built by Samuel Bootman and his wife. Their two sons were drowned while fishing. Their daughter, Elizabeth, married John Coffin, Jr. of Port Clyde and the couple lived with them until building their house a few yards west of her parents' home. These houses have long since gone but the cellars are discernible.

The next house north, was built by James Obed, Jr. and his wife, Elizabeth, daughter of Steven Smith. Their children were, Guilford, who married Jessie Thomas; their children were Irma, who married Trueman Thomas with no issue; Ida, who married Clifford Thomas and moved to Thomasville, their children were David, Marie, Joyce. Jesse, who married Odessa Swaine of Cape Negro, was a school teacher at Blanche. Jesse was in charge of the Salvages Fog Horn for many years and suffered a heart attack and died there. They had one daughter, Verna, who married John Matherson, Jr. and lived at Cape Negro. Reine, who married Walter Myrick, Sr., was working in the U.S.A. where they were married. They later moved to Blanche and their family history has been listed above. After the death of James Obed, Jr. his son, Jesse, maintained the house but on his death his widow moved to Cape Negro and the house was taken down.

The next house north was built by James Swaine, son of James, a descendent of Chapman Swaine, Jr. His wife was Margaret S. Their children were Wilbert, Harold and Edith. They all moved away from the Blanche area. When Margaret died James married a widow, Nelly Swaine, of Cape Negro and moved there. The house was sold to Joshua Selig who married Jenny Thomas a daughter of Howard. Their children were Everett, who moved to the U.S.A. and Phoebe who married a Williams and moved to Jordan Bay. Joshua Selig was killed in an accident in the Halifax Shipyards. His widow, Jenny, later married Frank, son of Walter, Sr. and Reine Myrick. They moved to Cape Negro. The house was sold and taken down. A hunting camp built by Sanford Nickerson is built near the old cellar.

Returning to the east side of the main road is the house built by Marsden Thomas, who married Fidelia Arey, a sister of Joseph Arey of Slateville. They had three children. Lerman, who married Ella, daughter of Ernest and Ida Perry; they moved to the U.S.A.; Leroy, who married Blanche, a daughter of Edgar and Etta Swaine; they had no issue. Albert, who died young. Upon Marsden's death his widow,

Fidelia, lived in the house many years, until her death, then the house was sold to Albert Simmons of the U.S.A., who used it as a summer home. The house has only recently been sold to Paul and Helen Jean Nugent.

The next house west, built by Austin Thomas and later purchased by Ernest Perry of Cape Negro Island, brother of Franklin, who married Ida, a daughter of Paul Swaine, Jr. They had two daughters, Ella, who married Lerman Thomas and moved to the U.S.A., and Eileta, who married John Thomas of Thomasville, having one daughter, Lola, who married Whitford O'Connell of Smithville. Ernest died and his widow married Walter Myrick, Jr. Ida died and Walter, Jr. still lives in the house.

The next house north was built by James Swaine who married Margaret (Maggie), a daughter of Paul Swaine and sister of Ida Perry, who lived next door. They had one son, Maurice, who married Ethel Snow of Port La Tour. She was a school teacher at Blanche. They had one son, Carrol, who married Katherine, a daughter of Mitchell Ross of Port La Tour and they moved to Seal Point. On James Swaines' death the house was occupied by a number of families, Carrol Swaine, Joseph Ross, Basil Hensler, and is now owned and occupied by Hugh Jones and his wife, Bruce Blakemore.

The next house east was built by Guilford Obed, son of James, Jr. who married Jessie Thomas. They had two daughters, Irma, who married Trueman Thomas, with no issue and Ida, who married Clifford Thomas of Thomasville; their children were David, Marie and Joyce On the death of Guilford the house was sold to Lloyd, a son of Franklin Perry of Cape Negro Island and his wife, Gertrude Nickerson of Clyde River. Their foster son, Frank, now resides in Ontario. On Gertrude's death, Lloyd Perry built a house and moved to Port Clyde. The house was sold and now occupied by a Nickerson family.

The next house west was built by Edgar Swaine, who married Etta, a daughter of John and Deborah Thomas. They had two daughters, Blanche, who married Leroy Thomas, son of Marsden, with no issue. Liza, who married Albert, a son of Gilbert Ross of Port La Tour. They moved to the U.S.A.

Edgar moved to the U.S.A. but in later years he returned to Cape Negro and died there. Leroy and Blanche Thomas occupied the house until it was sold to Arthur Moors, who took it down. The property is now owned by Hugh Jones, who uses the barn built by Edgar Swaine as a wood shed.

The next house east was built by William Lyle, a son of Seth and Sarah Lyle, who married Margaret (Maggie) with no issue. William kept the post office for many years. On the death of William the house was sold to George and Elizabeth (Libby) Drew, who with their son, John (Jack), moved from Montreal. On the death of George and Elizabeth Drew their son, John married Francis Smith and lived there some years before moving back to Montreal. They had two daughters, Caroline and Judy. The house was sold to Claire and Nan Price from Montreal, who still reside there.

The next buildings north are the community hall on the west and the school and chapel building on the east. These buildings are recorded in detail in another section of this book.

North along the main road, past the Keel Grove Hill and the Witch Rock is Jimmy's Road that leads to the east to the shore. This road was ditched and used by horse and oxen wagons at one time. It is now overgrown and not used. At the shore are a number of cellars. Chapman Swaine and his wife lived here at one time, also Paul Swaine, Sr. and later his son, Paul, Jr. and his brother, Francis Swaine, who later lived at Purgatory Point. Paul Swaine, Jr. and his wife, Ann, had four children, Frank, George, Ida, who married Ernest Perry and Margaret (Maggie) who married James Swaine. A little to the north of where the Swaines lived is a cellar where Nickersons lived. He was called "The Old Chairmaker". This family later moved to Wood Harbour. The Swaine houses were all taken down after the old folks died. Today there are no buildings here and it is called "Jimmy's Old Place".

The next house is north, above the Gooseberry Pond at Purgatory Point. The Perry's have always lived here by tradition. The last to do so was Anthony Perry, who was called Tone. He had two sons, Claude and Bradford, who married Helen Thomas and lived at Thomasville, having a son, Carl. Tone Perry's house was the last house remaining here, when it was long deserted and derelict, it blew down in a storm on May 20, 1933. Other families that lived north of the Perrys and their cellars may be located among the trees were, Lorenzo Messenger, who married Katherine, a sister of Dave Flemmings, Sr.; their children were Leona, Bertha, Ethel, Francis, Lee and Douglas. Their house had been built by Stan Greenwood, who moved to Port Clyde.

The next house north was built by Francis Swaine, son of Paul, Sr., and brother of Paul, Jr. his son, Winslow. On the death of his father they took the house down and rebuilt it on land purchased from Joshua Pierce at Cape Negro.

The next house north was built where there are several cellars I have not identified. One was the site of the residence of Isaac King. His son, Thomas King built a house near his father's. He married Elizabeth, daughter of John MacKillop. His son, William, occupied this house. He married Martha Perry of Blanche. Their children were, Archibald, Benjamin, Alexander, James, Jane, who married Francis, a son of Paul Swaine, Jr., Margaret, Martha and Elizabeth who married Alexander Perry of North East Harbour. On the death of William this house was taken down.

The next house north was built by Alexander Perry of North East Harbour, brother of John and Isaac Perry, who married Elizabeth King, daughter of William King. Their children were Elsie, who married Godfrey MacKay and moved to Thomasville and Leighton, who married Violet who came from England. Their children were Burdett, who never married; Fred, who died young; Betty and Leta, who married and moved to Dartmouth; Minnie Marie, who married Edwin Smith, a son of Captain John Smith, and they lived most of their life in the U.S.A. After Alexander's death, Leighton and his family occupied the house. After the death of Leighton the house was sold to Glendon Bunch and family of the U.S.A. and is used as a summer home.

The next house north was built by Captain Alexander Smith, son of Reuben and Cynthia (Swaine) Smith, married Susan, daughter of William Perry. Their children were Albert, Smith, son of Reuben and Cynthia (Swaine) Smith, who married Susan, daughter of William Perry. Their children were Albert, Mina and Ella. He was a captain of sailing ships. The to Edwin

Smith. In recent times the house has had several owners and is now derelict and presently for sale.

The next house north on the by-road east to Stone Wharf are several cellars where houses once stood but have long been taken down, and are now overgrown. The first house was built by Samuel, son of Jonathan Smith, who married Ruth, daughter of Chapman Swaine. Their son, Samuel, married Nancy, daughter of John Smith, and built a house next to his father's. His son, John, married Anna Schrage and lived with his parents until he built a house across the road. These Smith houses were taken down when the old folks died.

The next house west across the road was built by Captain John Smith, son of Samuel. He married Anna, daughter of Dr. Schrage of Barrington. This house was very large and well appointed and the property also consisted of a barn, with a store and separate carriage house built across the road. Captain John Smith had large fields cleared and kept cattle and horses. He also had warehouses and a large wharf on the east side of Eel Bay, where his sailing vessels came to unload cargo. He had an extensive trade in salt fish with the West Indies. This property was connected to his home and store by road , which came just south of the barn. Many local people were employed as seamen on his sailing vessels. The store building was sold and moved to Captain Zephaniah Nickersons at Port Clyde. The large carriage house, containing wagons, buggys and sleighs burned when tradesmen stopped there for lunch and dropped a cigarette in the mid 1930s. Captain John and Anna had two sons, Bert, who died young, and Edwin, who married Minnie Marie, daughter of Alexander Perry. They had no issue. On the death of his parents Edwin owned the property but lived in the U.S.A. until retiring and moving home. On the death of Edwin, his widow lived in the house alone a number of years. Upon her death the house was sold to Ray and Amy Thibeault, who operate the property as Deer View Farm and Riding Stables.

The next north is the Haul Over and a separate section is devoted to the history of this canal.

Having completed the east side of Blanche Peninsula, it's necessary to retrace and return to the west side, towards Green Point near the Peg-A-Nols. Peter Conk who was married to a daughter of Frederick Slate lived here for awhile before moving to Slateville to care for his father-in-law.

The next house north are several cellars where the following families lived. Alexander Lyle, his sons, James, George and Isaac also Andrew and Ransom Chatwynd. Alexander was a son of John Lyle of Port Clyde, brother of Seth, who married Eunice Blades. They had two sons, George, who married Ruth, daughter of Richard Smith and Isaac, who married Margaret (Maggie) Messenger. George Lyle's widow, Ruth, later married Andrew Chatwynd. These people moved to Cape Negro, Reynoldscroft and Port La Tour and houses all taken down in the early 1900s. The move was prompted due to the lack of suitable harbour. Only small boats could be kept and pulled out of the water in the event of storms. Also the road which was started was through mainly swamp and never useable to any extent. It began at or near Seth and Alexander Lyle's property on East Side and came to what is now called "Lyle's Old Place". In the early 1900s an elderly woman died and her body was carried on a litter up beach to Knowles' Old Place thence up the road to Keel Grove Hill where they met the undertaker. Now only the stones of the cellars, some overgrown fields and stone walls running between the trees remains of where these families lived.

The next house north, which is called today "Knowles' Old Place", is just south of Little Harbour. This house was built by James and Mary Ann Swaine. Their children were: Arthur, who married Alice Towner; Knowles, who married Florence Towner; James, who married Margaret Swaine;and Edgar, who married Etta Thomas. On the death of James, this house was sold and taken down. A road from this property to Keel Grove Hill was ditched and used by horse and ox wagons in earlier times; it is now overgrown. The stones of the Swaines' cellar surrounded by quite a large field of cleared grass land is still discernable.

The next house north was built by Knowles Swaine, son of James, Knowles married Florence Towner, daughter of Silas of Cape Negro. They had one daughter, Josie, who married Douglas Ross and moved to Upper Port La Tour. After Florence died Knowles married Mary Atwood of Clyde River, who was a school teacher at Blanche. On Knowles' death the house was sold to James Brown and only recently resold to Peter Reynolds of the U.S.A., a descendant of John Reynolds for whom Reynoldscroft is named.

The next house north was built by Arthur O. Thomas, who's wife was Cynthia (Aunt Tint). Their children were Oscar, who moved to the U.S.A. and Allie, who married Sandford Slate. They had two daughters, Millie and Neima. On the death of Arthur the house was sold to Wilma Obed, son of Archelius, who married Louise, daughter of Fendwick and Grace Perry. Their children were Lucy, Maxine and Emily. Wilma died several years ago and Louise only in late 1986 and the property is now owned by the family.

The next house north is a new house of modern construction, built on land purchased from Wilma Obed. It is used for a summer home and is owned by James Smith. His wife is a descendant of the Robertsons of Shelburne.

The next house north is a small house of recent construction built by Cecil, son of Fendwick and Grace Perry, who married Lorretta Smith of Baccaro. They lived here a number of years and the house was sold to a family in the U.S.A. The house has not been occupied for many years and remains vacant today.

The next house north, is a cellar by the shore, where a house once was built by James Obed, Jr., after he was ship wrecked on Cape Sable Island. He married Elizabeth, daughter of Robert Barry Crowell. Their children were James Jr. and Archelius. James, Jr. married Elizabeth, daughter of Steven Smith and moved to Blanche Village, Archelius built a house next door nearer the road.

The next house north was built by Archelius Obed, Sr., who had the following children, Archelius, Steven, Cordelia. When Archelius, Sr. died his son, Archelius, Jr. lived in the house. He married Genevieve, daughter of Silas Towner of Cape Negro. They had two children, Wilma, who married

Louise Perry and Dorothy, who married Coleman Ross. On Archelius, Jr. death, the house was sold to Fendwick Perry, who had been living for a time at Slateville having come from Birchtown some years previously. His wife was Grace Towner; their children were, Louise, who married Wilma Obed; Olson, who married Ruby Perry; Edna, who married Herbert Thomas; Cecil, who married Lorretta Smith. On the death of Fendwick the house was sold to Sydney Grasbill and his wife, Janet Jardine, who presently use the house as a summer home.

The next house north, which was called Slateville, was the house occupied by Aldo Smith, who married Eva, daughter of Stewart Swaine. Their children were Harold, Cecil, Lewis, Ernest and Ivy.

The next house was occupied by David Slate who married Annie Larkin. Their children were Herbert, Wilbert, Ira, Percy, Lester, Elma, Lamont, Annis, Debra, Winnie and Annie.

The next house was occupied by Benjamin Slate, who married Sarah Christie. Their son, Sandford, married Allie, daughter of Arthur O. Thomas. Their children were Millie and Neima.

The next house was occupied by George Slate, who married Martha Thomas. Their children were George and Lenard.

The next house was occupied by David Flemmings, who married Mercy Slate. They moved to Port La Tour.

The next house was occupied by Lester Slate, who married Grace, daughter of William MacKay of Thomasville. Their children were Marion, Bessie, Doris, Lillian, Ida, and Eva. In the 1930s Lester Slate and his family moved to the U. S. A. His daughter, Marion, married John Thomas in the U.S.A. and returned to live in Thomasville. Only recently her two sisters, Bessie and Doris have also returned and purchased the house formally owned by Captain Zephaniah Nickerson at Port Clyde.

The next house was occupied by Joseph Arey, son of Henry, who was a son of Nicholas Arey, the early settler who came from Ireland. Joseph Arey's sister was Fidelia, who married Marsden Thomas of Blanche. Joseph's first wife was Mary Slate, his second wife was Abbie Brown. Joseph Arey had one son by his first marriage, Walter, who married Stella Purdy of Yarmouth. Their children were Arthur, Everett, Gordon and Ernest. This family moved in the mid-1930s to Upper Port La Tour. The house was taken down and rebuilt at Upper Port La Tour by Douglas and Josie Ross.

All the Slates are descendents of Frederick Slate who came from La Have. Most members of the Slate families moved to the U.S.A. When all the above mentioned families lived at Slateville they had a post office. The road down to the homes had been much improved and Joseph Arey had one of the early cars, which was before 1930. The houses have all been taken away and only the stones of the various cellars, the stonewalls and the overgrown roadway remains of where these families once lived.

The next house north were two houses built by the Sholds' families. The first house close to the shore was built by Frederick Sholds, who married Charity, daughter of Zephaniah Swaine. Their children were Samuel, who married Mary, a daughter of Smith Nickerson, Zephaniah, Peter, Ann and Charity. George Sholds, who was a son of Samuel, built a house next to his father's, which was nearer the road. He resided here some years and then moved his family to the U.S.A. The house was then occupied by Samuel, son of Stewart Swaine, who married Leah, daughter of Captain William L. Ross of Port La Tour. They had one child, Lottie. After Samuel's death the house was sold to Charles Thomas, who married Merle, daughter of James and Nellie Swaine. Their children were, Kenneth and Herbert, who both have families and live at Cape Negro. The Frederick Sholds' house was taken down, but the cellar is discernable near the shore. The other remaining house is still owned by the Thomas family.

The next house north of the Haul Over was occupied by Daniel Matherson. This property consisted of extensive cultivated farm lands, with many stone walled paddocks, well organized orchard and a large house with a number of outbuildings for accommodating livestock. Much of this land had been cleared and cultivated by the French, and after their expulsion was taken up by Knowles. The stones of a number of cellars and evidence of where other buildings had once stood atests to the French occupation. Daniel Matherson came from Malagash to manage a lobster factory at Woods Harbour. He married Temperance Swaine and moved to Cape Negro. He was a well educated man with a Scottish accent. He was a school master at Cape Negro for many years. He held one of the first teachers licenses for the Barrington area about 1860s. His wife, Temperance, was a daughter of John B. Swaine. Their children were, William, who moved to the U.S.A. and John, Sr., who married Anna MacKinnon, of Malagash. They had one son, John, Jr., who married Verna, daughter of Jesse Obed of Blanche. They had two foster children, Herbin and Rowena Pierce. The Cape Negro School was next to the Daniel Matherson property and his well cultivated apple orchard. He made an agreement with the school children, if they did not bother his orchard he would give them apples when they were ripe. The children respected the agreement, and each fall he came to the school with several pails of apples for the teacher to distribute to the children. He did this every year up to his death in the mid 1930s. On Daniel Matherson's death the house was occupied by his son, John, Sr. until his wife, Anna, died, then he went to live with his son, John, Jr. For some years the house remained empty. One fall night the house and the attached outbuildings burned and everything was lost. The property is now overgrown and deserted and only the stone walls denote where the large orchard and the various paddocks of cultivated and pasture lands once were.(See photo of Daniel Matherson's house, p. 69)

 The next house south of the road, down a long lane way flanked by stone walls, right near the shore is the cellar where Joseph Swaine, son of Joseph, and grandson of Chapman Swaine,Sr. occupied the first house. There is some evidence that this land had been occupied by the French, and indications that this was the site of the Priest gardens as described in Denys' History which is outlined in first chapter of this book. At least one other member of Joseph Swaine's family built a house near the shore, prior to his grandson, James Freeman Swaine, who married Mary, daughter of William Patterson. He built a house further from the shore and his son extended the house, making the structure into a double house. Joseph Freeman Swaine, married Carrie Hills and their children were Florence, Mysie, Gertrude and Stanley. Captain Joseph Freeman Swaine was a captain of sailing ships and was engaged in the West Indies trade. They were a prosperous family and well educated. Both Florence and Mysie were school teachers. Gertrude was the church organist and Sunday School teacher for many years. On the death of Captain Joseph Freeman, his two daughters, Gertrude, who never married, and Mysie Gardner, who was a widow, lived alone in the house for many years. They moved to Shelburne and the house was sold to George Ross. The house burned and he then built a small house at the top of the lane by the road with material from the Cape Negro Temperance Hall. This house is now owned by Burdett Perry, who is not married, lives there alone. Immediately across the road is the school building which now serves as a community hall and to the west the stone foundation of the Temperance Hall.

The next house west was built by James Swaine, who married Nellie Burgess, who came from Liverpool, England. Their children were, Howie and Lawrence who died young, twin daughters, Merle, who married Charles Thomas, and Kate, who married Roy Snow and moved to Port La Tour. Another daughter, Lilly, married Bertram Hill and lived many years in the U.S.A. On the death of James, his widow, Nellie, married James Swaine, a widower from Blanche. On the death of Nellie, her daughter, Lilly, returned from the U.S.A. and occupied the house until the death of her husband, Bertram. The property was then sold to Eric Newell, its present owner.

The next house north was built by Seth Snow, who married Mercy, daughter of William Dowling. Their children were, Debrah, Mahala, George, Olivia. On the death of Mercy Snow the house was occupied by Foster Swaine. When he moved to the U.S.A. it was occupied by Steven and Lucy Obed. They moved to Seal Point and the house was occupied by Frank and Jenny Myrick. On Frank's death the house was occupied by John Shediac, who moved to Liverpool and the house was occupied by Kenneth and Linney Thomas.

They built a new home and the property was sold to John and Edris Baczewaki of the U.S.A. Edris is a daughter of Bertram and Lillie Hill. They occupy the property as a summer home.

East of this house, toward the old Temperance Hall was a road running north to the shore at Swaine's Cove. There are a number of stone cellars near this road and along the ridge at the shore. Bryants lived on the ridge near the shore. Several were occupied by Swaines who's identity is now obscure, and some of the stone foundations are evidence the land was occupied by the French settlers.

For the next house north, its necessary to go down the road past the church and the Old Burial Ground to "The Point" or "Swaine's Point". The first house was built by William Henry, son of Henry and Mary Swaine, who married Laura Slate. Their children were, Foster, Eithel and Edwin, who married and moved to the U.S.A., also Lucy, who married Steven Obed of Blanche; Odessa, who married Jesse Obed of Blanche and Mary (Mammie), who married Page of the U.S.A. William Henry was brother to Stewart Swaine who lived nearby and Sarah Ann who married William Smith of Blanche. On the death of William Henry and Laura, the house was closed and only occupied briefly by their daughter, Odessa. When she became a widow, she lived here about two years and her daughter, Verna and husband, John Matherson, Jr. lived with her. Her sister, Lucy, having died she cared for her two nephews, Kenneth and Eithel Obed while living here. Odessa bought the house of Captain Matthew Swaine and the house was again closed. The property was retained by the family living in the U.S.A., who still retain ownership, the house now being derelict. The property is much overgrown and only the stonewalls attest to the once cultivated fields, gardens and large orchard.

The next house north was built by John Smith, son of Benjamin, a son of Nathanial, Sr. of Port LaTour, John who married ???????????????.Their children were, Aldo, who married Eva, daughter of Stewart Swaine; their children were, Harold, Cecil, Lewis, Ernest, Ivy, who lived at Slateville. Edward who married Sarah Jane, daughter of Joseph Swaine. They had three children, Ernest, who married and lived in the U.S.A., Murray who married Neima, daughter of

Stanford and Allie Slate, Nan who married Albert Swallow and lived in the U.S.A. Edward and Sarah Jane occupied the house on the death of his father; they were affectionately known as Uncle Ed and Aunt Jane. When Nan's parents were elderly she returned from the U.S.A. with her husband, Albert Swallow and cared for them until their death. On the death of her husband, the property was sold and she moved to Port Clyde. The property was bought by a Captain Nicholson from the U.S.A. who was stationed at the Baccaro Radar Base. They lived there some years and the property has recently been sold to a family in the U.S.A.

The next house north, being the last down the point, set in a large field with apple trees and a good view of the Clam Creek and Cape Negro Harbour, was built by Henry and Mary Swaine. Their children were, William Henry, whose geneology appears above, Sarah Ann, who married William Smith of Blanche, Stewart, who married Mary Swaine, a daughter of James Freeman Swaine and sister of Captain Joseph Freeman Swaine. Their children were, Samuel, who married Leah, daughter of Captain William L. Ross, Everett, Clinton and Joseph all moved to the U.S.A. Walter married Lyda, daughter of Arthur Reynold, Herman married May MacLellan, Eva married Aldo Smith, Bessie married Percy Thomas and lived at Port Saxon, Sadie, who never married. Following the death of his father, Stewart Swaine lived in the house. When quite elderly he moved to the U.S.A. where most of his family then lived. He remained some years, but later returned with his daughter, Sadie to Port Clyde where they lived until he died. Sadie then returned to the U.S.A. The family in the U.S.A. retained ownership of the property and it became derelict and the house eventually blew down in the early 1940s. Stewart Swaine was a very kind man and much respected community leader. He raised a large family who were all very successful in the U.S.A. where many descendents now live.

The next house west of the church hill, opposite the Flag Swamp, was built by Ezra Swaine and his wife, Josephine. They had a foster son, Lester Smith, who was a son of Bigelow and grandson of Enoch Smith. Lester married Violet, daughter of James Snow of Port La Tour. They had one child,

Bessie, who married William Maule, and lives in Oshawa. When Captain Ezra Swaine died Lester continued to live in the house until his death. Then his widow, Violet, moved to Oshawa to live with her daughter, Bessie. The house was sold to Mary (Mammie) Page, daughter of William Henry Swaine, who had been living in the U.S.A. She lived here a number of years to be near her sister, Odessa Obed. When Mammie returned to the U.S.A. the property was sold and occupied by Toby and Barbara Raisbreck from the U.S.A. Ezra's Island which is just off the boat landing of this property was named for Ezra Swaine.

At the east of this property by the salt meadow a well built road runs to the shore, to a small cove and boat landing. To the west of this area a house was built, the cellar stones still being discernable, by James MacKay, a relative of the MacKays of Thomasville, who married Levina, daughter of James Swaine, Jr. Their children were Maude, who married Collin Smith and had one son, Jamie. When a widow, Maude married Walter Thomas, of Port Saxon, who was a widower with several children. Hilda, who married Harry Attwood of River Head where they lived most of their life except for several years in Joshua Pierces' house at Cape Negro. James MacKay as a widower lived alone in his house and one morning in 1928 when he was away working on the highway, his house burned to the ground with all lost. He spent his last days with his daughter, Hilda in River Head or as a boarder with relatives in Thomasville. The property is now overgrown.

The next house north was built by Samuel Smith, who married Sarah, daughter of Heman Horton. They had no children. They kept the post office for many years and he drove the mail to Blanche. In their old age they had as housekeeper to care for them, Fred Flemmings and his wife, then Basheba Snow held the position for awhile. After their death the property was owned by Libby Parsons. When she returned from the U.S.A. Libby who was a daughter of Knowels and Lydia Swaine of West Blanche, lived here as a recluse, with all doors locked most of the time and seldom venturing out of doors. She was cared for by Allie Slate Christie, who lived across the road. On her death the house was owned by Allie Christie and was sold to a family of Greenwoods of Shelburne, when the house was still being renovated it caught fire and burned to the ground. The Greenwoods moved back to Shelburne, and the land was sold to Emerson Thomas who used it for a number of years as a cow pasture, until selling one half of the lot to Maynard Myrick of Blanche who has built a cement block basement on the site of the house that burned. The other half of the lot is still owned by Lottie Thomas. To the south at the line fence separating this property from the Raisebeck property was a road of sorts and short cut to the ferry to Burn Island, this roadway is now long overgrown.

The next house east was built by Murray, son of Edward Smith, who married, Neima, daughter of Stanford and Allie Slate. The house was constructed from the house of Neima's parents moved from Slateville. They lived here a number of years before moving to the U.S.A. The house was then occupied by Neima's mother, Allie Slate, who as a widow had married Sydney Christie a widower with a son, John. They lived here a number of years before moving to Port Clyde. The house was then sold to Herbert, son of Charles and Merle Thomas, who married Edna, daughter of Fendwick and Grace Perry of West Blanche. Their children are Beverley, Mavis and Elgin. The Thomas family still reside in this house.

The next house west, across the road, was built by Captain Matthew Swaine, son of Joseph and Ellen Swaine, who married Lilla, daughter of Vincent Attwood of Port Clyde. Their children were Joseph, Cassie, Lloyd, Aldred, Helen, Sydney and May.

Captain Matthew was master of sailing ships engaged mainly in trade with the West Indies. Many local seamen sailed with him. He was a successful and well respected gentleman. On his death his widow, Lilla lived alone for a number of years . On her death the property was sold to Odessa, daughter of William Henry Swaine, who was the widow of Jesse Obed who had died suddenly on The Half Moons fog horn. The Salvages, at Blanche. Her daughter, Verna and her husband, John Matherson, Jr. lived with her. Their foster children were, Roeena, married a Bower and lives in Shelburne, Herbin, married Violet O'Connell of Baccaro. Following the death of Odessa Obed and the Mathersons, Herbin and his wife, Violet, live there today. Captain Matthew Swaine owned the property that extended to the shore. At the south west corner of the shore property the stones from the wharf can still be seen, which was where the ferry operated across to Ferry Point and Burnt Island, before the bridge MacDougals were built. The roadway, called the "thoroughfare" went north from ferry wharf along the fence line through what is called the short cut, then through what is now the ball field along what was called the old road where it joined what is now the present highway. Also in this ferry landing area is evidence of French settlers occupation. Within living memory this area was all cleared and cultivated fields and vegetable gardens. Now it is all overgrown with the stone walls running through heavy forest of trees.

The next house, across the road was built by Heman, son of Henry Swaine, who married Mary, daughter of Howes Smith, and sister of Esther Pierce. They had one son, Clifford, who died young. Captain Heman Swaine kept a store, and also had a horse and grocery wagon and peddled groceries to the nearby communities. He also used his horse to pull the hearse, which was kept in a building south of his house and is now Herbert Thomas garage. The hearse was moved to building near the church. Mary was church organist for many years.

On the death of Heman and Mary Swaine the property was sold to Joseph, son of Captain Matthew Swaine. He later moved to the U.S.A. and the property sold in 1925 to Emerson, son of James Thomas of Blanche and his wife, Lottie, daughter of Samuel and Leah Swaine. They had one son, Llewellyn, who married Helen MacKinley of Moncton, N.B. and they have one son, Derell, and they now live in Yarmouth. Emerson was an industrious man, having worked in the U.S.A. a number of years before establishing himself as a fisherman, boatbuilder and many other endeavours. His wife, Lottie at one time operated a store from the front of her house. The old Heaman Swaine store was moved and is now the wood shed at home of Herbin Pierce. Emerson purchased a garage from Winslow Swaine and moved the building to the site of the old store. Lottie, being a widow, still resides in this property. At the bottom of the cleared field of this property going east is a road leading to Cord Wood Point. This road at one time was not only for hauling salt hay from the meadows and the winter wood supply, but it also provided access to goose and duck shooting on the Clam Creek. It was also a handy short cut across the meadow to Swaine's Point, as the road continued on the other side of the salt meadow and came out by the Edward Smith garage.

The next house west of the road and nearly opposite the Old Rife Club building now used by the Quilting Club and the new ball field, is a new house recently constructed by Kenneth, son of Kenneth and Flora (Dash) Ross of Thomasville, who is married to Madonna Nickerson and son Barrett Tyler. They have only recently moved into this new home.

The next house west is also a new house constructed only a few years ago by Walter, son of Kenneth and Flora (Dash) Ross of Thomasville. He married Judy, daughter of John (Jack) and Francis Drew of Montreal and granddaughter of Reuben and Leah Smith of Blanche. Their children are Tammy and Jason. They still reside in this home.

The next house north, up the main highway, on the Clam Creek, the first house down by the shore, was built by Richard, son of Abram and Batheshba Smith. He married Thankful, daughter of John Reynolds of Reynoldscroft; this was the family home, when the parents died the house was taken down and used to construct a barn. Their son, Samuel, had built a house on the next hill west towards the road. He married Mary, daughter of Joshua Nickerson of the Ponds. Their children were, James Harvey, who married, Hattie, the daughter of James Swaine; their children were Clarence, who never married; Frank who married Clara Miller and lived in Yarmouth. Their children were Ronald, Glendon and Muriel, Anna Jane (Jenny) who married Captain William L. Ross; their children were, Burley, George, Allison, Joseph Randall and Alva Jean, Alberta, who married Robert Brannen and lived in the U.S.A. They had one daughter, Marie. James, who married in Florida with no issue. Anna Jane, who died young and Charles married Alice Olilver with no issue lived in the U.S.A. After Samuel died James Harvey Smith occupied the house until his death, then it was sold and taken down and rebuilt at Port La Tour by Harry Perry. The land was vacant for some time and used as a cow pasture by Grant MacKay, who sold the property to Kenneth, son of Charles and Merle Thomas, who married Elina Williams of Lockeport and their children were Merle, Armound, Owen. He built a new house only a few years ago on the site where Samuel Smith's house once stood. The Thomas family live there today. A few years ago, Thomas, son of Bradford Lowe and his wife, Seattle, daughter of John Nickerson, a merchant at Port La Tour built a new home at the shore near where the original Richard Smith house once stood. The Lowes still live there today. James Harvey Smith was a fisherman and as the Clam Creek was very shallow a boat could not be floated at low tide, making it necessary for him to have fishing shanties nearer the fishing grounds, he had these shanties at the Haul Over and at one time on Ram Island and Slateville. He would remain there during the week while engaged in fishing or lobstering and return home on the weekend to replenish his grub box with baked goods.

The next house north, a short way in the Swaine's Road, which begins near the Clam Creek bridge, George Ross was in the process of building a new house when he died. The house was sold to a Crooks family of Toronto, but is unoccupied most of the time.

The next house south of the corner of the Blanche Road, is a house built by Jerome (Rommie), son of Jonathan and Matilda Smith, who married Ella Smith. Their children were Neima and Ethel. They moved to the U.S.A. and the house was sold to Lloyd, son of Captain Matthew Swaine, who married Florence (Flossie), daughter of Zephaniah Nickerson at Port Clyde. Their children were Hazel, who married Fernwood Lowe, Dorothy, who married George Smith and moved to U.S.A. and Allan, who married Marion, daughter of Walter Perry, the lighthouse keeper on Cape Negro Island. Their children were Linda, who married Dr. Jefferies and lives in Halifax, and Darrell, who married Jane Weeks of Barrington Passage. Lloyd Richard Swaine and his wife, Florence, lived in the U.S.A. a number of years before purchasing the Rommie Smith house and returning to Cape Negro to live. He built the blacksmith shop on the west side of the road across from his house. The building contained a forge and a hand operated air blower. He was a highly skilled blacksmith and made the shoes which he used to shoe horses and oxen, being in great demand for this service as customers came from distant communities to have this done.

He was able to manufacture on the forge, parts for engine repair and many tools and items used in local work. In the mid thirties he made from iron rods all the bolts, spikes and metal fittings required for the rebuilding of the Haul Over. When cars started to become more common he built a garage where he repaired and serviced cars. His son, Allan, having moved the building across the road, now operates a Honda sevice there. The garage having a cement floor with a grease pit also had a Delco engine which not only supplied electric lights of 32 volts to the house but was used to recharge car batteries and later radio batteries. The electric lights from the Delco batteries were in operation 20 years before the electricity came to Cape Negro in 1939. He operated the garage and black smithy all his working life, and when quite elderly he made parts for antique muskets and guns which he also collected. When his son Allan married, the house was divided and the two families lived there until Marion died and Allan remarried Lillian Rodgerson and moved to Port LaTour. The house is now occupied by Allan's son Darrel, and his family.

The next house south was built by Jonathan, son of Joshia, who was a grandson of Jonathan Smith. He married Matilda Hopkins. Their children were Jerome, who built the house next door, later owned by Lloyd R. Swaine, and William, who married Jesse MacDonald. They had two children, Donald and Francis. On the death of Jonathan, his son William and his family moved to the U.S.A. and the house was sold to Captain William L., son of Thomas Ross, Sr. of Port La Tour. Captain William L. had previously lived at Reynoldscroft with his wife, Dora, in a house he built next to the Patterson property. That house was later owned by Bradford Lowe. Captain William L. was engaged as master in sailing vessels to the West Indies. Later after becoming a Master Mariner, he sailed steamships across the Atlantic to England on a regular basis and also one six-month journey to Australia. He was a captain in the Canadian Navy during the first war, and was decorated with a medal from the Duke of Connought, who was then the Governor General of Canada. He was active at sea all his life, making his last voyage at the age of 89, when he piloted a motor launch which came from Montreal. He boarded at Shelburne harbour and took the ship to New York then to the inland passage enroute to Florida. Captain William L. on the death of his wife, Dora, remarried Anna Jane (Jenny), daughter of James H. and Hattie Smith. Their children were, Burnley, who married Phyllis Brannen of Baccaro, George, who married Jean Isobel MacDonald of Eastern Passage, Allison, who married Marie VanDe Hurk of Neijmegan, Holland, Joseph Randall, who married Susan Jane (Peggy) Baltzer of Berwick, Alva Jean who married Gordon Jones of Stormont. The land to this property extended behind the Pierce property adjoining the Captain Matthew Swaine land boundary, being the old thoroughfare for the Ferry Point, Burnt Island Ferry. At the shore is considerable evidence of early French occupation. On the death of Captain William L., the family moved to Halifax and the property was purchased by Ada Goodwin, later sold to Edgar Swaine and is now owned and occupied by the Gerald Mailman family.

The next house east at the beginning of the old short cut, which in early years was the old thoroughfare, was a house on a square parcel of land of about 3 acres. The property is bounded on east by a stone wall.There was a large house with an ell kitchen and nearby a large barn. The house at one time was occupied by Emaline Fitzgerald and later by an elderly woman named Belle Isley. In later years an elderly negro woman lived there and cared for her. On her death the property was purchased by Captain William L. Ross, who later sold it to Albert Swallow, who did not take up residence there and the house became derelict and blew down in the mid 1930s. In front of the house was an extensive flower garden containing many different types of flowers as well as lilac bushes and also a spreading green and yellow leafed plant that covered the lawn. The latter was built up having a stone surround. There was also a large Hawthorn tree of the flowering type and nearby a large hop vine, which was used in preparing yeast for bread making. The property is now overgrown with only the cellar and stones of the house and barn disernable.

The next house west was built by Winslow J., son of Francis Swaine of Purgatory Point, who married Florence, daughter of Captain Joseph Freeman and Carry Swaine. Their children were, Hedley, who married Mary, daughter of Arthur Reynolds, Myra, who married 1st Frank Hutchins, 2nd Roland Wood, Albert, who married Ellen of the U.S.A., Ralph, who married Mary Reid of U.S.A. Winslow J. Swaine took down his father's house at Purgatory Point and built his house on land purchased from Joshua Pierce. He and his wife, Florence, lived in the U.S.A. a number of years before returning and constructing a store across the road from their house. They operated the store and a horse drawn grocery wagon for peddling to nearby communities. He also kept cattle and was noted for his vegetable gardens and cultivating strawberries. Florence was a school teacher before her marriage, having taught at Upper Clyde where she boarded at home of Chris Ryer. On the death of Windlow J. the property was sold to William Monk, who with his wife lived their until their deaths, then the property was sold to Richard Swaine and his family who still reside there.

The next house south was built by Captain John Pierce, who married Hanna King Snow. On their death the property was owned by their son, Joshua, who married Esther, daughter of Howes Smith. Their son, John Howes Pierce married Mary Ryer of Middle Clyde, and moved to the U.S.A. On Joshua's death the house was sold to Arthur, son of James H. and Mary Swaine of Blanche, who married Alice, daughter of Silas Towner. Arthur was drowned and his wife, Alice remained a widow, working at the Grand Hotel in Yarmouth for many years. The house was sold to Harry and Hilda Attwood who remained here only a few years before moving to River Head. The house was sold to John, son of William and Sarah Ann Smith of Blanche. He married Izola Brown of Bear Point. When they moved from Blanche they had two school aged children. Florence, who died when a young girl and Laurie, who married Alice, daughter of William

MacKay of Thomasville who was a school teacher. They lived at Thomasville. John was a fisherman all his life, keeping his boat in the small cove just below his house. This property extends along the shore joining property of Captain William L. Ross. At the shore on the ridge is evidence of early French occupation. On John Smith's death the house was sold to Merlin Williams and his family who still live there.

The next house south across the big bridge (Mac-Dougalls) is a house built by Silas, son of Job Towner. His wife's name was Margaret. Their children were. Alice, who married Arthur Swaine of Blanche; Jane, who died young; Florence, who married Knowles Swaine of West Blanche; Genevieve, who married Archelius Obed of West Blanche; Standford, who married Hattie Lamrock of Villagedale. They had one foster son, Russell Hallett Towner, who now lives in Toronto. Bernard, who married Iza, daughter of John Thomas of Thomasville; their children were Foster, who lives in Halifax and Anna, who first married Ross Perry of Ingomar, and second married Cal Young of Shelburne. Silas Towner went to sea as a young man on sailing vessels to the West Indies. He also had a large barn and kept cattle. As an old man he had a white beard. He was industrious and hard working and much respected in the community having raised a large family. On his death his son Standford and his wife occupied the house. On their death the property was sold to Merlin Williams. The house is now derelict and the property much overgrown. The gardens, fenced cow pastures of Silas Towner have all disappeared and only the shell of the house remains.

The next house north at corner of Silas Towner property on a road running north west for nearly a mile and leads to the house built by Enoch, son of Richard and Thankful Smith, who married Jane, daughter of Howes Snow of Port La Tour. Their children were, Sophia, who first married Elias, son of Thomas Banks, and second married Crowell, son of Benjamin Smith. Benjamin married Louisa, daughter of Arron Spinney, Bigelow, who first married Rebecca, daughter of James Gardner, second married Emma Harris, and third married Sophia, daughter of John Nickerson. Enoch and his family lived here some years before moving to Port La Tour, selling the property to Isaac and Margaret Lyle of West Blanche. Their children were, Edgar and Gladys, who died young, Agnes, who married Corey in U.S.A., Sadie, who married Greenwood of Port Clyde and moved to U.S.A., Mary, who married Gray, Winnie, who married Locke Larkin of Pubnico. Their children were, Ariel, Margaret, Leroy, Malcolm. George, who lived in Shelburne and Arthur, who never married, later occupied the house on his parent's death. On Arthur's death the house was owned by his sister, Winnie, who lived in Pubnico. Winnie having died only recently, the house is owned by her son, Malcolm, who uses it as a summer home. When Isaac Lyle's wife, Margaret (Maggie) who was a Messenger, still lived at Lyle's Old Place, West Blanche, she used to stand on a large flat rock that extended out from the shore and catch by hook and hand line pollock and scrod cod fish, for salting and drying. The rock is today called 'Maggies' Rock'. The Lyles had large well-tended vegetable gardens and some cattle. Near the house were extensive salt marsh meadows, where cranberries grew in abundance. The woodlands extended up and beyond large and small birch hills and north as far as China Meadows.

The Cape Negro School District covered what today is called Cape Negro and also Slateville and the first three houses of Thomasville, being MacKay, Nickerson and Thomas. The history of Thomasville has been well documented in the History of Port Clyde and is not being repeated here, other than to relate that residents of Thomasville have always been closely associated with Cape Negro. The school district extended south to the little bridge. Reynoldscroft was a part of the Upper Port La Tour district. The people of Reynoldscroft were however associated with the Cape Negro Methodist Church and had family plots in the Sea View Cemetery. As the history of Reynoldscroft has not been recorded a summary of some of the inhabitants is listed here.

Immediately across the little bridge, to the west of the road, may be located three overgrown cellars, with only the foundation rocks now discernable. The houses did not survive past 1900 but previously had been homes of the Wilson, Warmer and Brown families. They had cultivated fields and pasture lands that extended to the meadows and west to the brook; all has now returned to nature.

East of the road, across the expanse of salt meadow, just south of Burnt Island, on a point of land lived Russel and his wife, Violet Farmer. They had a large family which have now all moved away. Russell was a hard working man. He had oxen which he used to work for hire by pulling firewood, plowing gardens and other tasks. The Farmers are buried in Hillside Cemetery, Cape Negro. Their property is now derelict and overgrown.

The next house south was owned by Charles Willie Hurbert and his wife, Maude. Their children were Ivy, Clint and Peter. The Huberts had the contract to drive the mail from Cape Negro to Blanche three times a week. At first this was done by horse and wagon and later by car. The car was driven by James Farmer. The Hurberts are buried in Seaview Cemetery at Cape Negro and the property is overgrown and deserted.

The next house south, on west side of the road, was bought by Clinton Hurbert, son of Charles Willie and Maude Hurbert. His wife's name was Florence and they had a large family, who have all moved away, except a son, Manny, who lives in a mobile home across the road from his father's house. Clinton died a number of years ago and his widow, Florence, lives in Yarmouth with a daughter. The house is unoccupied.

The next house south and east of the road was occupied by Thomas, Jr., son of Thomas Ross, Sr., who married Bertha (Sis), daughter of George Lyle of Lyles' Old Place, West Blanche. They had one son, Delbert, who married Annie Symmonds of Clarks Harbour. Their only son, Floyd, married Isobel Brown, a minister's daughter and they lived in Shelburne. When Thomas Ross, Jr. died his widow, Bertha, remarried Captain Samuel Patterson. Delbert Ross and his wife, Annie, lived in the house until they died, then it was sold to George O'Connell.

The next house south was built by William Patterson, who also operated a store by the road. He also had a wharf where his vessels could discharge supplies for the store. His son, Captain Samuel Patterson, married the widow, Bertha Ross and lived in the house until they both died. A daughter, Effie, was the second wife of Bradford Lowe, who was a widower with children. I have not ascertained the present owners of this property. The store has been taken down, the house is presently for sale.

The next house south was built by Captain William L. Ross. When he moved to Cape Negro the house was sold to Bradford Lowe of Cape Sable Island. William L. Ross and Bradford Lowe sailed together on vessels to the West Indies. Bradford Lowe was married to Anne ????????? Their children were, Grant, Kenneth, Lorne, Thomas, Fernwood and Margarette. Since Bradford Lowe's death the house has been sold several times.

The next house south was built by Levi Reynolds. The geneology of the Reynolds' family is recorded elsewhere in this book, all being descendants of John Reynolds, the founder of Reynoldscroft. Levi's son, Robert, lived in his father's house for a period and has recently built a new home across the road. Another son, Norman, bought the store of Winslow J. Swaine and rebuilt it as a house across from his father's; this house burned some years ago.

The next house east, down the roadway to the shore of Eel Bay, a house built by John Bethel, which was later owned by Grant Lowe and his wife, Mildred, who was a daughter of Geodfrey and Elsie MacKay of Thomasville. She was a school teacher; they had no children. The house burned some years ago. Also by the shore was a house owned by John Howard Reynolds. His family have moved to other areas and house is now occupied by Donald Lyle and his family.

South down the road from Levi Reynolds' house, the road was straight and on both sides of road was heavy growth of spruce trees; this was called Eli's Woods, making the narrow gravel road dark and scarey at night and provided an excellent excuse for young men to offer to escort the young ladies home after church or a pie sale.

The next house south was built by Arthur Reynolds. The Geneology of this family is continued in the records of John Reynolds in this book. His descendants live in the U.S.A. but his daughter, Mary Swaine and niece, Virginia, make regular visits here in the summer. The house has been remodeled and only recently sold.

Good Days and Old Ways

When the New Englanders came, they first built houses some of which were of logs but others brought on their vessels timbers, lumber and windows from their old home. In very short time they were reasonably comfortable having also brought with them their cooking pots, looms, spinning wheels and other equipment used for country living As most occupied land that had been cleared and cultivated by the French, in the matter of a season they could grow a garden, make and store hay and be reasonably well organized.

Most of the men possessed small boats that they could row, possibly similar to the type we now call a skiff, about 16 to 18 feet long. They did not have to row far from shore to catch fish and even the few that had much larger boats and sailing vessels did not remain over night on the fishing grounds. The men rowed out fishing in the morning, baited and set one or two hand lines, which had sometimes more than one baited hook to a line. They would hand line fish from first light of morning until noon or a little after and return home at mid afternoon, beach and clean out the boat, split and salt the fish, retaining the livers in a barrel for the oil, which was used in lamps. If they had nets set they would be made from cotton twine, and nets attached to ropes. The nets were anchored in place by killocks. These were made by hand from a large oblong rock with curved wooden base and two green saplings which extended from base to be tied at top to grip rock in place. These could be made any size by employing a rock heavy enough to anchor what ever you wished to hold. Nets were looked once, sometimes twice daily, the herrings or mackerel taken out and net cleaned of sea weed and debris. A great disaster struck when a seal, usually chasing herring would become entangled in the net, destroying the meshes and requiring weeks to repair the damage. On occasion the net may become so full of fish the bobbers could not hold up the net and the net would sink, becoming all balled up and a terrible mess and sometimes resulting in it having to be removed, taken ashore, dried by spreading on the field and repaired. Herring and mackerel were salted in barrels and sold as wet salted fish. The fish caught by the hand line, after a few days of being salted were taken out and placed on somewhere flat with a weight to press out the water. Again in a few days they would be placed each morning out on fish flakes to dry. If it was very hot in summer they had to be turned or they would become sun burned, the fat in skin spoiled making them useless. Therefore they were turned several times a day, until they became dry and very hard. They were then piled end for end into kintels, which were tied with twine and ready to be sold. When the men were out fishing the women and the children, if at home, went to the shore and spread and turned the fish. Should the fog start to come in, they would run collect the fish, as the salt absorbed the moisture and the fish could be spoiled. The heads and offel from cleaning and gutting fish was usually spread on the hay field to make grass grow. Excess herring was also used as fertilizer.

When cotton nets were used it was necessary to remove them from the water, spread on the field to dry in the sun, remove any sea weed and debris, then tan the nets. A tan pot was filled with water which was boiled by making a wood fire under the pot. When boiling, kutch, purchased from the fish dealers, was put in the water. It was like a brown dye. In early times tree buds that had white sap on them was collected and boiled and this was used, but discontinued once kutch was brought from the West Indies.

After tanning the nets were spread on the field to dry. Any holes were repaired and rope surrounds checked before resetting. Nets, if left in water over Sunday, were tied up with twine so they would catch no fish, which would spoil because nets were not looked on Sunday.

Lobsters were caught for home use only, by the first settlers. Not until well along in the 1800s when tin cans were introduced and the lobster factorys organized was lobster fishing made a commercial enterprise. At first all size lobsters were taken, from Jumbo to Jinks, and this practice continued until along in the early 1900s. Just before the first war, the government issued instructions and a gauge for the size of lobster to be retained. Each boat had a brass gauge and the lobster shell was measured from the eye to the bottom of the shell. This taking of adult lobsters only, more or less was the end of the local lobster factory.

Lobster pots were constructed of wood with the three or four bow trap which are still used today for that purpose. The heads were of knitted mesh from twine, ballast being beach rocks, a wooden spindle in the center for bait. The bottom runners, the bows and a lot of the bottom cross sections were hand hewn from saplings where as today lathes from the mills are available. Some times a young man just starting out would have pots completely made from hand hewn saplings. The lobster pots, as today, had wooden bouys, of different colors and stripes, for identification of the owner. As the fisherman rowed out to pull his pots, there was a definite limit as to how far he could go in a day. Often certain rocks and shoals were reserved for certain individuals, such as Uncle John always set two pots at that rock. This casual ownership was usually respected. A man rowing to attend his lobster pots would have a string of 35 or 40 or in some cases possibly 45 pots, which he pulled and re-baited by hand. From such an undertaking he would earn possibly sixty five dollars a lobster season, which would be considered a fair living.

Herring from the nets was not only salted in barrels for sale, but was placed in barrels, with very little salt, for lobster bait. The fishermen used skulpins and other cull fish for bait when available but had to have 8 or more barrels of what was called salt bait for those times fresh bait was not available, usually in the winter. Because this salt bait was not heavily salted, in the heat of the summer some of the fish oil melted out as well as the fish itself became partially rotted, resulting in a very unpleasant odor. The fishermen made bait bags which were knitted into mesh from twine or if available old crocus bags were cut up into suitable size pieces and sewn into bags. These bait bags had to be filled by hand and to remove the terrible odor from ones hands was practically impossible. A person with only a drop of this on the clothing, could be smelled all over the room. Housewives went to great lengths to eradicate this smell from being brought home to their kitchens, not always successfully. Not only the lobster was attracted to the bait on the pots, but crabs, eels co-hogs and sand fleas as well. They often ate the bait, resulting in a poor catch. The fishermen used wooden plugs to put in the claws to prevent the lobsters from damaging one another. They were then held in a floating wooden crate which was near the landing where he kept his boat.

The Fisherman

The fisherman as a rule rowed his boat, but usually had a main sail and,depending on the size and shape of the boat, may also have a jib. These he would use when returning home.He would put up the sail and using an oar for a tiller to steer, with good wind sail up harbour and home. If it was a head wind then he had to row and buck the wind.

Shortly after the first war, the Acadia engine, the old Make and Break, Put-put-put, became more available. The Make and Break was a one cylinder engine that was started by kicking a pin in the fly wheel or spinning the fly wheel by hand. These engines were of very simple construction, having very few movable parts to break down and were easy to maintain and repair. With the Acadia engine, boats became larger and distances travelled to the fishing grounds became further. Eventually fresh fishing was possible as the fisherman could fish all day and then take his fresh catch to the fish dealer. In this area the dealer was at Seal Point, Cape Negro Island or North West Harbour. At one time Reuben Smith bought fish and lobsters for the Seal Point operation and the produce was collected by truck. The Acadia engine was eventually replaced by the car engine and the industry has progressed to the many machines and equipment of today.

The fisherman was engaged in his trade of fishing in summer and lobstering in spring and fall but in winter his efforts were directed not only to replacing and repairing lobster pots, knitting heads and bags which was usually evening work, but the year's wood supply. At Blanche,wood was cut on near by wood lots and the distance to bring it home was reasonably short. At Cape Negro many of the wood lots extended to Towner's Bunch and beyond, and the men went there and cut birch and other wood. If they did not have a horse or ox they would engage someone with one to pull wood to their home. To go to Towner's Bunch it was necessary in late January to cut brush or limbs from evergreen trees and brush the tracks of the wood road whereby ice would built up thick enough to carry the animal and the wagon load of wood. This was not always successful, resulting in the animal falling through the ice and becoming mired in the swamp, resulting in unloading the wood, extracting the animal, moving the sled or wagon to higher ground and then reloading the wood. Eventually, however, the fire wood would all be collected at home and then it was necessary with a hand saw, later a Swede saw, or cross cut saw for large pieces to cut wood into blocks. The wood was then split and stacked in a pile to dry. In summer when dry it was carried into a building out of the weather. In later years Joseph Arey and his son, Walter, had a saw engine and they would saw the wood into blocks for five dollars. This was a great help. Wood splits quite easily if there is frost in the blocks. Most fishermen obtained a year's supply of wood in winter when they were not that busy, and when the fishing season started they did not have to concern themselves with getting firewood. Storing the dry wood in the building was usually done by the women and the children old enough to help. Boys went fishing with their fathers in the summer at an early age, usually by 12 years a boy knew most of the chores required.

Another chore the fisherman had to perform each summer, usually in August, was hay making. A supply of hay had to be put into the barn for winter feed for the milk cow, the ox and other cattle. The fisherman would mow the hay with a hand sythe in the evening. The next morning the women and children would spread the hay with a fork so it would dry. If the fog came in or when night fell, before the dew came, the hay was raked and put into hay cocks. During the night the hay would sweat which helped the drying process. This procedure was carried out morning and night usually for three days. On the last day the hay was turned at mid day by a wooden hay rake, then in the late afternoon again raked and cocked and carried into the hay mow of the barn. If an animal was available the hay would be loaded on a wagon and taken in and pitched into the mow. If no animal or wagon was available, it was polled to the barn. Two smooth poles were pushed under the hay cocks and a person on each side would carefully lift the hay cock and carry it stretcher like into the barn. When salt meadow hay was cut this method of using hay poles was used to transport the hay off the salt meadow before the tide came in, as the salt meadow would not support a wagon or animal. The salt hay was usually poled to a wagon, then taken home and spread near the house so the women could process it until ready to be put in the barn. When making hay in the hot days of August, which were called locally Dog Days, making and storing hay was a hot task and a cool drink was always most welcome. Having no soft drinks in those days, the man swinging the sythe usually had under a nearby spruce tree in the shade a jug of "Switchel". The following is Haymakers Switchel: 1 gallon of water, 2 cups brown sugar, 1 cup mollasses, 1½ cups vinegar, 1 teaspoon ginger. A very refreshing drink. Sometimes this was kept lowered in the well on a rope so it would be very cool.

Some fishermen did more gardening and farming than others, but all had to do some gardening for the staple vegetables for winter. Usually the potatoes were plowed in by oxen in the spring. The furrow was made by a plow, one row filled with rock weed and the next furrow the children would drop the potato seed, then the furrow was covered and the process repeated for another row. The main crop of potatoes were grown in this method. However, some made hot beds of eel grass for potatoes, usually used for early and new potatoes. One could collect the potatoes by reaching in the eel grass with your hand and extracting the large potatoes without damaging the plant. Some men hoed the potatoes in the summer. Some others had a strong wife or older children that did it. The summer vegetable garden, once plowed and planted, was usually the woman's responsibility to the greatest extent. Rock weed was used as fertilizer for planting potatoes, but the cow and pig manure was used for the vegetable garden. The horse manure was usually spread on the hay fields as it was not considered suitable for gardens. The manure pits onside of the barn, were the result of cleaning out the animal stalls in the winter. These pits received, besides manure, all the old hay and straw, pumpkin vines, and other discarded vegetable matter, and were the fore runner of the now, compost heap.

The pig or pigs were kept in log pens and usually fed by the women and children. The slaughter in fall was done by several men, who in turn helped one another. The pig was stuck with a knife in the throat, (later years shot with a rifle in the head). The blood was saved in a basin for processing into sausages etc. The pig was placed in a wooden trough and boiling water poured over it. It was covered and allowed to steam, then the pig was hung up by its hind legs, usually to a nearby apple tree, and the bristles scraped off the skin. The pig was gutted, saving the intestines for sausage coverings. They were later soaked in salt water and cleaned. The pig was allowed to hang and cool for 2 or 3 days then cut up. The hams were salted and later processed with brown sugar and salt peter and then dried or smoked. The belly fat was rendered by putting it into water and boiling it on the stove. When the fat melted the water was drained off, resulting in pure white fat. This was packed into earthen crocks and lightly salted, then placed in a cool cellar for winter use. The pig meat was eaten fresh and the rest salted for winter in pork barrels kept in the shed. The head, feet and other bits and pieces were processed into head cheese, which could be kept for a month or so in a cool cellar. The pig's bladder was blown up and dried and used by the children to play with like a balloon. Everything on the pig was used and processed one way or another, except the ears and they were usually fed to the dog.

Some fishermen kept more cattle than others, but all kept one or two cows for milk for the family. In the summer the cows were milked in the morning and turned loose in the road. All day they would graze in any direction, travelling a number of miles in a day. In late afternoon some young person would have to go find the cows and bring them home. Usually one watched in the morning to see which direction they went, or if you met someone walking on the road you would ask if they saw the cows. Once you knew the direction, one would travel along and listen for the bells. Each householder knew the sound of their own cow bells. With this method you could usually track them down, but it may mean going across salt meadow and through alder bushes to collect them together. Sometimes this took a long time and before the cows came home it was dark, or nearly so resulting in taking a kerosene lantern to milk the cows. The milking of cows was almost exclusively done by women. Some men might learn to milk when young, but they would be on the fishing grounds when the cow was milked. They would possibly resume the practice when they were an old man, or be forced to do it if the woman was sick. The cow was kept in the barn at night and milked in the morning before being turned into the road again, repeating the process. The barn was usually cleaned out by the older children. If they neglected the chore, they heard about it when mother went to do the evening milking and were possibly sent with a lantern out to the barn to do the neglected chore. A new born calf was allowed to nurse the cow for three days to permit it to obtain what was called the Beaslings. The first milk contains the necessary elements that protect the calf from some diseases, such as scoures. Then the calf was fed from a pail, which was called weaning the calf. The person feeding the calf put their finger in the calf's mouth and, as the calf sucked the finger, put its mouth into the pail, thus teaching it to drink. Calves were kept in a pen in the barn and not turned out of doors until several months old. At 6 weeks a calf could be butchered for veal, if the owner did not wish to raise it as a heifer or ox.

    A fresh cow (one with new calf) would give a water pail, 10 or more quarts, of milk each milking, morning and night. The milk was placed into creamers, which were tall tin pails with spigot at the bottom. The creamer was lowered into the well on a rope or placed in the cellar where it was cool. When the butter fat had risen on the milk, which usually took about 12 hours, the skimmed milk was drained from the spigot at the bottom and then the thick cream collected. If a creamer was not available, the milk was placed in earthen bowls and allowed to cool, then the butter fat was skimmed off the top with a tin-creamer, (a large flat scoop with little holes). The cream was kept in crocks until it was placed in a churn and made into butter. In the summer when the cows gave a lot of milk from eating fresh grass the extra butter that was not used was salted into crocks and kept in the cellar for winter. Most families had several crocks of salted butter put aside by fall for winter use. The skim milk was used to feed the family, the calves, and any extra was given as swill to the pig. Sour milk was put in a large pot and set on back of the stove and if not boiled turned into curds and whey, now called Cottage Cheese. If the curds were properly salted and processed they could be kept a long time in the cool cellar, and the children usually ate curds with molasses as a sweetener. Buttermilk and skim milk were used for baking cakes, breads and delicious hot buttermilk biscuits. Hot biscuits and molasses or rhubarb sauce was a children's treat. In later years hand operated cream separators came into use. They consisted of a large bowl with a collection of skimmers which milk went through, with milk coming out one spigot and the cream the other. It was operated by a large heavy crank handle, which had to be turned at a certain speed for the bell to ring. If it was not turned fast enough the seperation of the cream was not satisfactory.

The wives of the fishermen and the women of the household besides drying fish, making hay, tending the vegetable garden and milking cows, had a separate routine that followed usually like this as weather permitted. Monday was wash day, Tuesday was ironing, Wednesday mending, Thursday weaving, spinning or quilting. Friday was bake day, Saturday scrub the floors. Washing was an all-day operation, especially if quilts had to be washed which happened at least twice a year. The night before the older children, the man if he was agreeable or the woman herself, drew from the well many pails of water and filled the containers to be put on the wood stove to make hot water, plus the pails and tubs that contained the cold water later used for rinsing. The wood fire was started very early to heat the water in morning to facilitate an early start. The wash tub, which was a large wooden (later galvanized) tub was set up on a bench or two chairs, filled with warm water and the clothes to be washed were soaped (the soap was made from pigs fat and wood ashes, but later soap was available in stores), then scrubbed on the wash board. A wash board was a flat wooden frame with a metal section with ridges in it where by rubbing the clothes were scrubbed. When properly washed and rinsed the clothes were hung on a rope line or spread on nearby bushes to dry. Clothes pegs were made of straight pieces of wood, later spring clothes pegs were available. The rope line which would stretch and sag had one or more poles near the middle and as the rope sagged it was necessary to adjust the line to keep the clothes from dragging on the ground. Quite often white clothes were left out all night in dew to whiten. Linen flour bags were often bleached in this way before being processed into kitchen curtains, bed sheets and little girls' bloomers. If the weather was fine the clothes would all dry and at evening be taken into the house and after the cow was milked and supper cleared the clothes could be folded and aired behind the wood stove if necessary. The following day some time within the schedule of children, fish, cows and hay the woman heated usually three sad irons on the wood stove and ironed the shirts, cotton dresses and anything that had wrinkles. Aprons, table clothes, curtains and collars of Sunday shirts were starched. Starch was prepared by cooking white flour and water with a little salt and thinning with warm water then soaking the part of the clothing to be starched. This method had good results except it would mildew if stored in a damp cupboard. Later commercial starch was available that contained blue granules and was easier to prepare. The next days of mending, weaving, quilting and etc. followed the usual process, but Friday's baking was slightly different than today. The first settlers grew hop vines and hops were used to make yeast for bread making. Later commercial yeast became available. Bread was mixed or done up in the evening. The big pot or bowl containing the sponge was covered by a blanket and set by the wood stove over night. In the morning the sponge was done over into loaves, allowed to rise again and then baked before noon, with good greasing of pig fat on hard crust while the bread was still hot. Most women tried to plan so they made bread only once a week, which meant they had to make from 8 to 15 loaves of bread and buns depending on the size of the family. While the bread was baking usually the woman prepared several pies for the oven for when the bread was finished. Besides bread, pies, loaves of cake and biscuits were made usually for a week, plus molasses cookies and sugar cookies if the sugar was available. By cooking ahead on Friday the woman had only to prepare vegetables and cook meals and possibly the odd pan of hot biscuits. Unless company came then an extra pie or something would be prepared. In some poorer families it was not uncommon for the wife to rise early and bake a pan of buns for the children's breakfast, or to fry some of the bread dough like pancakes to provide a good meal before they went off to school. On Saturday the older children would clean and scrub the floors of the bed chambers upstairs and the women would scrub the floors down stairs. If the floor had painted canvas it was quite easy but if only rag mats they all had to be taken out of doors and cleaned and the floor scrubbed before they were brought back again. Usually the door step was scrubbed off as the last chore.

In the summer months the women and children had to find time for berry picking. Blueberries, gooseberries, raspberries, blackberries and cranberries were the usual ones gathered. Those family members that could be spared from the operation of the home would early in the morning walk up Swaine's Road or John Seamon's Road to the blueberry barrens taking with them a number of Indian baskets and picking tins. An adult could pick 10 to 12 quarts of blueberries in a day. In later years the blueberies could be sold for about 4-5 cents a quart and put into crates of 32 quarts and shipped on train to Boston . The women used the blueberries fresh for pies but also had to preserve many bottles, if available, otherwise crocks sealed with wax, and stored in the cellar for winter. The blueberries were stewed down (boiled) with enough sugar to keep them from spoiling, and were very nice in mid-winter. The other berries were picked in season much the same way and then preserved and processed for winter. Cranberries were dried out of doors on a blanket in the sun and some families would have a ferkin or half barrel at the start of winter. Crab apples made good jelly and were preserved whole with sugar and spice and also sealed in crocks or bottles.

The women made a lot of the clothing. The first settlers had looms and wove cloth for making shirts and other clothing. They also knit long drawers for the men and boys, long socks, sweaters and different kinds of mittens. Sewing and knitting was usually done in the evenings by the light of the oil lamp, while the children did their school sums on the nearby table. Later years when sewing machines of the treadle type became common, sewing became much faster and easier, and clothes could be cut down and altered which made hand-me-downs practically new clothes.

    The older boys, after the first fall of snow, had rabbit snares set, usually along edges of swamps, where runs were easily located. The snares were usually looked or visited on the way to or returning from school. If successful the rabbits were skinned and cleaned and hung up to freeze, they were eaten in stews, stuffed and baked and occasionally fried, but once 20 or more were accumulated, they were usually cut up and boiled. The meat was taken off the bones, put through the meat grinder, ground apples, suet, raisins, spices and molasses added and the large pot cooked on the back of the stove for a day or more which resulted in a number of crocks of mincemeat, which was used for pies, tarts and turn overs. Often if a deer was killed some of the meat was added to rabbit meat and processed the same way.

    Most cellars in the fall were stocked with some or all of these items. It depended of course on the industry of the whole family, how much was grown, picked, processed and stored for winter use. Potatoes, carrots, turnips, onions, pumpkins and squash, dried beans, containers of pickled beet root, sweet and also sour cucumber pickles, green tomato chow chow, jams, jellies, preserved berries, citron, crocks of salt butter, crocks of pig fat (lard), beef tallow, eggs preserved in water glass or heavy salted water, peeled, sliced and dried apples. A large jug of vinegar which would contain a mother, the mother had to be fed to keep it producing vinegar, usually by putting in juice from sour apples. The first settlers used the sap from birch trees. It was necessary to have a large quantity of vinegar as its use was the easiest method of preserving food. In the odd cellar may also be found a jug of dandelion or choke cherry wine, kept strictly for medicinal purposes, of course.

The shed near the back door usually contained barrels of salted pork, firkins of salt herrings and mackerel, salted whole scrod cod or haddock and possibly some salted beef or deer meat. The salt dry fish were stored in the hay mow, as the dry hay kept the salt of the fish from absorbing moisture, which would cause it to spoil.

The first few warm days of March heralded the beginning of spring cleaning. Starting upstairs bedrooms all the wood work, ceilings and floors were scribbed. The rope beds would have fresh hay put in the straw ticks, making them nice and high until it became packed down. The feather ticks were taken out of doors put over the bars of the fence in the sun to air. Every room in the house had a thorough going over, all curtains washed, restarched, ironed and rehung at the clean windows. When possible some painting and papering was undertaken.

The old outside privy toilet, or as called locally the "Back House", was not overlooked. It received its spring cleaning as well, with possibly some left over paint and paper from the house. The privy toilet was a small wooden building over a dug pit, the most common type being a two holer. The seat was constructed of wood and had two holes as seats with fitted wooden covers. No back house was complete without the out-dated Eatons catalogue hanging from a nail by a piece of cod twine. A cold drafty experience in the winter

In the summer when the housewife became tired of a diet of baked, boiled, fried fish and also chowder, she could always send one of the children off to dig a couple of pails of clams, which would be turned into fritters, chowder or a type of clam casserole baked in the oven. When tired of this, one could chop the head off one of the older hens that was past laying, or go onto one of the islands and get a few pails of gulls eggs which could be turned into several interesting dishes. Therefore with a little imagination the diet could be quite varied. In the winter this was harder to achieve. After the salt fish, pork, rabbit stews and etc. for a variety or in desperation if the larder was practically empty. The staple was "Scouse" great pots of hot steaming scouse greeted the children when they returned from school. Scouse was made by frying salt pork scraps and onions, then adding water, diced potatoes, turnip and carrots. When cooked thicken with flour or add dumplings. With the sailing ships trading with the West Indies some of the nearby stores from time to time had a supply of Tamerons. This was a very tart fruit that was similar to pressed figs. Tamerons were stewed and eaten as a dessert or made into a drink in the summer. Tamerons have a distinctive taste; once tasted never forgotten.

The New Englanders at first taught their children at home. Once a school was built and a school master installed the children attended school which may be several miles from where they lived. School hours were usually from 9 in the morning until 4 in the afternoon. After the walk home the children usually had chores, such as taking into the house the supply of fire wood, a number of pails of water from the well, cleaning the barn and putting fresh bedding down for cattle if it had not been done in the morning. Then someone had to go find and bring home the cows. After supper there was school home work and most everyone would be in bed and lights blown out by 9 or 15 to 10 at night. Morning came early for the fisherman, usually 3:30 or 4 in the morning and usually by 6 or shortly after the household was up and active. The cattle were seen to , extra wood or water if necessary was brought in. If time permitted a trip to the rabbit snares and then the walk to school. Summer holidays had several added chores, potatoes to hoe, garden weeded, hay to make, help the father with the boat, the salting of fish and in spare time different kinds of berries had to be picked. By 6 years of age children had chores. Over the years these chores increased until at about 15 a youth could perform most of the adult tasks. Some boys went as seamen at 14 or 15, and girls hired out as "Serving Girls" (household help) from the age of 13 onwards. Girls often married at 16 and raised families, their husbands being 17 or 18 and working as full grown men.

When spring arrived one could expect to shortly receive a visit from a peddler. These peddlers, both men or women would come on foot, walking from one community to the other, with large packs on their backs. When they came to the door, they were invited in. Putting their pack on the kitchen floor, they would open it and spread the items about for the household to look at. They had print goods, needles, thread, variety of buttons, some novelty items of fancy nature, linen goods such as hand towels, ladies' cotton stockings, elastic in different sizes and color. After a little bargaining the purchases were made and possibly tea or a meal was offered; at night time a bed would be offered as well. These peddlers made their rounds usually at the same time each year. You got to know them, and they arranged their schedule so they arrived to spend the night at the same friendly household each year. Besides the variety of peddlers selling different things there was the visit from the organ grinder, who had an organ that was operated by turning a crank. He usually had a monkey and you gave the penny to the monkey and he played a tune. There were also the tramps, some good ones, others not so good. The good ones were known and may split wood or do some simple chore for a meal. Otherwise they were given a cup of tea at the kitchen table if they looked safe, but if rough looking, they sat on the doorstep and were given tea and cookies, cake or pie what ever was ready. Once these were passed out to him the hook was put on the screen door, until he departed. Most of the tramps were professional tramps, travelled from place to place and were harmless. Given a cup of tea they went on their way and not seen until making their rounds again the following year. In later years the peddlers were replaced by Norman Nelson who had a truck with a large box, and the wooden shelves were crammed with rubber boots, stockings, bolts of cloth, table oil cloth, many other items. He usually came in the fall when all the children needed lumberman rubbers for winter. Women could hook rag mats with flowers or other designs on them and he traded table oil cloth, curtain material and such things for them.

    Since early times doctors or mid-wives have been available first at Barrington, then later the Drs. Densmores, first father then later the son at Port Clyde. The doctor was not called, however, until all the old natural remedies had failed, which meant that person was very sick or dying before the doctor was called or arrived. The usual childhood catchable diseases such as measles, mumps, chicken pox, whooping cough, scarlet fever and pink eye made their rounds periodically. There were also the more dreaded diseases of small pox that came on the sailing ships quite often from the West Indies; diphtheria, which was also a dreaded disease and took many lives. Consumption, which is tuberculosis caused many deaths especially in young adults. Cases at home were not isolated and the other occupants of the house were exposed to the disease. Another problem that claimed many young women was childbirth. Deaths attributed to this in many cases were from neglect or improper care, from the old records it seems that retained afterbirth or hemorrhage were the two main problems.

Some of the problem was aggravated by the woman's Puritan upbringing ond outlook, or modesty. Most babies were delivered under the blanket, resulting in the mid-wife not being aware of what was happening, and preventing proper examination. Pneumonia which was called the 'Old Person's Friend' usually was cause of the death of the elderly. Once injured or becoming ill and confined to bed the natural process was pneumonia and death.

It was somewhat of a common practice of those with horse and wagon to take several wooden pails or even larger quantity of salt herring and salt dried fish and go inland to Upper Clyde to MacGills, MacKays or Bowers and trade the salt fish for apples and other vegetables. Sometimes one could even trade for a haunch of moose meat. This was usually done late in the fall when supplies for winter were being stored.

The first cars at Cape Negro in the early 1920s were brought from the United States by Edwin Smith, Lloyd Swaine and Willie Matherson. The first cars were open or touring cars, with canvas top that went up and curtains with izenglas windows clipped around to close in the car in bad weather. At one time Willie Matherson had a Stanley Steamer that was rather noisy and certainly different. A few years later Model T's and Model A's appeared. They were quite reliable, some what difficult to choke manually and turn crank to start. Some times the car engine would kick back and injure your arm if you were cranking to start it. Later in 1930s cars became more common and even the women took up driving. Some early drivers were Lottie Thomas, Verna Obed, Hazel Swaine and others. Some of the early cars had solid rubber tires. Later tubes and tires and wire wheels were introduced. The tubes required constant patching due mainly to the rough gravel roads, and changing tires was a common occurrence.

To the best of my knowledge one of the first radios in the area was a box type, one with earphones brought from Boston to Captain Joseph Freeman Swaine. In a few years radios with large horns appeared. Over a period of time the horns became cabinets, then part of the radio itself. All the first radio's operated on 12 volt wet car batteries plus other large dry cell batteries all hooked together. The wet cell batteries could be recharged at Mr. Lloyd Swaine delco, but the dry cells had to be replaced. The first radio station heard in this area was Boston. In between the voices fading in and out one could listen to a church service from Tremont Temple in Boston, or Uncle Elmer's request program, which was a choir and sang hymns, and later came Bert Pearl and the Happy Gang. Before the coming of the radio the entertainment in the home was sing songs around the parlour organ. The gramaphone was operated by winding it up with a crank and putting on a round cylinder record or later a flat celluoid one. The music came from the large horn on the top and it was necessary to change the needles frequently. One of the first makes of gramaphone being "His Masters Voice" - RCA Victor and trade mark was a white dog looking into a horn of a gramaphone.

Each community or school district was responsible for shovelling the snow in winter and keeping the roads open. After a snow storm the men cleared the road in their district. If there was an emergency at night and one needed the doctor, it was necessary to go around and wake up the neighbours to secure enough men to clear the road to enable the doctor to get through. When the doctor came by horse and sleigh it was somewhat easier, although the horse could not get through very deep snow drifts. In later years when he came by car, the roads had to be cleared. If the doctor living at Port Clyde was called to Baccaro, all the communities on that route would have to turn out and clear the road. There was no financial renumeration for shoveling snow or fighting forest fires until after the second war. It was a community responsibility.

The residents of Cape Negro had educational opportunities not available in some other country areas. John Matherson, Sr. had attended the Music Conservatory in Boston and was a qualified music teacher. He returned home to Cape Negro and taught many in this area to read music, whereas before they played by ear. The Cape Negro church had a library, which was open during the period of Sunday School. They had possibly a hundred books of different types and variety of subjects on loan to local residents. Also the local school received each fall, a wooden trunk of books under the travelling library scheme. The books were kept for a year then sent to the next school when fresh supply received. These books were available to local residents.

Hand Ringer, Scrub Board, Creamer, Churn, Butter Bowl, Butter Print, Butter Crock, Sad Iron, Vinegar Jug, Molasses Jug, Chair with Rope Bottom, Chair with Rush Bottom.

Gramaphone with horn, muzzel loader gun, butter crock, kerosene lamp, two women's rockers.

Alladin Kerosene Lamp

The grindstone turned by handle while another person sharpened sythes, axes, knives and other tools. Stone was kept wet by pouring on small amounts of water.

Treadle Sewing Machine

Horse or Ox single furrow plow

An Organ

Spinning Wheel & Wool Skeiner

Ruby Smith and fine pair of oxen.

Herbert Thomas and Reuben Smith with load fire wood at Blanche.

The Myricks poling hay.

Wagon load of hay.

John Smith, Kenneth Thomas, Jonn Matherson, Sr. and Jr. unloading herring.

"Now or Then"

You often hear the old folk say,
   Our time was better than to-day.
But gaze with me into the past,
   And see which places are first and last.

Milk, butter, cottage cheese and more,
   May now be purchased at the store.
Gone are the milking twice a day,
   Creamers, churns and making hay.

Grandma started at the dawn,
   To see that water would be drawn.
Heated, poured into the tub,
   With lye soap and washboarad to scrub.

Rinced and hung out in the sun,
   The work on wash day still half done.
For "sad irons", sad indeed were they,
   And wrinkles hard to iron away.

The "wash day blues" we now can beat,
   With washers new and driers heat.
While synthetics, no-iron clothes and knits,
   Cuts ironing time to little bits.

In winter ice was cut and packed,
   With sawdust tight in every crack.
No fridge, or freezer, so twas nice,
   To store the perishables on ice.

At sundown outdoor work must cease,
   But still for busy hands no peace.
By lantern men worked in the barn,
   And lamps lit women spinning yarn.

While round the table bent small heads,
   Before they scurried off to beds.
In lamplight's glow to work or play,
   And study lessons for next day.

No recorders, stereo or TV,
   To pass an evening like you and me.
The gramaphone it must be cranked, you know,
   Or listen to the battery radio.

I leave to you the choice you'd make,
   But as for me there's no mistake.
I'll happily put my pen away,
   And count the joys we have to-day.

                By Mrs. Walter Young

The boat Emerson Thomas built in his barn and launched into Eel Bay. Emerson and Lewis Brown at Blanche Wharf.

Daniel Mathersons House Cape Negro.

John Matherson Sr. & Jr. and unnamed youth, gutting fish.

Mildred Cameron, Millie Slate, Lerman and Fiedel Thomas, Allie and Sandford Slate, Monte Slate.

Winslow, Florence, Flossie, Allan, Lloyd Swaine and Nancy.

Olson Perry and Reuben Smith loading telephone cable into perry boat, prior to laying cable to Half Moons Fog Alarm.

Reuben Smith with two stakers ankle deep in herring

Savages Fog Alarm Jesse Obed, Elizabeth Drew, Odessa and Verna Obed, George Drew.

Blanche School and upstair Chapel.

Blanche School and Chapel.

When the first settlers established their homes in this area, they were often at some distance from their neighbours. During this early period, teaching of the children was carried out in the home by the parents as best they could. As more homes were built and a semblance of villages emerged, schools were built, usually of log construction. The school teacher was a man with varying qualifications for regular periods. Most of these more or less temporary teachers worked under the half board, half pay system. Most did not tarry long in any one place, therefore the education was sporadic. About 1835 the Government in Halifax decided to first license well-educated ladies of good character. This brought into the system a more permanent and dedicated base for the development of the educational system in the smaller communities. With the licensing of teachers also came grants which were used as part of payment of teachers salaries, eliminating the part board element and putting Teachers on a more professional footing. The remainder of the Teachers salary was raised through collection of direct school tax, and raising money through public Fétes. School Inspectors were appointed by Government and the system developed as we know it today.

The first school at Blanche was built in a clearing near Jimmy's Old Road. The building was placed there because the majority of the people at that time lived at West Side of Blanche and Jimmy's Old Place.The village of Blanche developed later. How long this school operated I have not determined, but by the mid 1850's the population had increased at the Blanche Village and a more convenient site for the new school chosen.

The new school, built in late 1850, was of timber construction and finished plaster walls. A two storey building with school downstairs and the chapel up-stairs. The deed for this new school was processed on May 19th. 1862, and indicates the building was already constructed. The deed was issued by William Swaine,Sr. and his wife Rebecca, to Thomas O.G. Thomas, Knowles Swaine and Harvey Slate, trustees.They granted the land on which the school house is now erected and built, measuring fifty five square yards, fronting on the main road for the purpose of a school house, and also to accomodate the inhabitants religiously. Where they can have a Sabbath School, the preaching of God's Holy Word, Prayer Meetings, Class Meetings, and other such services as the Wesleyan Methodists may wish to hold, providing always that such services shall not interfere with the day school. The deed is signied by William Swaine and Rebecca Swaine and Witnessed by Martin Thomas and Seth Nickerson.

Except for special prayer meetings or services the regular service was supplied by the minister from Upper Port LaTour who came usually once a month on a regular basis. He would usually have a service at Cape Negro before or after being at Blanche. Regular church services were held until 1965, when the chapel was closed for regular services. The chapel is still maintained by the residents of the community and a heritage service is held every summer.

Each School district had two or more Trustees and a secretary --treasurer appointed by the tax payers in the district. In the Spring the Trustees would receive a number of applications seeking a teaching post. Some of the applicants would hold permanent teaching license and other may have a permissive license only. The latter would be permitted to teach in small schools for a year or two to obtain the funds whereby they could then attend Normal Teachers College, in Truro. The Trustees would review the applicants and if their present teacher was not staying on for another term, which most did not, the Trustees would choose a teacher. The Secretary would advise her of the decision and the details of the school, the wages and the availability of suitable boarding places in the community. If the teacher confirmed acceptance of the post the date of arrival would be anxiously awaited and the boarding place made ready.

The teacher arrived the first week of September, and would live as a member of the family at the chosen boarding place. I may note it was considered something of a status symbol to board the School Teacher in a small community. The teacher, when not engaged in her school activities took part in the social life of the community, which may consist of skating on nearby frozen ponds, trips in small boats to neighbouring communities, and attending church services, Temperance Meetings, pie sales, dances, all helped fill the teacher's spare time.

The school, heated by a wood stove, with a supply of fuel stacked in a nearby corner, also had a pail of well water with several enamel mugs in the porch for drinking purposes. There were also a number of black boards, usually on every side of the room, where the teacher at each break interval would write out school work for the various grades and levels of pupils. The students in turn copied onto their slates and did the sums or solved the prescribed problems. When teacher has corrected the slate work they would be wiped clean and ready for another blackboard of problems. The teacher having students from beginners up to grade 8 or 9 had to spend considerable extra time out of normal school hours preparing work for the different levels. Slow learners and mentally handicapped students had to be accomodated in the school program as well, making it rather taxing for the teacher if the number of students was great. They taught not only the 3R's but had to convey some understanding of penmanship, Art and Design, Music, Singing and some Home Economics. There were special occasions as well. The Christmas Concert was only one, when the teacher practiced and trained each child in recitations, singing, parts in humourous skits and plays. This was much looked forward to and enjoyed by child and parent alike, the parents appreciated seeing their children perform and developing new knowledge and talents. Early in December the students drew names and presents for each student were placed under the Christmas tree. The tree was decorated and waiting in the corner of the hall until after the concert and then Santa, who was a local man pressed into this duty, gave out the gifts with a few candies as well. Quite often these Christmas concerts ended with a pie auction or box lunch sale and the proceeds were used to help pay the teacher's salary.

Some teachers were better able to cope with the varied responsibilities of teaching school in a small community than some others, but most were dedicated and hard working and a contributing asset to the small community in which they lived. Three of the female school teachers coming to teach at Blanche found husbands, married and raised families in the community. Odessa Swaine of Cape Negro married Jesse Obed and lived many years on the Salvages Fog Horn. Ethel Snow of Port La Tour married Maurice Swaine and lived a number of years at Blanche before moving to Seal Point. Mary Attwood of Clyde River married Knowles Swaine and lived at West Blanche.

Josie Swaine Ross remembers some of her teachers when she attended Blanche School, Ida MacKay, Vera Ethel Snow, Virginia Chivers, Sylvia Gardner, Ada Smith, Jesse Christie. Josie lived at West Blanche and the children had a short cut through the woods from Knowles Swaines that came across the swamp and up the hill to the Keel Grove Road Children went that way to school except in the winter when they had to go the long way around by the main road.

The School was maintained and operated until 1950, at which time there were only two students, Mervin Perry and Elizabeth Swaine. Mary Attwood Swaine was the last teacher. At the fall term the two students went to the Cape Negro School.

After the school had been closed several years and as the hall across the road was in very bad repair, it was decided to construct a kitchen on the south side of the school building. In 1963 this was completed and since then it has been used as a community hall. Except for the new addition the main structure remains the same.

Clifford and Ida Thomas: Blanche

Taken from the Col. R.E. Thomas vol. | This Indenture made this 9th day
Registers 20th May 1868, on the | of May One thousand Eight hundred
Will of Martin Thomas | and Sixty two, Between William
Swim Senr and his wife Rebecca
he being a Fisherman and an inhabitant of Blanck, in the Township
of Barrington, and County of Shelburne & Province of Nova Scotia of the
first part: and Thomas O. G. Thomas, Knowles Swim, and Harvey
Slate, Trustees of the Second part: Witnesseth that the aforesaid William Swim Senr in consideration of the Sum of Five Shillings of lawful money of Nova Scotia, hath granted, sold and Conveyed and by
these presents, to the aforesaid Trustees, and their Successors in
Office, as they shall be appointed, in conformity with the Province
al School act, a certain piece or parcel of Land; on which the School
House is now erected and built, measuring Fifty five reasonable
yards fronting on the main Road for the purpose of a School
House, and also for the accommodation of the inhabitants religiously
where they can have a Sabbath School, the preaching of Gods
Holy Word, Prayer Meetings, Class Meetings, and such other services
as the Wesleyan Methodists may wish to hold, provided always that
said services shall not interfere with the Day School. And the
aforementioned William Swim Senr hath granted, sold and conveyed by these presents, to the above mentioned Trustees, Thomas O
G Thomas, Knowles Swim and Harvey Slate, and their Successors in Office all and every part of the land and premises aforementioned and described, with all the rights, privileges and appurtenances thereunto, belonging in law and at equity for the
purposes and intents herein set forth and described. And the
aforementioned William Swim Senr his heirs, executors, and
assigns will defend the right of the aforementioned
Trustees & their Successors to the land and premises herein described and by these presents conveyed, and every part of it forever.
In witness whereof we the parties to the first part of this
Indenture have hereunto set their hands and seals the day and
Year herein first written. N.B. The words, on the ninth line
from the top of the Second page – "and all other" were erased before
this Indenture was signed.

Witness, Martin Thomas   William Swar (L.S.)
    Seth Nickerson   Rebaca Swan (L.S.)

Deed: Muselew Thomas and others 62 This Indenture made
to the Inhabitants of Blanch School District Reg'd June 9, 1908 this twentieth day of
March in the year of our Lord one thousand nine hundred and eight Between Muselew
Thomas, James Swaine, Austin Thomas, James Obed, and Elizabeth Obed his wife
of Blanch in the county of Shelburne Province of Nova Scotia Yeomen, of
the first part, and the Inhabitants of Blanch School district and their heirs of the second
part in the county and Province aforesaid Witnesseth that the said Muselew Thomas
James Swaine, Austin Thomas, James Obed, and Elizabeth Obed his wife for and
in consideration of the sum of fifteen dollars ($15) lawful money of Canada and
certain Bylaws bearing date of this indenture made at a meeting of said Inhabitants
on the above date or before the executing and delivery of these presents the receipt whereof
is hereby acknowledged, Hath granted bold assigned enfeoffed released conveyed and
confirmed and by these Presents doth grant sell assign enfeoff release convey
and confirm unto the Inhabitants of Blanch School District and their heirs
that certain piece of land and buildings thereon situate lying and
being at Blanch aforesaid and bounded and described as follows. Viz:-
Beginning at a rock marked A on the west side of the public highway leading
to Blanch and running westerly eighty five feet to a stake marked B,
thence northerly forty feet to a stake marked C, thence easterly to the
public highway and a stake marked D, thence southerly by the highway
forty feet to the first mentioned bound. Together with all and singular
the buildings woods ways Waters privileges and appurtenances to the above
described premises belonging or in any wise appertaining with the rents
with the rents issues and profits thereof and the estate right title interest
claim property and demand at law or in equity or otherwise which
the said Muselew Thomas, James Swaine Austin Thomas, James Obed

370

... Elizabeth Obed his wife now have or hereafter on any have, of in to, upon or out of the same or any part thereof To have and to hold the land and building above granted with all and singular the appurtenances thereof to the said Inhabitants of Blanch School District and their heirs forever and we the said Marsden Thomas, James Swaine, Creston Thomas, James Obed and Elizabeth Obed, do, for ourselves our heirs executors and administrators hereby covenant promise and agree to and with the Inhabitants of Blanch School District in the manner following, That is to say, that the said Marsden Thomas, James Swaine, Creston Thomas, James Obed and Elizabeth Obed are now seized or [?] of a good and indefeasable of inheritance in fee simple in and to the said and hereditaments hereby conveyed and that the same are free from encumbrances & that we have good or the full power and lawful and absolute authority to sell and convey the same in manner as the same are hereby sold and conveyed and further that the said Marsden Thomas, James Edward, Creston, Thomas James Obed and Elizabeth his wife and their heirs doth warrant the said lands and premises with the appurtenances with the said Inhabitants of Blanch School District against the lawful claim and demands of all and every person and persons whomsoever shall and will warrant and by these presents forever defend. In witness whereof the parties to these presents have hereunto this hand and seal the hereinbefore set the day and year first above written.

Signed Sealed and delivered
in the presence of
William E Lyle

Marsden Thomas (Seal)
James Swaine (Seal)
Creston Thomas (Seal)
James Obed (Seal)
Elizabeth Obed (Seal)

Shelburne County SS.
On the thirteenth day of March one Thousand nine hundred and eight before me the subscriber personally came and appeared Elizabeth Obed wife of the within named James Obed whose names are subscribed to this Indenture who being by me examined separate and apart from her said husband did acknowledge and declare that she did freely voluntarily and not by and without fear threat or compulsion of force or by her said husband or otherwise seal and as and for her act and deed deliver the within Indenture, and as and for a full release of all claims with interest of power to the land herein described and for the purposes therein mentioned.

John A Christie a [Justice?] of the Peace in and for the County of Shelburne.

Blanche Hall

The deed for the Blanche Hall carrying the date June 9th, 1908 was drawn up between Marsden Thomas, James S. Swaine, Austin Thomas, James and Elizabeth Obed and the inhabitants of the Blanche School District and their heirs. That certain piece and parcel of land and buildings thereon, being roughly land 40 feet square. Witnessed by William E. Lyle and sworn before John A. Christie, Justice of the Peace.

I have not been able to discover why this deed was executed in 1908 which would be 40 or more years after the original part of the hall had been constructed. The hall was being used by The Sons of Temperance, Grove Division, in 1888. They also record at that time arrangement for reshingling the hall and replacing glass in the windows. As wooden shingles have a life of about 20 to 30 years depending on the exposure to weather, if the hall was being reshingled it is safe to therefore assume the original ones had been installed around 1860 which is the time the school and chapel were built across the road. During repairs to the hall undertaken in 1985-86 the state of the timbers and material in some respects indicate the hall is older than the school, and there is definite evidence the building had been sawn in the middle, the ends moved and center section built with used lumber from another building, as obvious join marks and other evidence bears this out. Therefore considering the state of the building material and the construction, one has to assume the hall originally was on some other site and rebuilt and/or enlarged when the deed was issued in 1908, for certainty I have not been able to establish which. An account book indicates trustees were appointed in 1904 and cash accounts kept for a number of years would indicate that when the Grove Division closed the community appointed trustees and took over the operation as a community hall.

The first records available on the Grove Division, No. 668, was the Dec. 26th, 1887 meeting, at which time officers were elected and installed as follows: Bro. Marsden Thomas, W.P., Sister Fidelia Thomas, W.A., Sister Florence Nickerson, R.S., Sister Jane Thomas, A.R.S., Brother Joseph Arey, F.S., Brother Josiah Thomas, Treasurer, Alfred Swaine, Chaplain, Brother Knowles Thomas, Con., Brother Alex Lyle,

I.S. Brother Ed Smith, O.S., Brother Austin Thomas, P.W.P. The business meeting consisted of Sister Mercy Thomas wanting her name removed from the books. The entertainment consisted of singing by Alex Lyle, speech by Paul Swaine, singing by Austin Thomas and Alex Lyle, reading by Addie Thomas. The attendance was 24, the receipts 12 cents, signed F.G. Nickerson, R.S. The Grove division appeared to have regular meetings every two weeks, and some of the minutes indicate the following.

January 16th, 1888, proposed for membership John J. Thomas, Asa Chawtynd, John J. Thomas was balloted and accepted, Asa Chatwynd having 7 black beans against him was rejected. They reballoted for Asa Chatwynd and he was accepted. Visitors were Harvey and Benjamin Slate of MacMurray Division at Cape Negro. Moved and seconded that Marsden Thomas be paid 30 cents for making the fire for three months. Several of the members then spoke out about paying out money that was not necessary. It was moved and passed a different person would make the fire on meeting nights. Levi Thomas was to make the fire and light the lamps for next meeting.

Number present, Receipts 12 cents.

February 6th, 1888, Sister Mary MacKay wished her name erased from the books. Mrs. Arch Obed proposed for membership Cynthia Thomas who was dulely accepted. Entertainment, a reading by Lillian Thomas, entitled 'Only a Woman Drunk'. Singing by Alex Lyle, entitled 'The Ship that Never Returned', Recitation by Florence Nickerson, Reading by Jane Thomas, Reading by Edward Smith, entitled 'How I Would Paint a Bar Room'. A dialogue by Austin Thomas. Alex Lyle appointed to make fire and light lamps. Attendance 20, Receipts 49 cents.

At later meetings it is recorded their decision to hold a Christmas party with a Christmas tree. They continued to appoint different members to light the fires and the lamps, at one point agreeing to pay 12 cents for kerosene or the lamps. The meetings are recorded until 1892, and the transcribed and typed copy is on display at the annual Blanche festival, for the public to inspect for more details of these meetings.

In 1903 and 1904 the hall was reshingled, new shutters made and hinges for the same purchased. In 1906 a special meeting was held, the chairman being William B. Smith, to decide matters of obtaining a deed of hall, apparently as Marsden Thomas name was on the bill of sale of the building. They agreed to pay him five dollars and he with the other trustees issued the deed to residents of the Blanche School District. In 1903 they purchased the following: 12 M shingles 12.00, 200 feet sheathing lumber 5.00, 50 pounds of nails 3.25, paid for hauling lumber .40 cents. Receipts were 21.06 the results of a pie sale. Reuben A. Smith was appointed secretary in 1906. The trustees were, Walter Myrick, Sr., James C. Swaine, W.E. Lyle.

The hall was used for all social occasions, tea meetings, dances, pie sales, Christmas concerts etc. An annual meeting with the appointment of officers and trustees took place each year. No major alterations or changes were made to the hall structure after the major repairs of 1904-05, except for roof repairs and replacemnt of glass in windows.

In 1958 the population of the Blanche Village had declined and the school was closed at a general meeting, called by the chairman, Reuben A. Smith. It was decided that the community could not maintain the school building and the hall. The latter was declared surplus, resulting in the windows being removed and the inside sheating from ceiling and walls taken and used in construction of the kitchen as an addition to the school building. The latter then became the community hall and the old hall was left unlocked and abandoned.

In 1985 the Blanche Village consisting of only 8 occupied houses, decided to restore the old hall for the purpose of holding a dance. The building was cleaned up and,through community support,the hall has been reshingled, windows replaced and inside resheated in building paper. It is now used each year for the entertainment and dance segment of the Blanche Festival, the latter consisting of a Sea Food Chowder Supper, Bag Pipe Music, Sing Song, and other entertainers. With nearly 300 attending the supper and the entertainments, a fund is being built up for the up keep of both community buildings — the School — Chapel and the Hall.

Blanch Mar. 14 1904

An account of the annual meeting of the Building Com. of the Public Hall of Blanch was held in the School room on the evening of March 14. 1904 G. S. Obed occupied the chair minits of last meeting read and approved the rec. of the Com made a report showing the debt to be $82.54 and credit $3.63 leaving a Ballance of $3.09. The Com. then reported that they had shingled the roof of the Hall and had seven thousand spruce shingles now on hand and 200 feet of sheathing now and ... but we still keep trying to finish the Hall, after which S. K. Obed asked to ...

relieved from the office of
Chairman of the Com. which was
granted. after which Ruben A.
Smith was elected Sec. & Treasurer
to the Committee for one year.
The following persons were
appointed Trustees of the Hall for
one year, Walter Myrick,
James C. Swaim, and W. C.
Lyle. after which it was moved
second and passed that the
Trustees shall not make any
charge to the use of the Hall
for Meetings or the Hall
made for Church or School
purposes. But for all other purposes
the fee shall be One Dollar.
moved as. that the Sec. get a Deed
of the Land on which the Hall
stands. moved seconded meeting
[illegible]   Wm. Thomas Sec.

Blanchm Mins Lt 1905

An account of a meeting of the Building Com was held in the Hall on the evening of June 2 1905. W. B. Smith in the chair minutes of last meeting read and accepted. The Sec made a report showing Credit for the year $28.95 and Deb $4.39 leaving a Bal on hand of $24.56. The Chair reported that the walls of the Hall had been shingled during the past year and shutters made for the windows moved and that the report be accepted as correct after which some little talk about continuing the repairs on the Hall moved seconded and passed that we keep on a-hand repairing the Hall after which the following persons were appointed Trustees of the

all, W. A. R. Smith, W. E. Lyle
and James S. Swan, also R. A. Smith
was reelected Sec & Treasurer. Motion
and passed that Lee Jos Hall hire be
Two Dollars for all purposes except for
Sale and the matings made for Church
or School purposes. Moved see meeting
adjourn.
                          M. Thurman Sec Pro Tem

Blanch Hall Feb 24th 190_

An account of the public meeting held in the hall on the evening of Feb 24 Alex S Lyle was appointed chairman. Minutes of last meeting read and excepted as correct. The Sec then made his report showing credit for the year being (43.5.6) And debt (2.5.6) leaving a Ball on hand of (41.00) Then James S Swain made his report about what Mr White told him about the bill of sale saying that Marsden Thomas Austin & James S Swain held the hall as their names was on the bill of sale. And said that Austin Thomas wanted (5.00) for his part some talk on the same followed. It was then moved and passed that a com of three be appointed to go see Austin Thomas if he would sign the deed for the sum of (5.00) James S Swain James Abeal & _____

Blanch Hall Jan 13th 1909
An account of a public meeting held in the hall of said evening Jan 13 Mr James Sivainie in the chair Reuben Smith sec. The minutes of the last meeting read and accepted as correct. The sect. then read his report of cr ($45.00) and dr ($14.59) leaving still on hand a bal of ($35.41) the sect report was accepted as correct then Howard Thomas was appointed trustee untill 1912. then Reuben Smith was then appointed again as sec for 1 year more then some talk on what to do first to the hall then Marsden Thomas was then appointed to hold the keys for 1 year then the price of ($1.00) be charged to shows or any thing that's not much money in them Alex Syle moved the meeting adjurned it was moved and passed

Reuben A Smith
Sec Tres

Lyle Lewis is appointed to go see him Marsden Thomas then moved that the meeting be adjourned it was then passed
Reuben A Smith Sec

Blanch Hall march 20th 1908

An account of a public meeting held in the Hall on Thursday morning march 20 James S Swam as Chairman and Reuben A Smith Sec. first Marsden Thomas asked James Obed if he was going to give us the land on which the Hall sets some talk on the bill of sale then followed. Then Austin Thomas wanted to know what they was going to do with the Hall before he would sign clear then Mr John Christie told us which way to go to work. It was then moved by Austin Thomas and sec by W A B Smith — that the deed of the Hall be signed to the people of Blanch and their heirs it was carried then some talk followed then it was moved and sect that the Sum of ($5.00) be put in the deed then Mr Christie read the way the deed wanted to be. the bye laws was then made it was there moved and sect that the annual meeting be held on the evening of the first Wednesday in January the bylaws was then addopted the trustees was then appointed first James C. Swain, second Marsden Thomas third William C. Lyle, then Reuben A. Smith was appointed Sect. for one year. It was then moved and passed that the sum of $2.00 be charged for all purposes except funeral preparty or anything for the section. It was then moved and passed that ... the day a oft be paid. It was then moved and passed that all the money in the hands of the old sect. be handed to the new one. The auditing Com. was then appointed Alex Lyle James S ... W. A. Smith the trustees shall at the annual meeting make out a full report of money expended and what is still on hand. It was then moved and passed the meeting adjourned.

Reuben A. Smith
Sect.

See one

Blanch Jan 12th, 1910

An account of the meeting held in the Hall on Wed evening Jan 12. Alex Lyle Chairman and Reuben Smith Sect. The minutes of last meeting was read and accepted as correct. The sect. then made his report of ($60.00) and debt. ($41.91) Giving a bal. of ($18.09) still on hand the sect. report was accepted as correct. Then Reuben Smith was appointed Trustee for three years until 1913. Then Reuben Smith was relected as sect. Tres. Then the sum of ($1.00) be charged for shows and the sum of ($1.50) be charged for sales or any thing that they was much money. Then the addor. be Alex Lyle. Josh. Selig. Charlie Lyle by the last for one to go out each year as they was appointed Then five was appointed to be _____ hold a meeting then Howard _____ _____ meeting adjorin

Reuben Smith

Blanch Hall Jan. 11 1911
An account of the meeting
held in the Hall on Wed. evening Jan 11th
Alex Dyle Chairman and Reuben Smith Sect
The minutes of last meeting was read
and was accepted as correct the sect then
then made his report of Cr ($33.78) and
Dept. ($39.25) leving no in Dept of ($5.47) The
sec report was accepted as correct. Then
John Smith was appointed Trustee for
three years untill 1914 then some talk of
what next to be done to the Hall. Then it was
moved and passed that the trustee do as they
see fit. moved and passed that Marsden Thomas
be added in Alex Dyle place moved and
passed meeting adjourned.

Reubin A. Smith
Sec. Tres.

Blanch Feb 29 1912

An account of a ... ...
held in the Hall on thur evening of Feb 29
Mars Thomas Chairman Reuben ponth...
... minutes of last meting ...
The ... they made the report of Cr. of 12.3... and
(6.47) leveing us Bal. on hand of (715)
The ... report was accepted ... Then
Alex S. Lyle was appointed Trustee for three
years until 1915. & Auditors ... ... 3 years
until 1915 & Wm Lyle until 1913 Josh Selig for 1914
and such meeting adjourned
                        Reuben A Smith
                                    Sect.

Blanch Jan. 15th 1913
            An account of a meeting
held in the Hall on Wed. evening Jan. 15 Alex Lyle
Chair. Reuben Smith sect. The minutes of last
meeting accep. as correct. The Sect. then made
his report of Cr. (13.15) and Dr. of (5.70) leving
us a Bal. on hand of (7.45) The Sect and Auditors
                                          report was
accepted as correct. Then Josh Selig was appointed
as Trustee untill 1916 Then Auddertors Josh Selig
untill 1914 James C Swan untill 1915 and Marsden
Thomas untill 1916. Then it was moved and
Sect. metting adjoined
                        Reuben A Smith
                                    Sect. Tres.

Money paid out for Hall 1903

April 21	L.12 M Shingles		$27	00
"	"	"209 ft sealing lumber	6	70
"	"	freight and cartage	2	88
"	"	50 lbs nails	3	25
"	"	commission		50
May 25	paid for hauling lumber			40
July 7	" " lumber and nails	1	79
Dec 24	paid for 7 M Shingles	11	55
	one book			20
	Det	$52	54

1904
May 25 – Paid Stewart Swain for hauling shingles .30
Aug 4   30 lbs galvge nails @ 6c   1.80
         eight penny   4   .20
Aug 15 2 " gal clinch nails @ 10c   .20
Oct 18 9 pair Hinges 9" & 9 hooks @ 18c   .99
    27 1 Padlock @ 25   .25
    "   1 clasp @ 5   .05
    "   4 lbs W. B. Green Paint @ 15   .60
                                   4.34

1904			
March 14			
Rec'd.	For Hall Hire —	$2.00	
"	Left from last year	3.09	
Oct 24	Sold the old shingles @	.40	
" "	" 6¾ lbs of galv nails @ 6¢	.40	
Feb 3	Rec'd from Brad Berry for Hall hire	1.08	
" 24	John Smith for Hall hire	1.00	
March 14	Received from Pie Sale	21.06	
	Cr. # 1	28.03	
	Dr.	4.39	
	Still on hand #2	4.36	

Cape Negro Church 1920

Cape Negro Church 1936

Cape Negro Church

The first New England settlers at Cape Negro, the Swaines, Nickersons and Smiths, did not hold regular church services, but read the Bible and said simple prayers in their homes. There were no churches in the area they could attend except the Old Meeting House at Barrington Head, which at that time did not have windows or doors and did not have a regular minister. The three founding families were of Puritan persuasion from the Plymouth general area.

The Rev. Freeborn Garretson, the ardent pioneer of Methodism and a converted slave owner of Maryland, came to Cape Negro on his way to Barrington. He stayed with the Smiths several days before travelling on to Barrington. He held religious services during this visit. On his return from Barrington he again stopped and stayed with the Smiths and he formed a Methodist Class of 16 persons, 10 of whom professed the spirit of forgiveness. Shortly after the organization of this Methodist class, the 10 converted persons and others built a log chapel, which was the first Methodist chapel to be built in Shelburne County. The log chapel was at the joining of the Blanche and Cape Negro roads, located on the old original road where the ball field is today.

The Rev. James Oliver Cromwell succeeded the Rev. Garritson as minister in Shelburne, and he reported a Blessed Revival on one of his frequent visits to Cape Negro. The Rev. James Mann was the next minister in 1789 and he made Cape Negro his home, and this was the center of the ministerial circuit until it was moved to Shelburne in 1795. After the Rev. Mann came the Reverends James Wray, Jessop, Stocker, and Fidler. The Rev. James Mann returned to the circuit in 1799.

The log chapel at Cape Negro was the only religious building between Shelburne and Barrington. In Shelburne at that time the Methodists were meeting in a sail loft and the Old Meeting House in Rev. Garretson's time was as previously stated window and door less. The residents from the Harbour, Clyde, Port Saxon and Port LaTour came to Cape Negro Log Chapel for Methodist services.

Around 1818 the log chapel at the turn of the road had been replaced by a frame building on the hill by the burial grounds, which is about the same site as the present church. This frame church was sold and taken down in the early 1850's and reconstructed as a house at Port La Tour. The new church which still survives today was built in 1853. The first trustees were Samuel Smith, David Swaine, Jr., John B. Swaine, James Swaine, Josiah Smith, James A. Nickerson, and Wm. A. Paterson. This new white church on the hill in Cape Negro could be seen from both harbours and was a navigational aide used by the local fishing boats returning to harbour. The building of frame construction with a high steeple, was on two floors. The main floor had boxed pews with doors, and the pulpit was a raised platform surrounded by an altar rail with two entrance gates in the front. The Sunday School Library was situated in the left corner on entering the church.At the front of the church on each side of the pulpit platform are special boxed pews used for Sunday School. The second floor was reached by stairs in the steeple tower and consisted of a balcony with boxed pews on three sides with view of the pulpit. the windows are cathedral shaped extending from first to second floor balcony. The back pews by the library were reserved for the Negros who attended services from the Renyoldscroft area. They were greatly respected for the quality of their singing.

    In the early days the church pews were sold and became family pews. Up until church union, which was about 1925, the older folk often spoke of their family pew in the church. This custom was a form of raising money for the church and minister expenses, as socials, etc. were not considered a proper method of raising money for God's work.

    The Cape Negro Church was largely attended with people coming from all the surrounding areas until the late 1800s and early 1900s when other churchs were then built. After the first great war the population began to decline, by the young folk going to work in the United States. As many married they made homes and remained there. From then until early 1930 the population slowly declined. During that year Sydney Christie was engaged by the Church Trustees to close in the balcony on the second floor. During the course of the winter this was done by employing the metal sheeting which is still in place today, and the second floor of the church has not been used since then. Along about that time the cathedral window behind the pulpit was removed and a much smaller color glass window installed. Later years the Sunday School Library was dismantled and room used as a choir changing room.

At a conference in Yarmouth in 1870 the Port La Tour Methodist circuit was organized. The Rev. Barry Mack was appointed the first minister, with the parsonage being located at Green Hill, next to the school. The circuit included Baccaro, Green Hill, Cape Negro, Blanche, West and Port Clyde. At the time of this organizing Cape Negro had a class of 22 members of which James Swaine was the leader. In 1937 there was a realignment of the charge. Baccaro and Clyde River were then attached to Barrington Charge. In 1928 the Methodist churches and Presbyterian church united to form the United Church of Canada. After this the Methodists ceased to exist as such, both being termed United Church. In the early 1960s the Clyde River Manse was sold and minister moved to new manse at Thomasville which was a new house having been built by Captain C.B. Kenny and his wife, Elva. Some years ago the circuit was again changed and Green Hill became a part of Barrington Charge and this charge became the Clyde Carlton Charge and North East Harbour and Ingomar were added to the circuit.

Ministers of the Cape Negro Church:
1786	Rev. Freeborn Garretson
	Rev. James Oliver Cromwell
	Rev. James Mann
	Rev. James Way
1790	Rev. Jessop
	Rev. Stocket
	Rev. Fidler
1799	Rev. James Mann
1870	Rev. Barry Mack
1872	Rev. J.R. Borden
1875	Rev. James Tweedy
1878	Rev. Robert MacArthur
1881	Rev. A. Hockin

Year	Minister
1884	Rev. R. Williams
1887	Rev. J.M. Mellish
1890	Rev. A. Daniels
1893	Rev. Jabez Appleby
1896	Rev. Hirman Davis
1899	Rev. J. Phalen
1903	Rev. W. Nightengale
1907	Rev. W. Boyd & Rev. M. Parker
1910	Rev. H.H. MacNeil
1914	Rev. H.P. Patterson
1917	Rev. A.J. Reynolds
1920	Rev. Alfred Thorpe
1924	Rev. W.H. Palmer
1925	Rev. J.R. Saint
1926	Rev. Thomas Constable
1928	Rev. D. McClark
1931	Rev. F.W. Swaden
1932	Rev. J.A.T. Hart
1934	Rev. Henry Brown
1936	Rev. W.H. Forsythe
1939	Rev. W.J. Domville
1942	Rev. Harry Bagnall, Student
1943	Rev. W.D. VanZoost
1946	Rev. C.G. Westhaver
1950	Rev. R. Williams
1955	Rev. William Collins
1957	Rev. Ronald Dempsey
1960	Rev. Gordon MacBeth
1962	Rev. Donald MacDougal
1965	Rev. Ross MacDonald
1967	Rev. Arthur Tobey
1969	Rev. Donald MacQueen
1972	Rev. A.J. Clarke
1975	Rev. David Pierce, Student
1976	Rev. B. Scott Young
1978	Rev. Derek Shelly
1982	Rev. David LeBlanc
1987	Rev. G. Symonds

Cape Negro Cemetery.

In 1770 Benjamin Barass donated land for a Burial Ground at Cape Negro. The plot was dedicated by James Barass, his son. This Burial Ground, which is now on the west side of the present church, is where all the first settlers were buried. It was not divided into lots or family plots as is done today, but as required the graves were made one on side of each other, in rows. These graves had only field stone placed at head and foot to indicate where the graves are. Without written records or a marker, it's impossible to tell who lies in the individual graves. This system continued until 1897, when a community meeting was called by the Trustees of the Methodist Church and plans made to enlarge and organize the Burial Ground.

The Cape Negro Cemetery does not belong to the church, which is the case in most other communities. The Cemetery at Cape Negro was incorporated as a Company and Seaview Cemetery operated as such being the property of the shareholders or lot owners. I am copying the list of original shareholders. Please note that these shareholders are from a wide area, from communities we know as Port Clyde, Reynoldscroft, Upper Port La Tour. Blanche never had a burial ground, although there were a few individuals buried on their own property, all funerals and burials have traditionally been held at Cape Negro. For Church purposes Thomasville and Cape Negro have always been one, for the use of the Church Cemetary and Community Hall.

In 1918 a horse drawn hearse was purchased. This was a 4 wheel wagon with the usual hearse type body that contained side glass windows and black crepe curtains inside. The driver sat on an elevated seat at the front. The hearse was painted all black. Heman Swaine and the horse he used for grocery delivery operated the hearse for many years. It was kept then in what is now Herbert Thomas's garage. Later it was moved to the hill by the cemetery and kept in the building now used to store equipment, which was located at what is now the northwest corner of the new hillside cemetery. The hearse was sold after the Second World War and wheels used for other purposes.

Those not having a cemetery share were charged 50 cents for the hearse's use. It was the local custom when the hearse was due to pass through the community all the window shades were drawn and the children brought into the house and all remained quiet. The last time the hearse was used, was for the funeral of Charles Willie Hurbert and was driven by Burnley Ross with the black horse called Old Jim.

In 1958 a new cemetery was organized which is south west of the church, this is laid off into well organized family lots, which have permanent numbers installed for each. The plot maps for both Seaview and Hillside Cemeteries are copied for this book, as well as lists of plot owners and burial lists after Seaview was organized in 1897.

Sea View Cemetary and Old Buriel Ground.

Owners of Lots.

1. James Berry.
2. George Mathers.
3. George Webb.
4. Bradford Perry.
5. James Mackay.
6. Elroy Thomas.
7. James MacKay.
8. Walter Myrick. Sr.
9. Slate & Jesse Obed.
10. Steven Obed.
11. Arthur O. Thomas.
12. Arch Obed and Claude Perry.
13. James H. Smith.
14. William E. Smith.
15. Elam Thomas.
16. Silas Towner.
17. Jonathan Smith.
18. William H. Swaine.
19. J.S.B. Swaine.
20. William A.B. Swaine.
21. James Obed.
22. Alexander & Will Lyle.
23. Winslow J. Swaine.
24. John Bethel.
25. Capt. John Smith.
26. Stephen Smith.
27. Eldred Nickerson.
28. Josiah & Knowles Thomas.
29. James C. Swaine.
30. Daniel Matherson.
31. James Ross.
32. Nathaniel Horton.
33. Marsden Thomas.
34. Matthew Nickerson.
35. Ezra Swaine.
36. Lester Smith.
37. Hanson Chatwynd.
38. John Reynolds.
39. John Ross.
40. Joseph Thomas.
41. James S. Swaine.
42. George Drew & Wm. E. Smith.
43. Isaac Lyle.
44. Gilford Obed.
45. Clifford Thomas.
46. Harvey Slate.
47. Benjamin Slate.
48. George Thomas.
49. Lloyd Swaine.
50. Thomas Ross and Durkee Chatwynd.
51. Emerson & Austin Thomas.
52. Stan Greenwood & Ernest Perry.
53. Bradford Lowe.
54. Captain William L. Ross.
55. Charles William Hurbert.
56.
57. Heman Swaine.
58. George Sholds.
59. Anthony Perry.
60. James H. Swaine.
61. George Slate.
62. Howe Thomas.
63. Joseph Arey.
64.
65.
66.
67.
68.
69. Samuel Snow.
70. Nellie Swaine.
71.
72.
73. David Flemming.
74. Braddock Swaine.
75.
76. Captain Joseph F. Swaine.
77.
78.
79. William Reynolds.
80. Josiah Snow.
81.
82. Lovie Keeling.
83.
84.

A1. James Swaine & family.
A2. Martin Thomas.
A3. Chapman Swaine.
A4. Samuel Swaine.
A5. James Howe Swaine.
A6. Charles Sutherland.
A7. Matthew Svaine.
A8. David Thomas.
A9. Joseph Freeman Svaine.
A10. John Nickerson.

A.
B.
C. Oliver Thomas.
D. Labert Thomas.
E. Walter Arey.
F. John Smith.
G. Seth Nickerson.
H. Reuben A. Smith.
I. Joshua Selig.
J. Captain Alexander Smith.
K. James P. Smith and Elizabeth Parsons.

PLAN SEA VIEW CEMETERY & OLD BURIAL GROUND.
CAPE NEGRO.

Hillside Cemetary - 1951.
Cape Negro. N.S.

180
1898

Record of Burials in "Seaview" Cemetery.

Date	№	Names	Age	Residence
1898 Mar 4	3	Mrs. Geo. Webb (col)	59	Up. Port La Tour
1899 Jan 29		Rebeccah Slate	993	Clanch
Oct. 28		Barbara Smith	82	Clauch
Feb. 3	55	Robert Millar (col.)		Up. Port La Tour
Mar		Ellen Patterson	68	Up. Port La Tour
Apl. 15	57	Clifford D. S. Swain	25	Cape Negro
May 14		Mary Swain	82	Cape Negro
June 17	37	Wilbert Chatwynd	2	Up. Port La Tour
July 16	16	Jane Lowler	23	Cape Negro
Aug. 11	60	George L. Slate	33	Clanch
Oct. 28		John D. Swain	94	Cape Negro
Dec. 10	25	Bert S. S. Smith	18	Cape Negro
1900 Jan. 15		Elizabeth Swain	86	Cape Negro
Mar. 27		Mrs. John H. Reynolds		Up. Port La Tour
Apl. 6	23	Infant of Jane Lowler (Col. 10mo.)		Cape Negro
May 5	51	Mattie Thomas		Blacked
Aug. 12	79	Hannah Reynolds	59	Up. Port La Tour
" 28		Abigail Snow (Aunt Nabby)	95	Up. Port La Tour
Nov. 27	18	Mary wife of Henry Swain	84	Cape Negro
1901 Feb. 11	39	John Ross		Up. Port La Tour
" 13		Esther Swain	80	Clanch
July 27		Paul Swain	7	Blanch
Sept. 4		Wilford Ross	22	Up. Port La Tour
" 7		Mrs. Horton (Aunt Tempy)	97	Cape Negro
Dec. 9		Alfred Swain	56	Blanch
" 14		Patience Bennet (col)	53	Up. Port La Tour

1902				
Feb	22	19	Henry Swain	79	Cape Negro
Mar.	2	1	Attie Berry		
June	7	2	Djanna Kelly (Col.)		
June		14	Maria Thomas		
Sept	3	73	Rosa Fleming		Blanch
1903				
Jany	2	32	Eliza Nolton		
	6	76	Levi Nickerson		
Mar			Infant Ada & Eva Smith		Blanch

1903	No			
Date	Lot	Names	Age	Residence
		41	Agnes Corry	22	Boston
			Rachel Swain	99½	Cape Negro
June	2		Albert Thomas	21	Blanch
			Siner Smith		Cape Negro
Dec	13	51	Carrie B Porter	36	Blanch
1904 Feb 22	114	Alexander Lyle	90	Blanch
1904 March 19	34	Martha Nickerson	75¾	Cape Negro
1904 April 23	114	Thules V. Lyle	3	Cape Negro
1904 Apl 30	114	Edgar R Lyle	9	Cape Negro
1904 May 14	58	Hannah Sholds	83¼	Cape Negro
1904 May 30	34	Mathew R. Nickerson	74½	Cape Negro
1904 July 16	51	Ethel I W Thomas	10¾	Blanch
Sept 27	3	Nett	11	Up. Port La Tour
48 Oct 18	61	Geoge Slate	68	Blanch
49 " 28		Lot et Reding (col)	84	Up. Port La Tour
50 Nov 1	2	Sarah Ann Williams (col)	83	"
51 " 21	35	Ezra Swain	58	Cape Negro
52 " 22	70	Howie Swain	8	"
53 " 29	70	Lawrence Swain	12	"
54 Feb 8 1905	1	James Berry (Col)	83	Upper Port La Tour

No.	Date	Age	Name	Age	Residence
55	Mar 13	70	Joshua Pierce	71	Cape Negro
56	Apl 14		Capt Joseph Swain	81	" "
57	Dec 19 1904	29	Benjamin E. Swaine	9	Blanch
58	1906 16 old ground		Capt Alex Smith	76	Blanch
59		56	Capt Stephen Thomas	66	Cape Negro
60	June 9 1906	50	Andrew Chetwin	68	Upper Port La Tour
61	July 7	26	Wm H. Nickerson	55	Cape Negro
62	Feb 17 1907		Child of Mr. D. Chatwyn	10 mo	Up. Port La Tour
63	June	20	Deborah Thomas	96	West Clyde
64	Sept	7	Wm Hosford Swain	21	Cape Negro
65	Oct	27	Samuel L. Swain	27 1/2	Cape Negro
66	Nov 26		Sarah A Smith	64	Blanch
67	Feb 23		Ralph L. Perry	5	Blanch

When	No.	Names	Age	Residence
1907 Dec 29	71	Martha Snow	59	Upper Port La Tour
1908 Sept 8	30	Sarah M Nursey	52	Blanch
July 1 1909	2	Allen S Young		Upper Port La Tour
Jany 29 1909	14	Jonathan Smith	71	Cape Negro
March 23 1909	41	Martha S. C Swaine	44	Blanch
May 15 1909	25	Capt John Smith	76	Cape Negro
Dec 16 1909	12	Archelus C Obed	70	Blanch
Jany 23 1910	21	Elizabeth S Obed	62	Blanch
May 22	46	Harvey Slate	73	Cape Negro
May 23	32	Mary Eliza Hopkins		Bear Point
Sept 10 old ground		Edward Smith	73	Upper Port La Tour
Novm 18 1911	32	Mrs Lizzie Kenney	71 1/2	" " "
Jany 22 1911 old ground		Sarah Elizabeth Slate	91 7/12	Cape Negro
March 29	51	Ostena Mae Slate	4-12 days months	Slateville

			Name	age	Residence
2	Oct 14	22	Charles Lyle		Blanch
3	Dec 21 1912	69	Samuel J. Snow	63¾	Cape Negro
4	Jany 14 1912	9 mos	James F. Swaine	9 9/12	Cape Negro
5	May 30		An unknown person		Picked
6	Jany 20 1913	16	Arthur V Swaine	41	Blanch
7	" 24 1913	old ground	Rachel Mills	74	Cape Negro
8	July 9	12	Mary Ann Obed	64	Blanch
9	" 12	78	Ester Pierce	84	Cape Negro
10	Aug 20	29	Willetta Swaine	33	Blanch
1	Nov 8	40b	Seth Nickerson	66	Cape Negro
2	" 21	Old ground	Sophia M Thomas	78	Blanch
3	Apl 16 1914	51	Matilda Thomas	82	"
14	Nov 3	old ground	16 Hannah Nickerson	74	Cape Negro
15	Feb 14 1915	11	Elizabeth Reynolds	73	Reynolds Croft
16	March 22	54	Dora Ross	34	Cape Negro
7	Apl 19	1	James Berry Col	67	Upper Pt La Tour
8	July 27	48	Wm H. Swaine	68	Cape Negro
9	Aug 4	20	Robert H. Smith	61	Blanch

Record of Burials in Seaview Cemetery

1915		No Lots	Name	age	Residence
10	Sept 1	31	Nancy Ross	87	Upper Port La Tour
11	Jany 23 1916	50	Reuth Chatwin	85	Reynolds Croft
12	March 4		Annie Lowe	27	Reynolds Croft
13	May 16	59	Anthony D Perry	81	Cape Negro
14	June 3	57	Capt Heaman Swaine	82	Cape Negro
15	July 28 1916	17	Matilda J Smith	75	Cape Negro
16	Aug 26	13	Hattie Smith		Cape Negro
17	Jan 19	50	Thos Ross Jr.	55	Upper Port La Tour
18	Jan 29		Mary Ann Thomas	84	Port Clyde

	date		Name	age	Lot
99	Apr	57	Mary R. Swain	75	Cape Negro
10	Apr 30	44	Eliza T. Nickerson	72	Cape Negro
1	May 25	40	Fanny Thomas	76	Thomasville
2	June 30	28	Knowles Thomas	64	Thomasville
3	Aug 25	47	Benj. Slate	74	Slateville
4	Sept 17	"	Ruby Thomas	8	Thomasville
5	Sept 27	11	Arthur C. Thomas	28	Blanch
6	Jan 6 1918	21	James Allied	78	Blanch
7	Feb	35	Josephine Swain	69	Cape Negro
8	May 31	50	Thomas Rosek	92	Rep. Ont. Fr. Vo.
9	Oct 2	28	Fena Thomas	30	Thomasville
10	" 23	29	F. Howe Thomas	64	Blanch
1	Nov 24	33	J. Marsden Thomas	11	Blanch
2	Dec 28	5	Austin Thomas	54	Thomasville
3	Jan 6 1919	25	Anna Smith	71	Cape Negro
4	" 23	B	Oliver Thomas	33	Cape Negro
5	May 31	40	Joe Thomas	73	Thomasville
6	July 13		Ann Swain	82	Blanch
7	Oct 8	24	Ellen Newell	88	Reynoldscroft
8	Nov 12	43	Mary S. Gray	31	Cape Negro
9	" 15	53	Effie E. Lowe	48	Reynolds Croft

	date 1920		Name	age	Lot
0	Apr.	11	Joe Henry Swain	39	19
1	Sept.	15	George Sholds	44	58
2	"	23	Susan S. Smith	89	C.
3	"	5	Mary E. Thomas	68	15
4	"	27	Margaret Swain	45	29
5	Oct.	5	Earl Newell	21	14
6	"	13	Infant of Geo. C.		
7	"	29	Joshua Seelig	38	

111

No.	Date		Name	Age	Lot
35	Nov	22	Mercy Thomas	97	33
39	Dec	21	Margaret Towner	72	16
40	"	27	Martha Slate	83	61

1921

41	Oct	14	Allen W. Thomas	13 mos	O.G.
42	"	22	Josiah Thomas	70	28
43	Dec	1	Seretha Mathews	48	2

1922

44	May	31	Sarah E. Lyle	86	O.G.
45	June	30	Abigal Arey	65	O.G.
46	July	19	Menard Myrick	2 days	
47	"	25	Laura A. Sunin	63	26

1923

48	Feb	12	Levinia McKay	65	7
49	Mar	1	Charles E. Nickerson	5	
50	Sept	2	Isaac Lyle	77	40
51	Oct	23	Sarah Slate	76	O.G.
52	Oct	28	Percy Earl Perry		52

1924

53	Jan	12	Williams M. Glouster	2 days	1
54	Feb	13	George W. Thomas	51	48
55	Apr	28	Sarah Smith	88	O.G.
56	Aug	3	Ileta Thomas	19	52

No.	Date		Name	Age	Lot

1925

7	June	17	Josiah Snow	77	O.G.
8	"	22	Sanford Slate	51	O.G.
9	Oct	18	Silas P. Towner	89	16
0	Nov		Clarence A. Smith	37	13
1	Dec	20	Cretoria M. Myrick	2 hrs.	
2	Feb 1926	18	Stanley Douglas L. Gardner	12	

3	May	17 John J. Thomas	48	
4	May	18 Mathew Swain	71	
5	Nov.	15 John Elton Bethel	11m. 6 day	24
	Nov.	15 Deborah Nickerson	89	27
7	Dec.	9 Sarah Ann Smith	82 9-24	20
8	Dec.	25 Margaret J. Nickerson	52	27
	July 1927	19 Merilla S. Selvage	27	47
	1928			
	Feb.	6 James H. Swain	84	
	"	9 William Reynolds	94	
	Oct.	16 Wm Arthur Bill Smith	79	42
	1929			
3	March	22 Florence D. Swain	7m. 8d. 49	
14	March	31 Martha N. Thomas	3m. 9do. 68	28
15	April	6 Claude Hugh Perry	49 yrs. 3m 19do.	12
6	April	17 Samuel S. Smith	90 yrs.	
	1930			
17	Jan.	Cynthia Thomas		14
18	Jan.	William E. Lyle		22
19	Mar.	29 Temperance Matherson	85 yrs 2mo. 25	30
10	Mar. 1931	3 Lucy Frances Abed	41 yrs	40
11	March	2 Charles Wm. Herbert	75 yrs	9.55
2	Oct. 1932	22 James Stewart Swaine	75 yrs	10 min
3	Feb. 1933	5 Charles Henry Arey	1 yr. 3 m	15 days
8	Sept. 1937	Jennie Tobin	37 yrs	2 m

Date		No	Name	yrs	mos	days
April 18	1932	40	Jesse Clayton Obed	53	4	10
Apr 20th	1932		Frank Myrick			new
	1934	42	George Drew			
Aug 24th	1938		Walter Myrick	65 yrs		new
		42	Elizabeth Drew	65	—	—
	1933	44	Guilford Obed	62 yrs	—	—
June	1933	52	Ernest Perry			

1931

Name	Age		
Still Born Child of Russel Farmer			
Bradford Perry	53 yrs	9 m	30 d
Daniel Matheson	100	4	13
Margaret A Lyle	83	6	6
Mardria Herbert	68	11	20
Anna Jane Ross	46	10	6
Samuel Smith Patterson	81	4	10
Annie Patricia Slate	75	10	12
William Lewis Ross	91	2	20
James Harvey Smith	82	6	7
Geneva Augusta Obed	53	3	27
Lydia Lorraine Thomas		5	4
Annie Gertrude Ross	61	8	28
Robert Archilaus Obed	54	2	14
Florence Elinor Swaine	69	7	27
David James Munroe	79	9	21
Fidelia A M Thomas	85	0	14
Joseph Henry Frey	87	9	22
Stephen James Obed	71	2	14

Drumpew Francis Thomas	40.11.24	
Kathalau G. Thomas	42.7	
Marie Rita Jacques	2.24	
Mable Thomas	64.6.22	
Winslow Johnson Swain	76.9.21	
Lebert Forrester Thomas	70.3.9	
Alexander Stillman Lyle	85.5.1	
~~Tray Peter Thomas~~	~~59.6.7~~	
Melissa Jane Thomas	88.1.1	
~~Ida Exelena Thomas~~	~~74.6.9~~	
Margaret Jennetta Lyle	76.6.20	
William Edward Smith	84.8.29	
Barbara Jane Herbert	2.2.16	
Lester Alton Smith	77.3.5	
Jessie Exelena Obed	90.5.28	
Charlotte A'wlda Christie	74.9.29	

James H. Smith House: Cape Negro

1955 — Old Cemetery
Record of Deaths and Burials

Name	Age (Yrs Mo Dys)	Died (Mo Dy Yr)
James C Swaine	86. 4. 8.	4. 7. 55.
~~Robert Mitchel Swaine.~~	~~me~~	~~1956~~
Joseph Arthur Thomas.	83. 4. 1.	1. 25. '57.
Maud Swaine (Barrington)	84 — —	8, — '62
Stanley Swaine (Barrington)	85 — —	— — '65
Reuben A. Smith. (Blanche)	84. 11. 26	8 5 '66
Gertrude H. Swaine (Shelburne)	88 —	'66
Bradford Lame (Reynolds Croft)	86 —	6 29 '67
Malena Odessa (Ved. Cape Negro)	81 — 13	4, 6, '69
Myie Gardiner (Shelburne)	84 —	2, — '70
John E. Matheson (Cape Negro)	90, 11, 24	11, 24 '71
Ida (Perry) Myrick (Blanche)	91 — 1 —	8. . '72
Stanford Towner (Cape Negro)	88 — 12 —	12, 72
Verna E. Matheson	67 years	11-27-77
Leah A. Smith (Blanche)	92 years	3-25-79
Hattie Towner (Cape Negro)		10-5-81
Sadie Swaine	58 yrs.	2-12-58
Violet Smith Oshawa Ont formerly Cape Negro	67.	7- -84
John D. Matheson (cremated)	75 yrs	10 - 85

Hillside Cemetary, Cape Negro.

Owners of lots.

1. Mrs. Helen Perry.
2. Emerson Thomas.
3. Clarence Price and Edwin Smith.
4. Peter Hurbert.
5. Bert Hill.
6. Arthur Moor and Jack Drew.
7. Russell Farmer.
8. John Thomas.
9. Blanche Thomas and Knowles Swaine.
10. Clint Herbert.
11. Clifford Thomas.
12. Clayton Thomas.
13. Albert Swallow and Olson Perry.
14. Clifford Perry.
15. Herbert Thomas and Charles Thomas.
16. Leighton Perry.
17. Lloyd Swaine.
18. Leander Thomas.
19. Grant MacKay and Harry Attwood.
20. Hilbert Thomas and Grant Lowe.
21. John W. Smith.
22. Fendvick Perry and Cecil Perry.
23. Henry Logg.
24. Laurie Smith.
25. George Ross.
26. William Monk and Milford King.
27. Lloyd Perry and Walter Myrick.
28. Kenneth Thomas and Bernard Towner.
29. Community Lot.
30. Carrol Swaine.
31. Arthur Lyle.
32. Wilma Obed.

Students Cape Negro School Class 1920. Back Hazel MacKay, Marion Matherson, Verna Obed, Mary Swaine, Mildred MacKay. Middle Thelma Swaine, Hazel Swaine, Lee Messenger, Harry Perry, Ralph Swaine. Front Evelyn Lyle, Annie MacKay, Hele Swaine, Ida Slate, Dorothy Swaine, Ernest Smith.

Cape Negro School House.

Cape Negro School — 1910.
1—2 Twins Hedley & Albert Swaine 3. James Smith, 4. Herman Swaine, 5. Myra Swaine, 6. Alberta Smith.

Class 1937. Front Leta, Fred, Betty Perry. Middle Burdett Perry, Alva Ross, Llewellyn Thomas, Allan Swaine, Cecil Perry. Back Geraldine Swaine, Teacher Mildred Sholds, Joseph Ross.

Cape Negro School

The first New England settlers that took up the French cultivated land at Cape Negro, taught their children at home as best they could. The parents had attended school in New England and could read and write to some degree. This knowledge was passed on to their children, along with some knowledge of the Bible, which in some cases would be the only book available to them.

About 1810 the first log school was constructed in Cape Negro at Craig's Road, which is on the ridge just south of barn of Captain John Smith's. The first teacher was a Master Craig who remained at Cape Negro a number of years. The next teacher that I have found a record of was Robert Tomson of Shelburne, in 1827. He remains several years, and was the surveyor and also the Secretary for the Committee who organized the building of the Haul Over.

There were many teachers over the years but unfortunately since the closing of the school the records are not available. We know that in 1840s the new school of timber construction was built at Cape Negro. One of the first school masters to teach in the new school was Daniel Matherson. Daniel Matherson came from Malagash where he owned a lobster factory. He became manager of a lobster factory at Woods Harbour. He married Temperance Swaine, a daughter of John B. Swaine and a sister of Herman Swaine. Master Matherson taught school for many years at Cape Negro and taught a number of students that also became teachers: Mysie Gardner, Florence Swaine, Odessa Obed. Master Matherson had one of the first teaching licenses for this area, issued in 1866 by the Nova Scotia Government and School Inspector.

The school served the children of the community over the years, accomodating at some periods up to 40 students. Many devoted teachers taught at this school but unfortunately I have not located the records. Several of the better known teachers are still remembered today are Mysie Gardner taught several terms, Mrs. Roy Matherson taught a number of terms. She and her husband lived at Green Hill (Upper Port LaTour) and she came up at 8:30 each morning with Mr. Edward Reynolds who drove the mail to the train station in Port Clyde. She would get off at the Cape Negro Post Office and walk to the school and return home with the mail driver in the evening. Mildred MacKay, who became Mrs. Grant Lowe, was a daughter of Godfrey MacKay at Thomasville but their house was within the bounds of the Cape Negro School District. She attended the local school for a number of years and then the Teachers Normal School in Truro. She taught school for a number of years, walking from her fathers home near the Clam Creek bridge. She was very kind and understanding and well liked as a teacher. She taught at many other schools in the district until she retired.

The Cape Negro School was closed in January 1951. The last teacher was Alice Smith. Students then went to Port Clyde by bus, operated by Allan Swaine, to the new school building which replaced the one burned in 1950. The Cape Negro School building has been slightly altered in its interior and is now used as a community hall. The exterior, being somewhat imposing, remains unaltered.

Cape Negro Hall and School from doorstep of Mercy Snow's house.

Cape Negro Hall after the pantry was added in 1935.

Cape Negro Hall

The Hall was built prior to 1866. The Sons of Temperance, MacMurray Division, was organized during that year. The hall was a long rectangular building, with a good smooth floor for dancing, and a large stage at north end of the building, where concerts and entertainments were performed. The stage had a large main curtain and two side curtains used as dressing rooms for the players. The front entrance had a porch partition which was used by the outside and inside sentinals when the meetings of MacMurray Division were in progress. The Division operated at Cape Negro and was very well attended from 1866 until the First World War, when it declined. It was reorganized in the late 1920's and carried on until the Second War, when it was finally closed due to declining population.

    The hall, besides the Sons of Temperance meetings, was used for other entertainments, dances, wedding celebrations, tea meetings, quilting parties and school concerts. When the school was closed the community decided that the two buildings could not be maintained. The hall was sold in 1960, taken down and the material used to build a house, today occupied by Burdett Perry, which is at the beginning of Captain Joseph Freeman's lane way.

School concerts were organized by the school teacher, who rehearsed the school children in singing, recitations, acting in skits and other entertaining tableaux which were usually held at Christmas time, were accompanied by a decorated tree and a visit from Santa. This would be followed by a dance to end the evening. Quite often the proceeds from the school concert were used to help pay part of the teacher's annual salary. The concert not only taught music and singing to the children, but coordination and cooperation among the children, as well. The proud parents seeing their children perform were indeed pleased. The pie sales were usually held in conjunction with a dance, as were Box Lunch Socials. Both worked on the same principal, that local girls brought pies or box lunches which were auctioned off after the first few dances had the festivities in the right mood. The young men would bid and try to purchase the pie or box lunch supplied by their girlfriend. It did not always happen that way, because often rival young men would increase the bidding. If the boy friend did not have enough money he would have to withdraw from the bidding and someone else would then share the pie or box lunch with the girl. The girl always sat with the person buying the auctioned article, regardless of how disappointed she may have been. It was a lark and lots of fun and very seldom led to any hard feelings. Quilting parties consisted of the local ladies setting up in quilt bars one or more quilts. The ladies then brought food, and would quilt usually all day, but sometimes just an afternoon and evening, depending on what the men folk were engaged in and if they could leave home. Sometimes women from other communities would join them. They worked, had meals from the food they brought, and had a good visit together, hearing all the latest news, making for very social and enjoyable times for all concerned. The quilts thus produced were usually sold and money used for church purposes. The money from Tea Meetings and Hot Suppers were used for the same purpose, and these usually ended with a dance once the tables were cleared and put away. A number of men in the area could play the fiddle, the banjo or accordian. In later years Ruby Smith played the guitar.

The dances were the traditional Crazy Eights, which consisted of 4, 6, or 8 on each side, sometimes ending in a break down, when the men would swing every lady on the dance floor. Some of the more ambitious ones tried to swing the girls off their feet, but the latter seldom happened. When the dance was over, if couples were courting or going together, the young man would have to walk his lady friend home. This could be a formidable undertaking if she lived at Blanche or Green Hill.

Some of the concerts could be three act plays or a variety type with different kinds of entertainment, singing, dancing and humorous skits. Some of the best concerts were put on by the Negroes at Reynoldscroft. In the winter if they were short of money they would organize a concert, being good singers and playing different kinds of instruments. They put on a good show which was always well attended, people coming from all the nearby communities.

Haul Over looking east with wooden bridge over the Blanche Road.

Haul Over looking west before the 1935 improvements..

The Haul Over

The Haul Over which the Indians called Oo-ni-gum-suk, was in use as a portage place to transport their canoes from Cape Negro Harbour to the Eel Bay and thence to Port La Tour Harbour and beyond, many hundreds of years before the French settlers, or the New Englanders came to the Cape Negro area. It is possible the French settlers followed the Indians' example in portaging their small crafts as well, as the French inhabited the area at the French Meadows and vicinity. It was not until some years after the New Englanders came, and established more commerce and fishing activities, that the need became more pressing for a less dangerous route than around the Blanche Point, for those wishing to go to the westward into the Eel Bay or Port La Tour Harbours.

It was therefore decided that a meeting would be called, for the purpose of discussing the possibility of cutting a canal through the French Meadows. The first meeting was held at the home of Jonathan Smith on February 24th, 1827, and Robert Thomson of Shelburne, who was the school teacher at Cape Negro, was appointed secretary. He recorded "Cape Negro, Township of Barrington. It has long been under consideration that great benefit would arise to the inhabitants of Cape Negro, Port La Tour and the whole neighbourhood around which is extensive by having a water communication between Cape Negro and Port La Tour across a narrow isthmus called the Haul Over, of the breadth of 450 yards or there abouts chiefly through soft ground." It is also recorded that after due consideration came to the following resolutions for the purposes herein named:

"First; That a committee be appointed as Directors of the business, to solicit subscriptions and to transact all such matters and things as may appear necessary more especially to obtain a deed, to solicit subscriptions and to consult upon every measure that may be deemed for the general benefit and from time to time as the business proceeds to call meetings and to consult with those concerned and that they appoint a secretary and treasurer. The Committee of Directors was appointed as follows: John Lyle and John Staker, Jr., Clyde River, David Swaine and William Patterson, Cape

Negro, Samuel Doane and Benjamin Perry, North East Harbour, James Snow, Port La Tour. It was resolved that notice be sent to those as directors who were not present requesting them to meet at Mr. Jonathan Smith's on Monday, 5th March next. Signed Robert Thomson, Clerk Pro Tem. Cape Negro. February 27, 1827."

The directors met again at Mr. Jonathan Smith's at Cape Negro on fifth day of March, with Robert Thomson the school teacher recording the minutes. "Agreeable to the foregoing resolutions, notice was given in writing to those appointed Directors who were not present at the first meeting to assemble on this day. Accordingly the following members were present; David Swaine, James Snow, William Patterson, John Lyle, Jr., and John Stocker, who after due consideration requested William Patterson and James Snow to wait upon the owners of the land through which the canal is intended to be made, who after a short absence returned and reported that Mr. Swaine agreed to give a deed of Gift to the Public of 20 feet wide across the Haul Over for the said purpose and to allow a privilege of as much ground as may be found necessary for the carrying on the business until it should be completed and then make no difficulty with the respect to said accommodation, which report being found agreeable to the wishes of the committee. Mr. David Swaine was proposed and unanimously chosen chairman and the following resolution agreed to: First, that the subscription papers be made out to the following persons requesting them, to solicit subscriptions for the purpose intended of making the canal in question upon the following terms. That is to say if a person subscribes a certain sum, it may be at his option to pay the money or perform work to the value there of at an equitable price, and the following persons were proposed and chosen: For the middle district from Mr. Gavin Lyle's to Blanche Point, John MacKillop. For Clyde River, James Nelson. From Solomon Smith to Charles Morrison's and thence on the western side to Mr. Gavin Lyle. For North East Harbour Stephen Perry from his own house to William Perry's, Jr. from the North East Meadows to North West Creek, Knowles Reynolds and from North West Creek to Baccaro Point, James Snow, and to request Mr. Benjamin

Perry to aid Stephen Perry in his applications and that Mr. Robert Thomson as Secretary to the Committee to make out subscription papers and forward to the different persons appointed, requesting them to go forward and make return on their proceedings as soon as possible to the Chairman of the Committee to meet to consult upon the measures there after to be adapted and the Committee do appoint Mr. Robert Thomson their Secretary, Mr. William Paterson will be pleased to solicit subscriptions in general where it does not interfere with the afore mentioned districts."

Later it is recorded the subscribers and their promised contributions, William King promised 10 shillings, John King seven shillings six pence, Thomas King seven shillings six pence, William Perry twelve shillings, Samuel King ten shillings. No further contributions are recorded but we must assume that all the districts solicited did contribute with money or by work as suggested.

Robert Thomson has recorded the following after he surveyed the land for the canal. Haul Over at Cape Negro course S 39°W 106 chains. N 20E between Swaine and A. Smith. 53½ chains to R. Smith fence from a rock marked R, on the shore of Dicks Point, course across the division E 2°S.

N1	26	13	
2	23	11½	E 2°S
3	29	14½	
4	28	14	

Later that same spring the work was begun, continued by various groups of men throughout the summer. Many worked at the low tide intervals in the late afternoon after early morning fishing. Shovelling and spading were done by hand and the help of various teams of oxen were used to remove the dug materials, as well as bring wagon loads of rock for stoning the corners and reinforcing between the crib work. After much effort the canal was completed and cut through the following summer.

The canal was in such order that boats could be pulled or poled through at high tide only at first. Over the next twenty years various improvements were carried out as the need arose and time permitted. Therefore for first twenty odd years the canal was maintained by contribution from the local residents.

By 1850 the crib work had been damaged by storms and ice and additional work had to be undertaken. The provincial government in Halifax agreed to give a grant of one hundred pounds towards that purpose under the conditions the local residents subscribe and spend twenty five pounds first. This was done, and considerable repair and improvements were carried out that summer. The following year 1851, the government again gave a grant of £25 as well. This was carried out that summer, and the canal repaired to a good standard.

Over the years the Haul Over has had repairs and replacements of various kinds, but its original size and character have remained unaltered to the present.

In 1935, under a contract from the provincial government, Mr. Sydney Christie, as foreman, with a crew of local men, replaced the log crib work and realigned the stone installations. The logs for the crib work were all cut and processed by local men. The iron work and long bolts and spikes were made by Mr. Lloyd Swaine in his blacksmith shop. Ox teams were also engaged to transport extra rocks and supplies, and the canal was returned to its original condition. This was the last major work carried out on this development.

The canal has been in continuous use since it was completed in 1828 by boats of various sizes. The only inconvenience was that boats had to lower their sail masts to go under the fixed bridge of the Blanche road which crosses the Canal. The canal is still used today by small fishing boats and pleasure craft as well. Since the mid-forties the number of fishermen in both these harbours has steady deminished, due mainly to the loss of the inshore fishery.

During a recent summer a youth group on some type of works grant attempted to restore some of the crib work, but nothing of a permanent nature was accomplished. The Canal is in very poor state of repair, requiring the crib work to be replaced and rock reinforcement realigned.

The Reuben Smith wharf at Blanche where he bought lobsters. Note break water on far beach, with inlet into creek, also the wooden lobster pots with lathed ends, the wrench at end of dock for unloading firkins of herring and fish. Far view is Cape Negro Island.

Blanche Lifeboat Crew.
William Smith, Coxwain, Alex Lyle, William Lyle, James Obed, Reuben Smith, Walter Myrivk, Sr., James Swaine.

Blanche Lifeboat

Since the French explorers arrival in the early 1600s there have been shipwrecks on the many reefs and rocks at the end of Blanche point, especially the ones where The Salvages is now constructed. Since early times an accurate count of the number of ships lost at this location is not available but it was many. These shipwrecks continued up to the very late 1930s. In the early days local fishermen would respond to the call of distress horns, usually in thick fog and stormy weather. When possible to launch the fishing boats they would go to the rescue, and bring back survivors. They would be cared for in the local homes, some remaining for months or all winter before obtaining transport back to where they lived. A number of unknown seamen are buried in the Cape Negro Cemetery. Their bodies having been picked up on the beach. In some cases no identification or other information as to their origin was available.

These shipwrecks resulted in many types of materials and goods being brought ashore by the waves as the ships broke up on the reefs. Clothing, bolts of cloth goods, tubs of lard and molasses, many different items were retrieved by the local residents after the storm had abated. Many of the local homes have tongue and groove lumber in their homes that came from such shipwrecks. The first floor coverings were the canvas sails of these wrecks. The canvas was fitted to the floor and then painted several times, usually with grey ship paint. Some with an artistic flair would paint flowers in the corners. Most houses for miles around had these ship sails for floor covering, especially upstairs in the bed chambers. The last ship wreck in Blanche, in the late 1930s, left hundreds of oranges and lemons floating and stacked on the beach, and large balls of lard as well, like big lumps of snow. The lard, once rendered, was quite good and used for cooking. The oranges unfortunately took on salt water and became terribly bitter and unpalatable.

Before the first war, about 1910, the Nova Scotia Government had built at Blanche a large building which was to house the lifeboat. The building had a two track ramp to the sea, where the boat could be not only more easily pulled out of the water but it facilitated the boat being launched in very rough weather. Some crew could be in the boat with oars ready and, as soon as it reached the water, start to row therefore keeping the boat from capsizing in the rough sea.

Once the lifeboat was built and established at Blanche, Mr. William Smith was the first Coxwain, with six men from the local inhabitants as crew. They were well organized and had regular training sessions, usually every two weeks. This consisted of launching the boat and practicing not only their rowing skills, but others as well, which involved the use of their equipment for life saving of the wrecked seaman such as rigging boswains and etc. There was a small stipend paid for their services. I have not been able to locate the log books for this period and do not know the total number of wrecks attended. I do know, by tradition it was quite a number and quite often William Smith, the Coxwain, housed quite a few of the wrecked seamen or saw that they were properly placed with other families in the upper village.

On William Smith's death, the lifeboat service was taken over by his son, Reuben A. Smith, as Coxwain, in 1931, and his Log Books are still available. The following are excerpts from them:

Took charge of the lifeboat on September 9th, 1931.
Reuben A. Smith, Coxwain.

Sept. 28th, 1931
Went to drill in lifeboat my first time. Wind east and good breeze. Went over to Cape Negro Island. Had a talk with the men on there. They reported times dull. Returned and housed boat.
R.A.S., Coxwain

Coxwain Smith held lifeboat drill about every two weeks, some of the comments made in his log are:

October 9th, 1931. Went to drill in lifeboat went up to Everett Nickerson's saw his new boat he built for Dave Doane. Trueman Thomas cut his foot so he stayed in the boat. November 7th, 1931. Spoke to John Matherson who had been gunning. He had three ducks. Landed at Uncle Tone Perry's old place. May 11th, 1932. Called crew together for drill, wind easterly. A little sea hove in the afternoon. Landed on Blanche beach. The crew present was Elroy Thomas, Walter Myrick, Amos Myrick, John Drew, James Swaine, Alex Lyle. All satisfactory. June 6th, 1932. With wind southwest and thick fog and raining called crew to go to drill. Went to Half Moons, the government ship Lady Laurier was landing supplies. I went on board and talked to Mr. Hougan who was coming here to see slip. Brought Mrs. Angie Thomas and George from Half Moons. We returned and washed out boat. July 4th, 1932. Went to Blanche Island then over to Half Moons. Happy (Everett Hersey) put a handle on the hatchet. July 28th, 1932. Went in lifeboat, wind southwest, and thick fog. Had Randall Myrick as a passenger. Water Myrick in Amos Myrick's place. August 15th, 1932. Went to Blanche Island and up in cove, and off to Shag Rock. Amos Myrick being absent had Floyd Ross in his room. November 14th, 1932. Wind southeast and good breeze and quite a sea running. Went over to Cape Negro Island and down to Southwest Point and then up to East Breakers. Saw Harry Perry and John B. Smith fishing. There was no fish. November 23rd, 1932. Wind light but quite sea running with fog. Went out to Shag Rock then up harbour. Walter Myrick had his gun and got 5 ducks. We returned and washed out the boat. May 21st, 1934. Wind southwest with quite a sea. Went up to the harbour. Saw Leighton Perry and Charles Thomas who had just got back from getting kiaks, 1400. I went aboard Everett Nickerson's boat who was hauling traps. July 20th, 1935. Saw Freeland Perry out fishing. He said there were plenty herring and lots dog fish. Sept. 4th, 1935. On our way back spoke to Will Matherson and Morton Nickerson going out fishing. October 30th, 1935. Went up the harbour. Trueman Thomas sick Arthur Moors in his place. April 30th, 1936. Called crew to go to wreck of M.V. Placentia. Captain Reuben Power from Yarmouth to Halifax, which stuck on Southwest Breakers, off Half Moons and is a total wreck. They had got ashore to fog alarm. Took them off and brought them to the station. Took extra men as crew. Crew: Alex Lyle, James Swaine, John Drew, Trueman Thomas, Walter Myrick, Sr., Elroy Thomas, Walter Myrick, Jr.

    The lifeboat was of wooden construction and had a

variety of equipment on the boat for rescue work and that function. The coxwain sat in the stern and operated the tiller The usual crew consisted of six men, two abreast on each thwart with a large wooden oar each, to row the boat. The Lifeboat Service was operated at Blanche until after the Second War, then the service was discontinued and the boat sold to Edward Crowell. It remained at his home at Port La Tour for some years and is now deposited at the Archeleas Smith Museum, Cape Sable Island. The horn which was used to call the crew together in an emergency, or for drills, was operated by hand crank and a bellows type of operation. Some of the artifacts from the Lifeboat Service are still retained privately.

Sheep Shearing Days

Sheep shearing pens at Blanche in the 1930s.

Alec Lyle and few sheep at Blanche.

Blanche Sheep-Shearing

When the Haul Over was built at Cape Negro this made Blanche technically an island. Due to its long narrow shape it was an ideal place for having free ranging sheep. The New Englanders, shortly after their arrival, realized the importance of keeping sheep successfully as their wool was essential for providing items of clothing and blankets. Keeping sheep at Blanche was a better organized industry than it was at some other areas, due mainly to the reasons previously mentioned, the canal and the shape of the land. At Blanche a large community sheep pen was constructed, first in the 1800s and temporary lead-in fences installed when needed. At the turn of the 1900s subscriptions and contributions were obtained and a large sheep pen was built on Blanche beach near Barss Cove. It was built of heavy wooden timbers for posts and boards and lumber for main surround walls. It was a large rectangular shaped pen with individual smaller pens along the east and west sides. There was always a keeper for the sheep pens and contributions obtained for its upkeep.

Sheep were allowed to run free on the peninsula of Blanche. The residents all had fences around their gardens and homes and sheep were fenced out. Each person owning sheep and keeping same at Blanche had a mark registered at the Barrington Municipal Office. Such a mark would be something like a hole and notch in the right ear and a slit and notch in the left ear. By these various ear marks the sheep were identified and, when rounded up, found by their owners.

Sheep shearing was usually the first week in June, being a foggy period weather wise. Local inhabitants usually referred to the heavy fog as Sheep Shearing Weather. On the day before shearing day Charles Thomas would start the sheep down from the Haul Over area. Leighton Perry would do likewise for his area. Sometimes it was possible to drive the sheep from Jimmy's Old Place down to the west side or bring them down. Sheep in Blanche Village were taken down across the beach and these smaller groups would be joined with the large drive the next day. Early in the morning of the drive the men would be assigned the area where they were to cover. Most men took with them their fog horns which were hand held horns that the dory fishermen used to signal their location in the fog. As the crew of beaters came down with these horns blowing, the sheep went at a run and the men keeping them going in the right direction until they reached Green Point. This was always rather a difficult spot as they had to turn, and usually a group managed to double back and escape. Once they were at the head of the pond, it was easier to keep them on the ridge of the beach and bring them into the community sheep pen. During the morning it was possible to listen to the fog horns being blown and to know the progress of the drive. Men were assigned posts at the end of the lead-in fences and those people who had collected at the sheep pens were forced to hide below the embankment and not scare the sheep until they were safely penned. It was a thrilling sight to lie on the bank at the sheep pens, as a young lad, and hear all the horns blowing and the large movement of sheep coming along the ridge toward the pens. There were usually upward of 400 sheep kept at Blanche. Not all the sheep owners lived at Blanche. Many were from distant places, only coming once a year for this event.

   Once the sheep were in the yard, and the gates securely locked, the sorting was begun. The older men would read the marks and say the owner's name, and the younger men and boys would take the sheep and put them into the individual pen of the owner. It was exciting and lots of fun. Once the sheep were sorted the unmarked lambs were all put in a separate pen by themselves. Once the shearing was completed the owners having ewes with milk in their udders drew a lamb As the system did not identify twin lambs, the extra ones left over were usually sold and money contributed to repair and maintenance of sheep pens.

   Once sorted the shearing began and continued all day. When owners finished their own sheep, they would help others with more to be shorn. When all were finished the wool was bagged and ready to be taken away.

   Before the sheep were released, lambs, which were drawn had their ears marked to identify their owners. The ram lambs were neutered, and all lambs detailed. If the latter was not done, as sheep lived in the wild, their long tail contributed to dirtying the wool. Once all the marking and doctoring was completed the gates were opened and the ewe sheep, after much blatting and running about, located their own nursing lambs. They were then started back down the ridge, minus the winter fleece, to have the process repeated another year.

Sheep buyers were present who purchased old wethers and the cull sheep. These were taken away, usually by skiff, to Reuben Smith's wharf. Ruby Smith had a tent erected just over the embankment from the sheep pens and throughout the day sold soft drinks, candy, gum, peanuts to the many onlookers. Blanche Sheep Shearing was a holiday, not only for Blanche, but the near communities as well. Many people came making the whole village into a holiday atmosphere. The Blanche residents cooked extra food and most homes had extra people for meals. Mrs. Leah Smith always had a large clam chowder ready for that day, with a variety of pies, loaves of cake and home-made bread. All day and well into the afternoon people kept arriving at her home for a chowder lunch and a visit. The visit was very important, because one saw folks they had not seen for a whole year, or possibly much longer. Usually by 4 in the afternoon, the sheep had been released and all would leave the sheep pens to walk to the village. Those who had been drivers and shearers would get cleaned up and changed into clean shirts and clothes, and go up to the hall where the pie sale and dance was held. Usually a couple of fiddles, accordion or banjo and the dancing was Crazy Eights with sets of 4 to 8 on each side. The dance would continue until mid-night.

The Blanche sheep shearing was held up until about 1951, when the Barrington Municipality brought in the animal act which prohibited animals from being loose in roadways and open ground. The sheep were rounded up and moved to Blanche Island or Cape Negro Island but the sheep industry did not flourish at these sites. Now no sheep are kept on Blanche Island and very few on Cape Negro Island.

The wool from the Blanche sheep at shearing time was bagged and taken home. During the hot days of summer the wool was washed and put out of doors to dry, then picked over with twigs and other foreign objects removed. Burrs were a particular problem. The wool was bagged and taken to the woollen mill in Barrington, where it could be traded for Barrington-made blankets or yarn. Instead of trading which was usually a fifty-fifty deal, it was possible to pay cash. The blankets produced in Barrington were very heavy and durable quality. The yarn, usually white or grey, was knitted by the housewife into a variety of articles to wear. In the early days women knitted long legged drawers for their husbands, lobster mittens which were double size and double knit especially for pulling the rope of lobster pots, socks of various length and the knee socks for boys, scarves, touques and sweaters, the vest type and ones with long sleeves. Before the Barrington Woollen Mill, the women washed the wool and then hand carded it. They used two carders, one held in each hand. When operated in an experienced hand the wool fibers became straightened and in one direction. They could then be spun on the wheel into yarn. Just how even the strands of yarn were depended on the skill of the operator.

Usually the local men at Blanche went onto Blanche Island the following week, taking the netting for a temporary pen. They would round up the sheep there and shear them. This was a much smaller operation and it was never known how many sheep would be found there, as they often came off to the mainland during the very low tides, by following the Blanche bar.

The sheep shearing at Cape Negro Island was organized by the families that lived on the island. Boat loads of men from Blanche went on there for this annual event, and the procedure was similar to what took place at Blanche and, as usual, ended with a supper and a dance. The families moved from the island shortly after the second war, and the practice of sheep shearing became a private and individual affair.

The Goose Shooting War

1. Unknown child. 2. Murray Smith. . Unknown. 4. Charles Thomas. 5. Walter Arey. 6. Stan Towner, Winner of the Goose. 7. John Matherson, Sr. 8. Unknown.

Fisherman Who Shoot The Goose

This was the title given an article written in 1964 by Cyril Robertson when he visited what is locally called a Goose Shooting. He further relates.

It happens every March and April, during the lull between lobster and herring fishing. Fishermen from Shelburne County shoulder their muzzel—loaders firearms and head for improvised shooting ranges to have themselves a rollicking time in a marksmanship contest called "shoot the goose".

All the weapons used in the 125 year old event are U.S. muskets brought into the country by the ancestors of the contestants, the Loyalists settlers who moved to the area after the American Revolution. The contest involves as many as eight matches, each held in different communities. The same fishermen usually take part in them all.

The match at Blanche brought out 42 fishermen who riddled six by six inch targets at 60 yards for 8½ shooting. No one seems to know just how the event got its name. Nobody really cares commented one of the fishermen as he rammed a 58 calibre lead ball down the powder charged barrel of his musket.

People come out to Blanche from miles around to get in on the fun, the women staged a whopping supper for everyone in the community hall, 150 yards from the shooting range. While the men were out shooting, the women played cards, whist or forty—fives and the children sang and played games.

Out on the range stocky ruddy—faced Hilbert Thomas took careful aim and fired. His shot went clean through the bull's eye. "You killed it, Hilbert;" the men shouted.

Hilbert Thomas's shot had earned him the role of collector under the contest's betting system. After that each competitor paid him two cents for the privilege of shooting. When another shooter killed the goose, he took over from Thomas. In addition, each man added ten cents in the pot for the final shoot off.

When the sun went down the men lit gas lamps and hung them on the branches of surrounding trees. Reuben Smith 82 year patriarch who had just come down from the hall, where he had been tending the fire, wanted to tell a ghost story. "Old Uncle Thomas used to play a tune on his fiddle and the ghost would beat out the rhythm on the wall of his house. People used to come from everywhere around to look for the ghost of Blanche. But they could never find it.

The only time it would never keep time to the music of the fiddle was when he played a hymn,.

Then Reuben began to tell about the longest goose shooting on record. Locally its called the Goose Shooting War.

Cape Negro men were competing against the men of Blanche. The shooting logs were set up east of Will Lyle's house at Blanche. The men were shooting in their regular turns when some disagreement developed and they all became disgruntled. The reason is obscure today and therefore it could not have been of major importance because it's lost to memory. Reuben Smith related that it took place in 1920, and it went on for nearly a week. "Four full days and four full nights", corrected Lloyd Swaine of Cape Negro, who had been one of the 25 contestants in that historic shoot. It was like some kind of grudge match; they kept on shooting right through a blizzard.

Others recall that one of the fishermen walked 30 miles for a new firing nipple so that he could continue the match with his own musket. The rivalry was so keen no one wanted to stop. A few walked to their homes for brief periods of sleep; others took cat naps hunched down at the shooting range. On the fourth evening, James Obed, a very old man and also the owner of the land where the shooting range was built, came to the group and demanded that they stop, saying "there will be no shooting on my land on Sunday." It was then late Saturday evening. The men respected his wishes and did the shoot off and Standford Towner of Cape Negro won the Goose.

The 1964 goose shooting at Blanche ended shortly before midnight and Llewellyn Thomas of Cape Negro won with 12 out of a possible 15 points in the shoot off. Clifford Perry of Blanche and Allan Swaine of Cape Negro tied with 11 points until Perry took the second shot in the deciding match.

" Best turn out we ever had," said Reuben Smith, as fishermen picked up their families at the hall and headed home. It was a big sucess and the women had earned $100.00 from the supper to pay for repairs to the hall.

Credit to The Standard Weekend Magazine, Cyril Robertson, for the narrative.

Captain Joseph Freeman Swaine and wife, Caroline Hills Swaine.

Evelyn Myrick, Verna Obed, Reuben Smith, Foster Swaine, John Matherson, Olson Perry, Bessie Swaine, Mamie Page, Odessa Obed, Roewna Pierce, Herbin Pierce, Leah Smith.

Lloyd Swaine, Bradford Perry, Charles Thomas, Emerson Thomas, Walter Arey, James Smith, John Matheson, Jr., John Christie.

Cape Negro Gun Club in 1937 with the winners of the Wilson Cup.

Bits and Pieces

The local area had a unique way of distinguishing women with the same name. To identify the five Sarahs, their husband's first name was added to theirs, in the event they did not have a suitable second name.

Sarah Ben	was Sarah Wife of Benjamin Slate
Sarah Sam	was Sarah Wife of Samuel Smith
Sarah Stewart	was Sarah Wife of Stewart Swaine
Sarah Jane	was Sarah Wife of Edward Smith
Sarah Ann	was Sarah Wife of William Smith

Being older and well respected members of the community they were often called Aunt. Aunt Sarah Ann was called that by most local people.

Some others had their husband's names added to theirs, i.e. Mary Heman and Carry Joe.

All women were addressed as Miss. If they did not have some other identification attached to their names, adults and children alike addressed or referred to them as such, Miss Hazel, Miss Florence, Miss Lottie. The same system applied to the men, i.e. Mr. Alex, Mr. John, Mr. Jimmy.

Nicknames were widely used as well, Alexander became Eck, Isaac became Ike, there was Snooter, Ben Snaggie, Tumbler Jim, Aunt Sackie, Long Division, Short Division, Nute, Dewy, Cotton Ears, Hink-Dink to name but a few.

At Christmas the young adults and children had an activity between Christmas night and the New Year called Santa Clausing. They disguised and transformed themselves by dressing in old clothes and adding pillows etc. They also wore women's cotton stockings over their faces for masks and the eye holes surrounded with black from lamp chimneys. Equipped with an Indian basket or a tin lard pail they went from house to house and after the occupants of the house attempted to guess who you were they would give you a treat, usually cookies, Christmas cake or candies. The older adults would act silly and try to make the people laugh orn run sit on the woman's lap and attempt to kiss her and she would act scared and in some cases they really were. It was lots of fun for those dressed up and Santa Clausing and a diversion for those being visited.

The older boys would often go long distances to go Santa Clausing, possibly down to Green Hill or even around the creek, where they were not known. They would have a basket of treats to eat on the long walk home. The smaller children would go to the local houses and when they were older would go further afield.

This was a bit of fun for most of the children but it also allowed the children of poorer families to obtain sometimes quite a collection of treats they otherwise would not have. Besides being fun it was a polite form of charity with dignity.

This custom is no longer observed in this area now being replaced by Halloween and Trick or Treat.

Halloween years ago was for scaring people, putting jack-o-lanterns with lighted candles up in the windows. If the person was not especially liked by the children, their gate, wheelbarrow or something that they had left out of doors, would be taken a mile or so away and hidden. Parents did not permit their children to do any damage, but innocent jokes were tolerated. All assumed they did not know who had taken Mr. Smith's wheelbarrow to the cemetery or exchanged his gate for someone's a mile or more away.

The older boys of course had a few more daring tricks. They would take a wooden spool from thread and make notches along the edges, then wind a piece of string around the spool, put a nail through the hole to hold on to, put this up to someone's window. Usually they found someone sitting near a window, possibly with a kerosene lamp knitting or reading and,holding the nail and putting the notched spool up hard on the window glass then pulling the string. It would make a terrible noise. Of course the occupants of the house would run out and the person who had done the deed had to be a fast runner and a long way away. If he was caught and his parents told then he was in for punishment. Usually only the larger boys did this when no smaller ones were around so they could make a fast get away with no informers about. This was called a Tic-Tac-Toe and a hush hush operation all around

The early settlers provided for their own needs and helped their neighbours who were sick or in need as best they could. But for those that did not have close relatives to look out for them, life was very difficult. Widows usually remarried as soon as it was considered proper for them to do so. Young girls who were orphaned hired out as serving girls at a very young age, some as early as 12. The very elderly that could not make any other arrangements would have to apply to the municipal poor officer and be admitted to the Poor Farm at Barrington.

One of the ways of helping those in need was by having "Pound Parties" which were enjoyed as a social occasion and not looked upon as charity. The neighbours of a widow, or a person in need, would send out word that they were holding a Pound Party and on the given evening people from far and near would come. Each one brought something, a pound of tea, pound of butter, salt, flour, lard, all the staple things required for country living and housekeeping. They also brought cakes, buns, cookies for a lunch. Some others brought their fiddle or a banjo. If the house had a parlour organ they could have a sing song. Everyone enjoyed themselves, had a lunch, left all their parcels and the receiver would have usually almost enough supplies for winter. What a happy and enjoyable way to provide charity with dignity.

Local Place Names

1. Clam Creek
2. Stewarts Point
3. Stoney Cove
4. Swaines Cove
5. Cordwood Point
6. Hawl Over
7. Buckwheat Cove
8. Lobster Factory
9. Salmon Rock
10. Stone Wharf
11. The Dyke
12. Purgatory Point
13. Gooseberry Point
14. Jimmys Old Place
15. Peaked Rock
16. Soukies Clam
17. Flat Rock
18. Scrubby Rock
19. Tamerons Ledge
20. Flat Rock
21. Bell Breakers
22. Dry Rock
23. Wig Wam
24. Green Point
25. Peg-A-Nolls
26. Trap Rock
27. Conks Rock
28. Sand Cove
29. Knowles Old Place
30. Little Harbour
31. Point of Cove
32. Conks Rock
33. Harve's Ledge
34. Slates Point
35. Slates Creek
36. Lyles Shanty
37. Capt. John's Wharf
38. Capt. John's Ledge
39. Sholds Island
40. Gerties Ledge
41. Joe Freeman's Point
42. Johns Point
43. Ezras Island
44. Ferry Point
45. Aunt Sakies Hole
46. White Brook
48. Cold Tar Hill
49. Flag Swamp
50. Grader Hill
51. Martins Hill
52. Treadles Hill
53. China Meadow
54. Keel Grove
55. Witch Rock
56. Jimmy's Road
57. Short Cut
58. The Old Road
59. The Ridge
60. Chap's Old Place
61. Sheep Island
62. Birch Hill
63. Giner Plum Hill

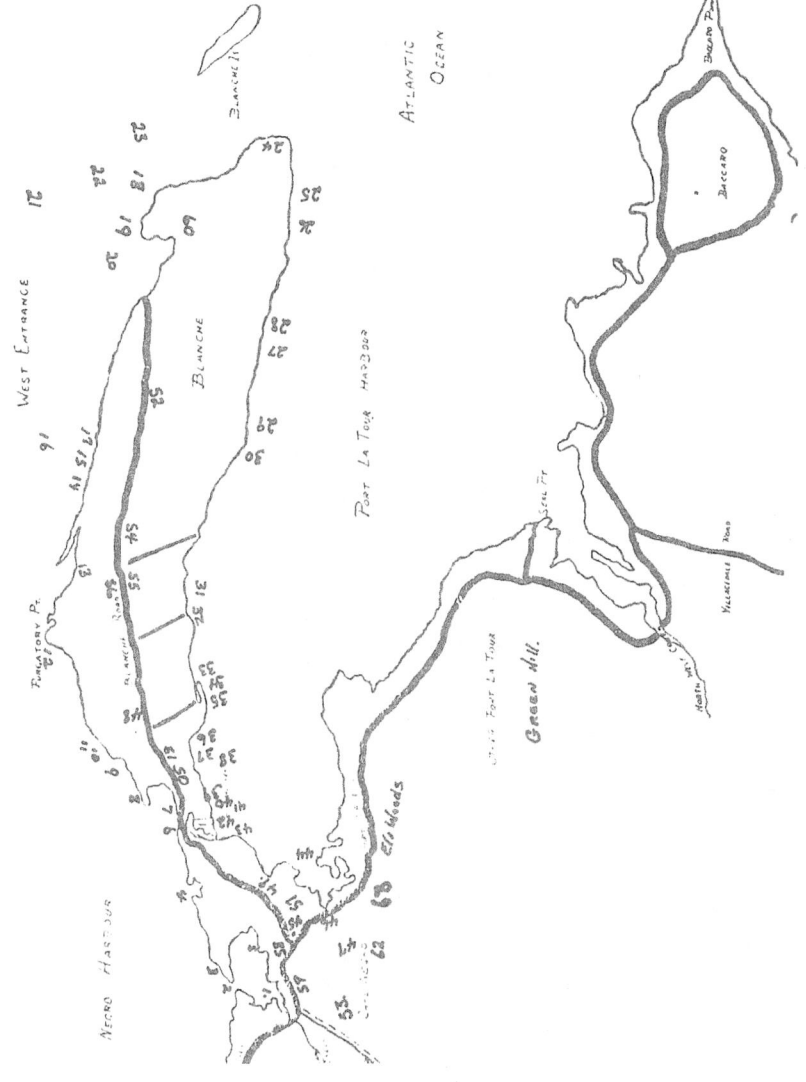

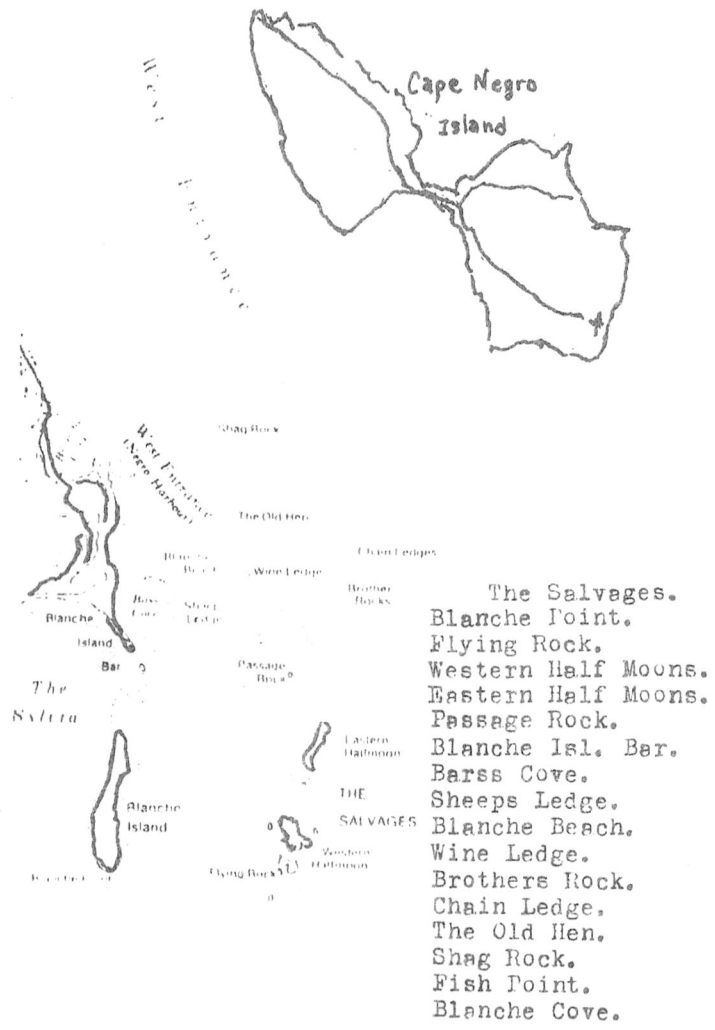

The Salvages.
Blanche Point.
Flying Rock.
Western Half Moons.
Eastern Half Moons.
Passage Rock.
Blanche Isl. Bar.
Barss Cove.
Sheeps Ledge.
Blanche Beach.
Wine Ledge.
Brothers Rock.
Chain Ledge.
The Old Hen.
Shag Rock.
Fish Point.
Blanche Cove.

Mr. John Nickerson in front of his store at Upper Port La Tour also the car used to peddle groceries at Cape Negro and Blanche.

The Consolidated Store at Port La Tour.

Stores

Jonathan Smith kept the first store in Cape Negro. It was on the east side of the Eel Bay, and in operation in 1783. He sold molasses, rum and other staples. How long this store operated I cannot determine. The next record was kept by his grandson, Captain John Smith, on much the same site. His vessels anchored near there and he also had warehouses for storing supplies brought by his vessels. A road from there went east and joined main Blanche road just below his barn. The store was opposite his house. When the store closed it was moved to Captain Zephaniah Nickerson's at Port Clyde who operated the store there. Captain Heman Swaine had a store which was located just about where Emerson Thomas's garage is now. This store was moved when Heman Swaine died and is now the wood shed at home of Herbin Pierce. After the Swaine store closed Winslow and Florence Swaine returned from the U.S.A. and built a store opposite their house. They operated the store for many years and also had a horse drawn grocery wagon which he used to peddle groceries to neighbouring villages.

When Winslow and Florence Swaine retired, the store was operated by Jenny, wife of Captain William L. Ross, who lived almost opposite the store, which was also the beginning of the short cut across to the Blanche road. She also kept the Post Office and operated a horse drawn grocery wagon for peddling. The store, under her management, was quite active and enjoyed considerable trade due mainly to the post office. Local people who came to wait for the mail in the evenings would sit around the fire, talk and socialize. In the winter the Halifax train may be three hours late resulting in a long wait. One fall evening Jenny's dog, called Old Bing, chased a skunk, which ran under the store's stone foundation. The resulting smell was a disaster, not only for the occupants of the store but most of the stock as well. The lard, which was in large wooden firkins and weighed out onto wax paper, the large crates of loose tea, sweet bulk biscuits and hard tack. Everything not in a tin took on the skunk odour and most of the goods were lost. The store was eventually cleared, cleaned and restocked. Only a short time later Jenny became ill, and the post office was moved to Lester and Violet Smith's. The store was closed and the building sold to Norman Reynolds. He built a house for his wife, Roseman Smith, which was on the hill opposite the home of Levi Reynolds. The Norman Reynolds' house in later years burned

Emerson and Lottie Thomas operated a store in the front of their house for some years. This was for local trade and they did not have a grocery wagon for peddling. This store was closed shortly after the second war.

There were other stores in the area, where one could walk for supplies. Stoddard Store, Port Clyde, started as a small store, eventually enlarged and became a wholesaler. Above there Fred MacLaren had a store and the main Post Office. Zephaniah Nickerson had a store for many years. At Port LaTour was John Nickerson's store, also The Consolidated. William Patterson at Reynoldscroft had a store as well. Some of these stores, such as John Nickerson's had a grocery wagon for peddling and came to Cape Negro and Blanche.

There are now no stores in this area.

The Old Road

The first road coming from Port La Tour came through Reynoldscroft, past Charlie Willie Hurberts and Russel Farmers to Burnt Island and Ferry Point. A ferry operated from this point across to Captain Matthew Swaine's, then the road followed the line fence to the "Short Cut" up through the present ball field, along the "Old Road" to the ridge and then to Thomasville and the ferry at Lyle's Falls.

William Patterson helped develop Patterson's Road which was cleared and ditched. This was the original route to Barrington from this area. Later, when MacDougal's Bridge was built and the road redirected there, the Swaine's Wood Road was developed and used as the route to Barrington.

Patterson's Road no longer was used. The wood road used by the Swaines was put through because it was higher ground requiring less material to build and maintain than Patterson's Road to Coffincroft, which was mainly through swamp or savanna as then called. Swaine Road over the years has been used as a short route to Barrington. However in recent years it has been neglected and no longer used.

The road from Shelburne to Clyde River was upgraded and paved in 1938-39. The road from Clyde River through Cape Negro to the then American Base at Baccaro was upgraded and paved after the second war. The upgrading of the Cape Negro Road removed "The Ridge" which ran from Clam Creek Bridge to James H. Smith's roadway. Also in the new construction has disappeared Aunt Sakie's Hole, which was at the N.W. corner of Lloyd Swaine's house lot. It consisted of a swampy area with a water hole in the south end, reported to have no bottom. The moss in the swamp protected ice and it was possible to go there in July, dig down in the moss and extract ice.

The road to Blanche from Cape Negro has received very little attention and is more or less in the same condition today that it was some 50 or more years ago.

Waiting for the Bride.

On a Picnic - Gordon & Beatrice Ennis, Stella Lyle, Lena Wood, Alvin Thomas.

William Lyle's car in front of his house at Blanche.

Swaines at Cape Negro

Ethel, Merle and Nellie Swaine.

Lobster Factory

Opposite Captain John Smith's house is a road leading to the shore. This road at one time was a public road, it ends at the stone wharf. Near this wharf was a lobster canning factory owned and operated by Captain Alexander Smith. The foreman was John Bethel, and George Webb also worked there.

Mr. Tone Perry operated the Catch which was a sailing boat. He went about the harbour and collected from the various fishermen the catch of lobsters, which he brought to the factory. The lobsters were boiled and then girls removed the meat from the shells and packed it into tin cans (some of the cans were manufactured at Captain Zephaniah Nickerson's). The cans after packing were sealed and then boiled to complete the sterilizing process. When this was finished the cans were labelled and packed in cartons for transport to Cann Boats that operated the freight service to Yarmouth, and then they were shipped to Boston.

Some of the girls who worked at the lobster factory were: Mrs. Nellie Swaine, Merle and her sister, Kate Swaine, Ida Swaine Perry.

The lobster factory was in operation for quite a few years and was very successful, until such time as the government brought into law the restriction on the size of the lobster to be retained and sold. Prior to this the fishermen had kept and sold to the factory all lobsters caught. The purchase of the large lobsters only, proved to be uneconomical and the factory was closed.

The lobster shells were ground up and used as fertilizer on the fields. The stone wharf still exists today but the road leading to it is much overgrown and long disused.

Railroad at Port Clyde

The railroad at Port Clyde was opened for business in 1906 and first passenger train from Yarmouth to Halifax was on December 20th that year. After the railway was established the mail was then brought on a regular basis as well as express and freight. Prior to this it was necessary for express and freight to come to the government wharf at Port Clyde, usually by the Cann Boats from Yarmouth. They came as a rule each week and the people could go to Port Clyde and with their horse or ox cart collect their goods when they arrived. The mail to this point was usually by coach between the larger centers, but was very unreliable. With the train the mail went once daily each way.

The service originated in Green Hill (Upper Port La Tour). The mail being collected there, the driver proceeded to Reynoldscroft, Cape Negro, Thomasville, West Clyde and Port Clyde. The mail bags were sorted at Mr. MacLarens Post Office and then placed on the train in the morning for Halifax in the afternoon for Yarmouth. The mail driver stayed in Port Clyde between the morning and afternoon trains from Halifax. After the latter arrived, he brought the mail and any passengers to the various post offices in reverse order from morning collection. With this system one could mail a letter in the morning at Cape Negro before the mail driver arrived and late that afternoon it was in Halifax. The same applied to Yarmouth.

Blanche operated under a different system. The mail driver was over years Captian Samuel Smith, Ezra Swaine, William and Maude Hurbert, Jimmy Farmer, John Seamon, John Matherson, Jr., Amy Thibeault. The mail was taken from Cape Negro Post Office to Slateville Post Office then on to Blanche. The mail was brought back after the driver spent one hour for the return mail. The mail to West Blanche was placed in a special box situated at head of their road, by the mail driver on his return from Blanche. This service was provided three times weekly, Monday, Wednesday and Friday.

The mail service now consists of a rural delivery from Barrington. The trains have all been discontinued and the tracks removed. The Port Clyde station house has also been taken down.

Telephones

In 1885 the Port La Tour Telephone Exchange was established with a line to Cape Negro and eventually to Blanche. The first manager was Captain John Nickerson of Port La Tour. The Telephone Exchange was organized as a company, with shares being sold to various investors. The Port La Tour exchange was eventually connected to Barrington and they had a line to Clyde River and Port Clyde. When Captain Nickerson moved away, Addison Huskins was the manager for many years. On his retirement Captain Joseph Nickerson became manager, and was succeeded by Captain Willard Nickerson.

The telephone system consisted of plain wire with glass insulators on wooden poles. Sometimes these poles were only trees along the road between the communities, with the bare wires. It was possible for limbs of trees to ground the telephone making it unusable. The telephone was a wall type with a crank. Each subscriber had a different ring, two long one short or some such thing. This was for calls on your immediate line, if you wished to call someone not on your line then you rang central and she made the connection. The central switchboard was usually in a woman's kitchen at Port

La Tour and she managed the board on a 24-hour basis. In an emergency at night it was necessary to ring long enough to awaken the central at the switchboard. When the lines were poor in winter, it was not uncommon to ask someone further along the line to repeat the message. As rings on same line came into all the houses, those of a curious nature would lift the receiver and listen to the others talking. If many receivers were lifted it reduced the transmission and the original recipient could not hear; it was then necessary to say "Would you please hang up so I may speak to my party". One may then hear several clicks. If you were talking to someone it was interesting to let them hang up first, then listen to the clicks to see how many had been listening into your conversation.

In the 1950s the Port La Tour telephone system was taken over by the Maritime Telephone and Telegraph Company. The bare wires have been replaced by cables, some being underground. The dial system is used, but as multi-party lines still exist the telephone system functions much in the same way as years ago.

What I Remember
By Hazel V. MacKay

Years ago most people in the community attended church and prayer meetings. At one time they came from Blanche, Upper Port La Tour and Port Clyde to the Cape Negro Church. I have heard my mother tell of people walking from Blanche, as they did in those days, they wore their everyday shoes, but brought their better shoes and changed them when they got near the church. This was mainly due to the muddy roads. People in those days did not have shoes that matched their clothes as they do today.

There were many different ministers for this church district. The list is contained elsewhere in this book. The church had a stove which burned coal. Mr. James Swaine was the janitor, he always had shoes that squeaked when he walked, and always about the time the minister would begin to pray, Mr. Swaine would get up to stoke the fire and maybe put on a little bit of coal. We had church services three Sundays in a month, one morning, one afternoon and one evening service.

I have heard my mother tell of going to prayer meetings when she was growing up. I have faint remembrances of Mrs. Heman Swaine being the organist, then Miss Gertrude Swaine, then later years Mrs. Odessa Obed.

We always had Easter and Christmas concerts, also Mission Band; it was usually the Mission Band members (they were children) and the Sunday School teachers who put on the concerts.

The colored folk from Reynoldscroft, who came and sat in the back pews, was before I remember to much about them, but I have heard others speak about it, also what good singers they were. We had a large Sunday School library around 1,000 books, each book was numbered and placed accordingly, each household had a little catalogue, with the titles and numbers of each book. We all had cards with our name on them, when we got a book the number of book put on the card, when we returned the book the following Sunday was was checked off. Captain Joseph Swaine was the librarian; he recorded the numbers of the books each person had out on loan. Later Miss Gertrude Swaine was the librarian.

When we went to church in the morning, quite often someone invited us to dinner, and we stayed down for Sunday School in the afternoon. The same when church was in the evening, and we attended Sunday School in the afternoon. Mrs. Ezra (Josephine) Swaine was the teacher of the Bible class. Mrs. Joseph (Carrie) Swaine taught the older boys.

When I went to school in the early 1920s there were no school buses, all pupils walked, some having as far as 1½ or two miles to walk. It had to be a very bad storm that we missed school. Mr. Lloyd Swaine drove his daughter, Hazel, to school, if we happened to be on the road we always had a ride. There was a belfry on the school house with a bell, which had been donated to the school by Captain John Smith. The bell was rung each morning by one of the boys at 8:45. If and when we heard the bell we realized we had 15 minutes to get to school and not be late.

The teachers I remember were: Dean Goulding, Agnes Baxter, Francis Reynolds and Mrs. Mysie Gardner. Some of the pupils were Jamie Smith, Evelyn Lyle, Hazel Swaine, Thelma Swaine, Millie Slate, Lillian Slate, David Slate, Lester Slate, Harold Smith, Cecil Smith, Louis Smith, Ernest Smith, Marion Matherson, Hedley Swaine, Albert Swaine, Mary Swaine, William Swaine, Helen Swaine, Merton Nickerson, Mary Nickerson, Ivan Nickerson, Arthur Nickerson, Ralph Swaine, Allie Nickerson, Flossie Nickerson, Mary Nickerson, Ivan Nickerson, Mildred MacKay. If we talked in school we often lost our recess and had to write on the blackboard "I must not talk" one hundred times. If we wished to leave our seats at any time, we put our hand up and held it there until the teacher asked us what we wanted, then we asked to be excused. We always had a Christmas concert and often another on Empire Day in the spring, and always exercises when school closed for summer holiday. We enjoyed getting ready for concerts, and practicing our parts each day. The blackboards were decorated with things each student made. Once or twice a year we had a visit from the school inspector, a Mr. Stanley Bruce from Shelburne. We did not look forward to his visits, as he was not very popular with we school children.

I remember Millie Slate from Slateville used to bring in her lunch, usually after Christmas, cranberry tarts her mother made by baking pastry shells in cup cake tins, which at that time was called patty pan tins, and filling the shells with stewed cranberies, they always looked delicious. In the winter when there was snow on the ground we were allowed to go during the noon hour coasting on Rocky Hill. The hill is gone now, following some roadwork a few years ago, it was lots of fun. Sometimes in the noon hour we were coasting a horse and sleigh would come along, we may get a short ride.

We often had our little spats, as children will, on the long walk home from school, resulting in not speaking with each other for a day or two, but there were also many good times. I do not remember there ever being itch or lice in the school while I attended but years later there were. Learning in school today is much different. I am happy about my school years and am certain I learned as much then in the little red school house as they do today even though they have many modern equipment and gadgets not even thought of or invented in my school days.

Walter Myrick and his bride, Lorena, taken at their marriage in Maine, U.S.A.

Happy Times in a Large Family
Ina Myrick Hogg

I was born at Blanche, one of eleven children. My father's name is Walter Myrick and mother's Lorena. My mother was working in the United States when she met and married my father. They came to Blanche shortly after they married and bought a Thomas house, which was very close to mother's father, James Obed. The two fields joined and we could run over to grandfather's house very easily.

Our house, which was near the sea, was not that large. It had the usual bed chambers upstairs for we children and our parents had a bedroom on the main floor. The house also had a large kitchen, pantry and hall with front parlour. The parlour was only used for special occasions, it was kept neat and tidy at all times and used if the minister or some important person cane to visit or at sheep shearing time when there were many callers and visitors to the house. Then at Christmas time we always had the tree there, which would be decorated and we kept the fire going so we enjoyed the use of the parlour at those times. There were usually extra people at our house at Christmas. My older married sister would come with her children and quite often there would be 18 or 20 of us together. Christmas was a happy time, as children we played together, shared what toys we had and played games, played in snow and had a good time. In those days most people were poor and for those with large families it was harder than others to have more than the essentials for living. Quite often at Christmas we would all have a present such as a hair ribbon, or some other thing. We enjoyed these small presents and cherished them, as I still have today some of those gifts. They meant so very much and we children enjoyed our Christmas to the fullest. One Christmas my grandfather, James Obed, bought a doll for me. It was a T. Eaton Beauty, he had sent away having ordered it from the catalogue. The doll had real hair, unfortunately before Christmas my mother had hid the doll under her bed, so I would not know anything about it until Christmas day, but some how our cat which was little more than a kitten and always playing with bits of yarn and things go under the bed and played with the hair on my Christmas present, come the morning and I received my doll I was ever so upset and cried to see my doll's hair ruined, but mother fixed it as best she could and I loved that doll, it was the only large one I ever had.

This is a picture of myself and my doll taken by our house with my brother, Walter. Please note my brother's pinafore; boys in those days wore this type of dress and some had long curly hair almost up to the time they went to school, then they had knee trousers and long stockings and had their hair cut.

My mother was a great seamstress, with so many children she was kept busy. She made all our clothes, dresses, underwear, slips and also knit our socks and mittens. We younger ones often had hand me downs, which mother would do over to fit us. If someone gave us clothing or a coat mother could take it apart and redo it, so it appeared like new. Mother also was a good cook. It seemed she made bread each evening and in the morning it was done over and when ready baked before noon, course there were biscuits and mollasses and sugar cookies as well as rhubarb and berry pies to be made at different times. In those days most people had the usual fish and potatoes, duck stews, rabbits and sometimes deer or even eels. When properly prepared these things all made good meals for hungry children. I think a hundred pound bag of flour, with mother making bread just about every night, biscuits and things, the bag of flour did not last much longer than a week.

We all walked to school, which was one room, with wood stove in the middle of the room. The older children kept the fire going and put wood in the stove. On Friday all the children cleaned the school room before we went home that day, sweep floors, clean black boards, dust window sills and tidy all books and papers. Our drinking water was a pail with a tin mug in the porch. Two of the children would take the pail and go to a brook for fresh water. I liked doing this especially of we could go during school hours, it made time go faster. We had a school inspector, a Mr. Bruce, he was rather strict and I was very scared of him. If we knew when he was coming I usually found some reason to stay home that day. Many of our school teachers were single ladies and once they arrived and became acquainted the young men sometimes may come up to the school, knock on the door so they could talk to teacher, possibly to invite her to a dance or pie sale. She would stand outside and talk to him and close the door. As soon as the door was closed we would be up to something, but always managed to be quiet by time she came back. A number of our school teachers married local men and remained in the village. Odessa Swaine married Jesse Obed, Ethel Snow married Maurice Swaine and Mary Attwood married Knowles Swaine are the ones I can think of now.

When we were older we went to the pie sales, hot suppers and the dances. I was about 12 when I first learned to dance the eights, but learned the fox trot and waltz later. The pie sales were a lot of fun, the girls put their pies in a box and decorated them with tissue paper and things real fancy and young men had to bid at auction for them. Sometimes a young man wanting to buy a certain girl's pie would have have to price way high and he would have to borrow money from his friends or miss getting his girl friend's pie. The girl was supposed to eat the pie with the young man and then he walked her home. It did not always work out that way, however, because my pie it seemed was always bought by a married man who ate the pie with his wife and I didn't even get a piece. It was good fun and we all enjoyed ourselves at these social functions.

When we were older in the winter it was fun to go to the pond by the beach to skate. The boys in evening would keep the bonfire going and everyone with skates would skate around. In those days the skates fit onto your shoes with clamps and if they did not fit you had to tie them on with heavy twine. By doing this they would come loose and you would fall when skating. It never seemed to work too well for me and I did not have a really good pair of boots and skates until I was married when new type of skates because available. Coasting on hills was lots of fun as well as two or more children could crowd onto a sled and it was lots of fun sliding in the evening moon light.

I forgot to add that when we were quite small we girls would collect discarded broken cups and other dishes and interesting items that had been discarded and we would assemble them all in a sheltered flat spot and play house. We would make mud cakes and decorate them with berries and cones from trees and play at keeping house and doing the things we saw our mother do. The neighbour's children would join in and we had lots of fun together.

My mother and father have both died and we eleven children have all gone to different places, married and raised families and only one brother remains near the old home place. Other folk have now bought and live in the old home but some of us still visit on occasions and its nice to see the places where we played and did different things as children and memories are all happy ones.

Evelyn & Sadie Myrick by James Obeds house

Back row:- Alice Smith, Marie Thomas, Mrs. Jimmy Stoddard, Allan Swaine, Cecil Perry, Fred Perry, Llewellyn Thomas, Burdett Perry.

Front row:- Izola Smith, Florence Swaine, Grace Perry, Merle Thomas, Lottie Thomas, Violet Perry, Flossie Swaine, Mildred Sholds, Verna Matherson, Myra Hutchins, Odessa Obed, Nellie Swaine, Betty Perry, Nancy Swaine, Rowena Pierce, Betty Perry, Herbin Pierce, Violet Smith.

The Runaway Horse

Ruby Smith Perry

In 1915 my grandfather, Ross, at Cape Negro had closed his house as his wife, Dora, had recently died, he left his horse and buggy for us to care for while he was gone. My mother, Leah Smith, used to take the horse and buggy and go to visit other people on errands. One day Mother, Aunt Izola Smith and Cousin Florence and I, left Blanche early in the morning with the horse and buggy and wnet to Green Hill to visit my great- grandfather, Thomas Ross, and his wife, Nancy. We had a few hours with them and then called at Uncle Jim's and Aunt Carry Ross's who lived near by. We left in late afternoon to return to Blanche and when we were on our way home the black clouds rolled in and it started to thunder and lightening and then the rain came down in sheets. Mother took the horse blanket from the back of the buggy and Florence and I got down by their feet and Mother covered us up and the blanket came up around their laps as well. It rained ever so hard and the lightening would dash across the sky and horse got right nervous and his ears stood back on his head and he started to gallop along. The harder it rained and more noise from thunder the faster he ran. Florence and I down under the blanket was scared stiff. Mother was bracing her feet and pulling on the reigns but she could only slow the horse a little, he was scared.Grampa Smith and dad was watching and when they saw the horse running down the road and coming across the beach they stood out and when he got near they grabbed the horses head and stopped the buggy.

The run away horse

Lester Slate's House the last house to be taken down at Slateville.

Lillian's Birthday Party. Marion Slate first row far right.

How I Remember Slateville
By Marion Slate Thomas

I was born at Slateville, which was a village on the east side of Eel Bay. The village name derived from my great-grandfather, Frederick Slate, who with his family came from La Have and settled there. During my time there were seven houses other than ours, all occupied by Slate relatives except two, one was Joseph Arey, the other Aldo Smith.

Our house was the usual large frame built house, which at one time had an ell kitchen but it was removed by my father and a porch added. the house consisted of four bedrooms upstairs, and two down, plus the kitchen, front hall and the parlour. The latter was the usual for those days, the parlour was neat and tidy and kept in good order all the time with the door shut and we children only allowed to go in on special occasions or Sunday afternoons. Our house was built on rather a high ridge, the nearest house to the shore, being somewhat south of the other houses, giving us a wonderful view of the Eel Bay and the lower harbour, and across to Ram and John's Islands as well. On a clear day one could see for miles out on the sea, and we could watch ships pass on their way to distant points as well as watch the local fishermen as they travelled up and down the coast to pull their lobster pots or the herring and mackerel nets. As a lot of the fishermen had sails they put up when they were finished their day's fishing would try to sail up the harbour and home rather than row, it was interesting to see them tack from side to side, beating their way up the harbour with cross wind.

Our house was heated by wood stoves and the kitchen was the center of all activity, especially in the evening with a good fire in the kitchen range. Mother and grandmother would knit, father would be making something such as pot heads or repairing something, while we children would do our lessons by the light of the kerosene lamp on the kitchen table. It was very convenient doing our lessons in this way because we could ask either of our parents to help us with homework if we did not understand it.

My father's name was Lester Slate, my mother was named Grace, she was a MacKay before marriage. There were six of us children, all girls, besides myself there was Lillian, the oldest, Alice who died young, Ida, Bessie and Doris was the youngest. Father when younger was a fisherman the same as all the other men there but when we girls were growing up father started to go over to the United States for what then was called 'Yauchting' — to work on boats for the summer months and this he did most of the time which meant that when he was away working we had various chores to do to keep everything going until he came home again.

My mother when we were of school age and when Grandmother Slate stayed with us, would go out to various homes as a practical nurse and would help the doctor for the birth of babies and then stay and care for the mother and baby until she was able to get about and do her own owrk, as a rule women stayed in bed two weeks when having babies those days so usually she stayed that period with them. We always missed her when she was away and we counted the days when she would be finished and could come home to us again. She was always very kind and helpful and in demand as a nurse because she cared for at least 35 mothers and babies when she was doing this type of work. She was the nurse for Miss Flossie when Allan Swaine was born.

The other families at Slateville lived much the same as we did at that time. Some of the men went to work in summers to the United States as father did and some others were fishermen who had boats of one type or another, some just rowed to the fishing grounds at the outer harbour or to their nets for herring and mackerel. Lobstering was mainly done during the cold weather in late fall or spring. The lobsters were sold to the lobster factory either at Smiths in the other harbour or up to Captain Zephaniah Nickersons at Port Clyde who also had a lobster factory. Later years they bought lobsters at Seal Point which was just across the harbour. My Uncle David and Aunt Annie, who lived up in the field more north of our house, they had 16 children. Their sons helped their father fishing when they were older and then grown all that family moved to the United States and made permanent homes for themselves over there. Stanford Slate and his wife lived in the next house to Uncle David's and they kept the Slateville Post Office. Abbie Arey, wife of Joseph Arey, had a store which was an extension onto the side of their barn. She sold groceries and things for Captain Hemain Swaine who had the store at Cape Negro.

My sisters and I would walk to school at Cape Negro, which was about 2 miles each way. We would walk up our road to Blanche Road and sometimes meet the two Messenger children an Harry Perry from Purgatory Point, and we children would all go along together. We did not as a rule play along the way going to school because we would be punished if we came in late, but on the way home in late afternoon it was always lots of fun, coming along by the Hawl Over we could catch gudgeons in the pond along there and usually manage to get wet. In winter we used to jump ice cakes and play on them on shore at Hawl Over until some grownup saw us and we were warned to stay off the ice as it was dangerous. We had the usual children's ups and downs on the long walks home from school, some resulting in not speaking to someone for a day or two, but nothing very serious. We played innocent pranks on one another and it was all good fun. On the way home we often took short cuts instead of the long way by the road way we would turn down Craig's Road and then by various wood roads arrive near my Uncle David's and then home. It was interesting to explore the woods, pick different kinds of flowers like Lady's Slippers and the first May flowers or sometime see strange birds or watch squirrels. This short cut was also a good opportunity to collect some spruce gum which was very easy to find in the spring. We could collect quite a wad of gum to chew as we went along.

The school teachers were interesting to say the least, some were good and some not so good. We had one man teacher who was very highly educated and could write out all kinds of problems on the slates but could not explain things very well and had no discipline. The boys used to do things and he would be very angry but not say anything. One of the big boys rolled a glass ink bottle down the aisle and it went up against his desk, he was very annoyed and upset, so he kicked the ink bottle, it went down the isle very fast and struck the leg of the old wood stove and broke into many pieces. Everything was quiet for the rest of the day.

The best times at school was getting ready for school concerts, which would be put on in the hall. We studied our verses and lines in skits and practiced our parts and it was all very exciting. Some of my teachers were Mysie Gardner, Francis Reynolds, Sadie Nickerson, Terrance Huskins and others I forget their names. James Swaine made fire in school in winter and he would be sitting by the stove and it would be red hot when we arrived in the morning, It was wonderful that hot stove in winter. When we arrived with cold hands and we could dry our mittens, because playing in snow made them wet. By afternoon they were dry and we could snow ball on the way home.

Some of the teachers allowed the girls and boys to play together at break time; then we could play ball and other games, but the teachers made the girls stay on their own side of the yard and boys on theirs. It was more difficult and someone was always in trouble by crossing to the wrong side. We were never allowed to go down into the pasture behind the school to play, but on Arbour Day when the windows were cleaned and everything done then we all went there for our picnic and then we played there after and it was lots of fun. One of the happiest times of my school years was our trip to Barrington. Hazel Hines, the teacher, engaged Brad Perry who drove Will Nickerson's horse and wagon with hat rack of hay and all the school children went in this through Swaine's Road to Barrington Head and saw a silent movie in the building which is today some community hall near the fire hall. A movie was moving pictures with no voices but music was played and it was very exciting. After the show we came back in a wagon to Mr. Lloyd Swaines and then we walked home from there, it was very late at night, but all very exciting.

Most of the people kept cows, we had one and at night time we had to go and find her as she was loose to graze in the day time. We would go to Jimmy's Old Place or up at Hawl Over and sometimes very long distances to find the cow, bring her home and then mother always did the milking. All cleared land was fenced as the hay was cut and made and put in the barn for winter. All fields had fences to keep out sheep, they came up along our fences all the time. Once the sheep came up near our place and a dog run after them and chased them out onto the bar, we children went to get them off before tide came in and they ran away leaving a very small lamb which was possibly only a day or less old. We carried the lamb to the main land and put it down but mother's sheep would not accept the lamb, so after a while our mother said if the lamb was left it would die so we children should bring it to the house, which we did and after finding a nipple and bottle we gave the lamb cow's milk and it became our pet and grew up into quite a big animal and was a pest because we played with it and it would not go away with the other sheep and was more or less a nuisance to mother. One day we came home from school and could not find our lamb, finally mother told us that she was forced to sell it because it became to much trouble about the property. We were all very sad indeed.

We girls could do all kinds of chores but it usually fell to me to do the unusual ones. I think I was the only one who learned to row the skiff. I could row across to John's Island and look for raspberries and more than once rowed mother up the Eel Bay to visit friends. I don't think she exactly enjoyed the trip too much but I managed quite well. Once when mother was away I rowed out to one of the rocks and pulled a lobster pot. We enjoyed the feed of lobsters, but I was told it was too dangerous and never to do it again. I never quite mastered the art of setting rabbit snares, I never had much luck with that venture.

My grandmother owned sheep and we always had wool from the Blanche sheep shearing in June. The wool was washed and dried and taken to the woolen mill in Barrington and exchanged for yarn. From this yarn mother would knit socks and mittens for everyone. Grandmother had several woolen blankets made in the Barrington Woolen Mill. They were very heavy and wonderful warm on the beds in winter.

Slateville was only a small village but we all had a good childhood with many fond memories of growing up there. My family later moved to the United States and the other residents there moved to other parts as well, the houses were all one by one taken down and no one lives there today.

All that remains are fond memories of folks long gone and our childhood there.

Ruby, Francis, Lottie, Reuben and Leah Smith.

How I Remember Blanche
By Lottie Swaine Thomas

I was born in my Grandfather Ross's house at Green Hill (Upper Port La Tour) and lived the first three years of my life with my parents in Sholds house by the Hawl Over in Cape Negro. My father was Samuel Swaine and mother's name was Leah. My father died when I was three and mother moved back to Green Hill with her grandparents and we lived with them until mother remarried. My stepfather was Reuben Smith and we moved to Blanche and at first lived with his parent's Bill and Sarah Ann Smith. Later Reuben built a house near his father's and with my two half sisters, Francis and Ruby we all grew up there.

    I was some years older than Francis and Ruby and when mother was not around I think I bossed them about a little as children will do but we always got along well together. We played games with some of the neighbours' children who would come down and I think the favorite was hide and seek. We would count and the children would run hide and then we would try and find them. There was a hay mow full of hay and many corners in the barn and places to hide making it very hard to find them.

When mother and I moved to Blanche I was about 5 years old or so and ready to start school. On my first day mother walked across the beach with me as I was the only child down there to go up to school. In the village we met other children and I went along with them. The first day, one of the first ones I met was Emerson who was 5 years older than I but we went along to school together with the others. I always carried a lunch to school because the distance home was too far to go at noon time. Some of the others did as well and we all sat around and ate together. In winter months when I would come home from school sometimes it was to bad a storm to walk the beach to get home and I would spend the night at Mrs. Ida Perry's. Her daughter, Ileta, and I were good friends. Storms seemed to be very bad in those days and the big ice cakes would pile up on the beach.

Sometimes I would get the urge to see my grandparents Swaine who lived on the point down the road by the Cape Negro Church. If I coaxed enough mother would agree that on Friday after school I could go visit them. After school I would walk the 5 miles along, when I got tired I would sit on a rock and rest then go on. Grandmother Swaine was always glad to see me and I enjoyed going up there for the weekend. On Sunday Reuben and mother would come up in the boat, they would stay and visit and have dinner then we would all go home before dark.

When we were older we used to go up to Mr. Will Lyles who kept the post office and listen to records on his gramaphone. He had lots of records and it was very exciting to listen to all tunes, time went so fast it was soon time to get home because we were never allowed to stay out late.

Some Saturdays we would all go in Reuben's boat over to the Consolidated Store at Port La Tour. I was never a good sailor and most of the time I was sea sick, but it was well worth the trip as the store was largest around in those days and we saw so many interesting things and always had a treat while there.

Other than playing the gramaphone and records we also

used to have sing songs at different houses in evenings if they had an organ or some music. Then the big excitement of the year was the Blanche sheep shearing. The men chased the sheep from Cape Negro, Slateville, Purgatory Point and west side and brought them around to shear yard at Blanche Point. The yard had separate pens for the men who owned the sheep and they would look at the marks on the sheeps' ears and then put them in the right pen to be sheared or culled or what ever was necessary. We always had a tent by the shear yard and sold pop, candy, gum and treats, because quite a large crowd gathered there. The supplies were ordered from Yarmouth and they would come on the old La Tour steamer and we would go out in his boat by Shag Rock and take the supplies off. She always blew the steam horn when she left which made a very loud noise. Mother was always busy 3 or 4 days before shearing cooking extra cakes and things because many people came to our house for their dinner, sometimes we would set table three or four times. Mother always made rheubarb pies for shearing time which was first Monday in June, it was always the first spring rhubarb and ever so good. After shearing in evening we all went to the hall for the supper and dance. There was always a lot of people and the hall crowded for dancing.

 When I finished school I worked for Captain Zephaniah Nickerson at Port Clyde. I clerked in the store and when not busy helped Mrs. Nickerson in the house. One winter I spent on Half Moons and taught grades 5 and 6 to Verna Obed. Her mother, Odessa had taught her that far but she was to homesick to stay away from her parents to go to school on the mainland. She finished those grades but next fall she came off to her uncles, Mr. Gilford Obeds, and stayed there and went to Blanche school.

 On December 2nd, 1924, I married Emmerson Thomas and we bought the house and moved to Cape Negro in 1925. I am now a widow but still live in the same house and have fond memories of my childhood on Blanche.

Emerson & Lottie Thomas, 1924.

Genealogy

JOHN SMITH

John Smith, the son of John Smith of Wymondham, Norfolk, England, was baptised on March 8th, 1618. He married Lydia Goath, the daughter of William Goath, who was baptised on September 24th, 1616. Both baptisms are recorded in the Register of the Parish Church of Wymondham.

John's father was a farm worker, and it is very easy to imagine John growing up and learning the farming skills which he put to such good use in later life, as this area today is still some of the best farm lands in England.

John and Lydia left England and arrived in Plymouth Old Colony in 1638. The early records indicate that he was a herdsman with a number of farm animals in his care. The records of the Plymouth Old Colony record his various endeavors as a herdsman over a number of years.

They remained at the Plymouth Old Colony until 1643, at which time they moved as the first settlers to Eastham, Mass.

They remained at Eastham, Mass. and raised their five children, until Lydia's death on July 21st, 1672.

Following Lydia's death John married on November 15th, 1672, one Jael Packard of Bridgewater, Mass., the daughter of Samuel Packard who came from Wymondham, England in 1638 on the ship Dilegent out of Ipswick, John Martin as Master.

I discovered no children born of this second marriage.

Both John and Lydia are buried in Eastham, Mass.

Author's note:

There were three SMITH families at Plymouth Old Colony, one being a Samuel Smith whose son, John, was killed by the indians at Hatfield Meadow on May 30th, 1676. Some of Samuel's descendants were Loyalists in the American Revolution and came to Preston, Dutch Village and Sackville, all near Halifax, Nova Scotia. Another family being Ralph Smith, who was born in Hingham, England in 1610, and moved from Plymouth Old Colony to Eastham, Mass., in 1657. A descendant of Ralph Smith was Archelaus Smith, the first settler of Barrington in 1760 and later Cape Sable Island... The other Smith family being John and Lydia, the subject of part of this book.

SMITH

(1) **John** B. 1618
Lydia B. 1616

Ch:

Hannah B. 1641
M. Frank Curtis

John B. 1644
M. Hannah Williams

	Isaac	B. 1647
	Mary	B. 1647
(2)	**Jeremiah**	B. 1654
	M. Hannah Attwood	
(2)	**Jeremiah**	B. 1654 D. 1706
	Hannah	B. 1649 D. 1729

Ch:
- 2-1 Mercy — B. Feb. 17, 1678
- 2-2 Abagail — B. June 1, 1681

2-(3)	**Jeremiah**	B. Aug. 18, 1685
	M. Abagail Smith, D. of Daniel (Ralph)	
	Hannah	B. Sept. 15, 1691
(3)	**Jeremiah**	B. 1685
	Abagail	B. 1683

Ch:
- 3-1 Simeon — B. May 10, 1712
- 3-2 Jeremiah — B. Feb. 22, 1714
  M. Lydia — B. July 4, 1718
  D. James Lincoln
  Ch:
  - Elkaney — B. Dec. 8, 1738
  - David — B. June 30, 1741
  - Heman — B. March 8, 1744
  - Phillip — B. Jan. 25, 1746
  - Lydia — B. Dec. 7, 1749
  - Mercy — B. March 5, 1753
- 3-3 Nathaniel — B. April 2, 1718
  M. Mary — B. 1720
  Ch:
  - Nathaniel

3-(4) **Jonathan** — B. July 19, 1725
M. Jane — Nov. 21, 1720
D. Thomas Hamilton,
married on Nov. 9, 1752, at Chatham, Mass. by the Rev. Stephen Emery.

Author's note:

Jonathan Smith's wife was named Jane but called Jenny. This practice was carried through the generations to Anna Jane (Jennie) Smith, 1893-1939.

Abagail Smith, mother of Jonathan was an aunt of Solomon Smith.

Jeremiah, the brother of Jonathan Smith, died in Eastham, Mass. on April 2, 1754. Three of his children came with their Uncle Jonathan to Barrington, namely Elkaney, who was married to Elizabeth, the daughter of Solomon Kendrick and Lydia, who married David Crowell, son of Jonathan Crowell, also Mercy, who married Neil McComisky, who came from Ireland. They lived at Neils Creek, Brass Hill, Barrington. Jeremiah's widow, Lydia Lincoln, was a cousin of Susanna Snow the first wife of Solomon Smith.

Jonathan Smith's wife, Jane (Mayo) Hamilton, was a granddaughter of Sgt. Daniel Hamilton of Rhode Island. She was also sister to Rebecca Hamilton, who married Solomon Smith, a cousin of Jonathan Smith, making them also brother-in-laws. Jane was also cousin of Samuel Hamilton who came to Barrington, also cousin of Mary Mayo who married Samuel Freeman of Liverpool, N.S., also cousin of Elizabeth Mayo who married Caleb Nickerson, the father of Joshua Nickerson who came to Barrington.

Jonathan Smith was a brother to Nathaniel Smith, a cousin and brother-in-law of Solomon Smith all of whom came to Barrington, N.S.

Jonathan Smith and his brother Nathaniel, his newphew, Elkaney and (possibly his cousin, Solomon) came in the summers from Eastham and Chatham, Mass., to Barrington Bay and Port La Tour harbours, where they spent the summer in fishing. In the fall they returned to their families with salt and dried fish and barrels of fish oil and results of their summer's work. They did this for a number of summers until in 1761 they built log houses which they made ready and their families came in the fall to live in Barrington. Jonathan Smith's first land was at Barrington Head about where the United Church now is situated. When they came to Barrington there were cleared fields and plots of land some with apple trees and a burial ground which had been left by the French settlers. One of the reasons that prompted the move to Barrington was the abundance of fire wood, which was scarce where they lived in New England and also the great supply of fish and game so easily obtainable.

Their first winters in Barrington apparently were very severe and although they had flour and grain brought from New England, plus the dried and salted fish they had processed themselves, they were reduced to many meals from the clam flats near Barrington. They could not get about easily in the deep snow neither were they experienced hunters, but eventually learned to shoot game, the odd moose, rabbits and ducks kept the larder better supplied.

Jonathan Smith helped build what is now called the old Meeting House in Barrington and attended church and civic meetings held there. His name is recorded in the records of the civic meetings and was involved in many ways with the original settling and organizing of the community and the life of this new country.

Jonathan Smith and his sons, Samuel, Jonathan and Abram, with the Swaines were the founding families of Cape Negro. At this time all the area on west side of the harbour was called Cape Negro. The villages of Port Clyde, Thomasville, Blanche came much later. The first houses were built of hewn logs with floors of pit sawn boards and windows brought from New England. Jonathan Smith lived on East Side of the Eel Bay and operated a trading store where he sold mollasses, rum and other staples. Abram lived at Clam Creek and Samuel lived at shore below what is commonly now called Captain John Smiths. Abram's first hewn log house was built on ridge by shore where Thomas Lowe's new house now stands. Abram's son, Samuel later built a frame house where house of Kenneth Thomas now stands; he also had a stone cellar type hen house built into the bank south to the house.

When the first Methodist minister walked from Shelburne to Cape Negro he stayed with Jonathan Smith for a week. During that time they became the first converts to Methodism in Cape Negro area. Later the first log church was built at corner of Cape Negro to Blanche Road, not the present corner but where the old road used to be that came out where the ball field is now; it was built on lands of Abram Smith of Clam Creek. The present church built in 1851 was built at the old burial ground, which is now called the Old Cemetery and is where all the early families are buried, Jonathan being buried here in 1805, his wife, Jenny in 1799. The records of the old burial plots no longer exist and as very few had head stones, the exact burial plots are not known.

Samuel Smith, a grand-son of Jonathan, was an original trustee of the Cape Negro Church when it was built in 1851.

(4) **Jonathan** B. 1725

Jane B. 1720

Ch:

4-1 **Samuel**
M. Ruth,
D. Chapman Swaine

4-2 **Jonathan**
M. Elizabeth,
D. Nathan Snow

4-3 **Abram**
M. Bathsheba,
D. Joseph Atwood

4-4 **Jane**
M. Samuel Perry,
of Black Point

4-5 **Abagail**
Unmarried

4-6 **Abijah**
M. Sarah Ring,
of Sambro

4-7 **Elijah**
Unmarried

4-8 **Phebe**
    M. Zephaniah,
        S. Chapman Swaine

4-1 **Samuel**
    Ruth

Ch:
4-1-1	Betha	B. 1795
4-1-2	Rachael	B. 1796
4-1-3	Samuel	B. 1797
4-1-4	Sarah	B. 1800
4-1-5	John	B. 1804
4-1-6	Anna	B. 1808
4-1-7	Deborah	B. 1812

4-1 **Samuel**
    M. Ruth, Daughter of
      Chapman Swaine

Ch:
4-1-1 Betha   B. 1795
    M. Richard, Son of
      Smith Nickerson

4-1-2 Rachael   B. 1796

4-1-3 Samuel   B. 1797
    M. Nancy, Daughter of
      John Smith

Ch:
(A) Deborah   B. 1828
    M. William Nickerson

Ch:
A-1 Joseph Nickerson, Capt.
    M. 1. Emily Ford
        Bessie Abbott

Ch:
    Osmond
      M. Helen
      James, Osmond

    Douglas
      M. 1. Isobel Hodges
        2. Veda Crowell
        3. Marie Goodick Thomas
    Lois

    Florence

A-2	John	
	M. Isora Tedford	
A-3	Selemma	B. 1866
	M. Edward, son of Josiah Reynolds	
Ch:		
	Jeannette	B. 1896
	M. Ernest Silvey	
	Elsie	B. 1898
	M. Kenneth Mirrell	
	Francis	B. 1899
	Unmarried	
A-4	Helena	B. 1868
	M. William Ross	
	Edna, Isora	
A-5	Florence	B. 1870
	M. Oscar, son of Josiah Reynolds	
	Floyd, John, Louise	
A-6	Cora	B. 1872
	M. George Brannen	
(B)	Samuel	B. 1833
(C)	John	B. 1834
	M. Anna Schrage	
	Edwin	
	M. Minnie Perry	
	No issue	
(D)	Joseph	B. 1839
(E)	Eleanor	B. 1840
	M. William, son of William Paterson	
Ch:		
	Samuel	B. 1858
	M. Bertha (Sis) Ross D. of George Lyle	
	No issue	
	Effie	B. 1874
	M. Bradford, son of Freeman Lowe	
	No issue	
(F)	Mercy	B. 1843
(G)	James	B. 1846
(H)	Adelaide	B. 1848
	M. Leander	S. Josiah Reynolds
	William	S. Wm. Sholds

Ch:
- Tressel — B. 1872
  M. Alfred, S. W.H. Matheson
  Keith, Alida, Helene, Bruce

- Kenneth — B. 1874
  M. Bertha Haines

- Herman — B. 1876
  M. Laura Neiss

4-1-4 Sarah — B. 1800
  M. William Shephard
  Cornelius, Susan, Nathan

4-1-5 John — B. 1804

4-1-6 Anna — B. 1808
  M. Elisha, son of
  Smith Nickerson

4-1-7 Deborah — B. 1812

4-2 Jonathan
  M. Elizabeth, daughter of
  Nathan Snow

Ch:
4-2-1 Phebe — B. 1796

4-2-2 Reuben — B. 1797
  M. Cynthia, daughter of
  Chapman Swaine

4-2-3 Mary — B. 1799

4-2-4 Howes — B. 1801
  M. Mercy, daughter of
  Eldad Nickerson

4-2-5 Elizabeth — B. 1803
  M. Abram, son of
  Abram Smith, Jr.

4-2-6 Lydia — B. 1811

4-2-7 Josiah — B. 1813
  M. Margaret, daughter of
  David Swaine

4-2 Jonathan Smith
  M. Elizabeth, daughter of
  Nathan Snow

Ch:
4-2-1 Phebe — B. 1796
  Unmarried

4-2-2 Reuben — B. 1797
  M. Cynthia, daughter of
  Chapman Swaine

Ch:
- Alexander — B. 1830
- James — B. 1833
- Phebe — B. 1835
  M. Davis Thomas

Ch:
(A) Walter Thomas
    M. 1st Adelaide McComsky
        2nd Maude MacKay, widow
            of Collin Smith

Ch:
- Genevieve — B. 1888
  M. Freeland Smith

Ch:
- Franklin — B. 1911
- Stanley — B. 1913
  M. Elsie Blowers
  Michael, Peter, Stephen
- Ethel — B. 1914
  M. Zedley Acker
  Chester, Thelma, Nellie

(B) Percy — B. 1890
    M. Bessie, daughter of
        Stewart Swaine

Ch:
- Eleanor
  M. Clayton, son of
      Capt. Fred MacLean
  Robert, Dorothy

- George
  M. Ruby Langthorne
  Cheryle, George, Dianne

(C) Fletcher
(D) William
(E) Kenneth

- Cynthia — B. 1838
  M. Elisha Perry
- Knowles — B. 1840
- Josiah — B. 1842
- Olive — B. 1843

4-2-3 Mary — B. 1799
4-2-4 Howes — B. 1801
      M. Mercy, daughter of
          Eldad Nickerson

Ch:
    Mary
      M. Heman, son of
        John B. Swaine

    Esther
      M. Capt. Joshua Pierce

    Prince
      M. Mary, daughter of
        Thomas Nickerson

    Deborah
      Unmarried

4-2-5 Elizabeth   B. 1837
      M. Abram Smith

4-2-6 Lydia   B. 1811

4-2-7 Josiah   B. 1813
      M. Margaret, daughter of
        David Swaine

Ch:
    1. Jonathan   B. 1837
      M. Matilda Hopkins

    1. Jonathan and Matilda Smith

Ch:
(A)   William   B. 1867
      W. Jessie MacDonald
      Donald, Francis

(B)   Jerome   B. 1869
      M. Ella Smith
      Neima, Ethel

    2. Samuel   B. 1840
      M. Sarah, daughter of
        Heman Horton

    3. Daniel   B. 1846
      M. Susan, daughter of
        Henry Brannen

    4. Susan   B. 1848
      Unmarried

    5. Alicee   B. 1851
      M. Capt. Wm. L., son of
        Thomas Ross, Sr.

Ch:
    Wilford
      Unmarried

    Lizzie
      M. David Horton

4-3	Abram M. Batheshba, daughter of Joseph Atwood	
Ch:		
4-3-1	Zeruiah	B. 1784
4-3-2	Richard	B. 1876
4-3-3	Susanna	B. 1788
4-3-4	Abram	B. 1795
4-3-5	Batheshba	B. 1801
4-3-6	Lettice	B. 1803
4-3-1	Zeruiah M. Howes, son of Nathan Snow	B. 1784
Ch:		
-1	Howes	B. 1807
-2	Harvey	B. 1809
-3	Jonathan	B. 1810
-4	Jemima	B. 1812
-5	Eleanor	B. 1814
-6	Jane	B. 1815
-7	Nancy	B. 1817
-8	Matilda	B. 1818
-9	Sophia	B. 1820
-10	Joseph	B. 1822
-11	Delma	B. 1825
-12	Mercy	B. 1828
-1	Howes M. Elizabeth, daughter of Heman Crowell	B. 1807
	Ch:	
(A)	William M. Sarah, daughter of Caleb Nickerson	B. 1840
	Ch:	
	1. Zipporah M. George, son of Francis Crowell	B. 1870

			Ch:	
			Lionel	
			M. Vera, daughter of	
			Lewis Crowell	
			No issue	
			Mertie	
			M. Marshall, son of	
			Herbert Ross	
			Clytie	
			M. David, son of	
			Churchill Dexter	
		2.	Edmund K.	B. 1873
	(B)		Andrew	B. 1841
	(C)		Edmund	B. 1847
-2			Harvey	B. 1809
			Lost at sea.	
			Unmarried	
-3			Jonathan	B. 1810
			M. Mary, daughter of	
			William Swaine	
			Ch:	
			William	B. 1842
			M. Catherine, daughter of	
			Samuel King	
			Ora, Oscar	
			Mary	B. 1837
			M. Hezekiah, son of	
			Isaac Huskins	
			Margaret, Eldora, Herbert	
-4			Jemima	B. 1812
			M. Warren, son of	
			Paul Swaine	
-5			Eleanor	B. 1814
			M. John, son of	
			John Smith	
			Ch:	
		1.	William	B. 1848
			M. Diadania, daughter of	
			Thomas Nickerson	
			John, 1882; William, 1884;	
			Ernest, 1885; Lloyd, 1887	
		2.	Sophia	B. 1852
			M. Elias, son of	
			Thomas Nickerson	
			Bigelow, son of	
			Enoch Smith	
			Effie, Essie	

-6

3. Jessie   B. 1854
    M. Jerusha Chetwynd

Jane   B. 1815
    M. Enoch, son of
       Richard Smith

Ch:
1. Sophia   B. 1840
    M. Elias, son of
       Thomas Banks
       Crowell, son of
       Benjamin Smith
    Emma, 1868

2. Benjamin   B. 1842
    M. Louisa, daughter of
       Arron Spinney

Ch:
(A)   Annie   B. 1883
        M. Willard, son of
           George Nickerson
        Maxwell, Marjorie

(B)   Ralph   B. 1888
        M. Florence, daughter of
           Joseph Nickerson
        Barbara, 1923

3. Bigelow   B. 1845
    M. Rebecca, daughter of
       James Gardner
    2. Emma Harris
    3. Sophia, daughter of
       John Nickerson

Ch:
1. Lester   B. 1876
    M. Violet, daughter of
       James Snow
    Bessie

2. Horrace   B. 1878

3. Reginald   B. 1879
    M. Margaret, daughter of
       John MacKay
    Jeannette

4. Althea   B. 1881
    M. James Doleman

5. George   B. 1884

6. William   B. 1886

4. Harvey D.   B. 1847
     M. Deborah, daughter of
       James Snow

Ch:
     Edmund V.   B. 1875
       M. Alberta, daughter of
         George Nickerson
     Alpheus, 1910

5. Jemima   B. 1849
     M. Henry, son of
       James Nickerson
     Eulalia, 1880; Dean, 1881;
     Ethel, 1884; Edna, 1892

6. George H.   B. 1857
     M. Annie, daughter of
       David Smith

-7   Nancy   B. 1817
       M. Benjamin, son of
         Nathaniel Smith
       No issue

-8   Matilda   B. 1818
       M. James, son of
         Theophilus Crowell

Ch:
     James   B. 1837
       M. Mahal, daughter of
         Seth Snow

Ch:
1. Wilhemina   B. 1866
     M. Nathanile, son of
       John Smith
     No issue

2. Seth   B. 1869
     M. Annie, daughter of
       Jonathan Crowell

Ch:
     Kenneth   B. 1902
       M. Veda, daughter of
         John Snow
     Aneta, Earl, Irma

3. Bernard   B. 1876
     M. Adeline, daughter of
       George Nickerson
     No issue

-9	Sophia	B. 1820
	M. Seth, son of	
	John Lyle	
	see 228	
-10	Joseph	B. 1822
	M. Wealthy, daughter of	
	William Spinney	
	Prince, Harvey	
-11	Delina	B. 1824
	M. Peter Dewade	
	No issue	

-12 **Mercy born 1826**
    M. Jessie son of Zephaniah Swaine
    Ch:
    1. Howes
        M. Sarah, daughter of
            Isaac Huskins

    2. Sarah
        M. William Snow
        Jesse Smith

    3. Lydia
        M. George Miller
        John, George

-4-3-2	Richard	B. 1786
	M. Thankful, daughter of	
	John Reynolds	
	Ch:	
-1	Jane	B. 1809
-2	Benjamin	B. 1811
-3	Enoch	B. 1813
-4	James Mann	B. 1815
-5	Rhoda	B. 1817
-6	John	B. 1818
-7	Samuel	B. 1820
-8	Richard	B. 1822
-9	Batheshba	B. 1824
-10	Ruth	B. 1826
-11	Lydia	B. 1829
-1	Jane	B. 1809
	M. Samuel, son of	
	Joshua Atwood	

		Ch:	
		1. Lydia	B. 1839
		M. Nemiah Doane	
		2. Sarah	B. 1841
		M. Neimiah Nickerson	
		3. Jethro	B. 1844
		4. Richard	B. 1845
		5. Samuel	B. 1847
-2		Benjamin	B. 1811
		Unmarried	
-3		Enoch	B. 1813
		M. Jane, daughter of Howes Snow	
		Ch: Enoch and Jane were cousins, refer to page 192, the -6 Jane family record, etc.	
-4		James Mann	B. 1815
		Unmarried Went to China did not return.	
-5		Rhoda	B. 1817
		Unmarried	
-6		John	B. 1818
		Unmarried	
-7		Samuel	B. 1820
		M. Mary, daughter of Joshua Nickerson	
		Ch:	
		1. James Harvey	B. 1859
		M. Hattie, daughter of Samuel Swaine	
		Ch:	
	(A)	Edgar Frank	B. 1884
		M. Clara Miller	
	A - 1	Ronald E.M. - Gladys Butler, Newfoundland. No issue.	
	A - 2	Muriel - Unmarried. Army Nursing Sister & Hospital Matron.	
	A - 3	Glendon William - M-Lorraine Martin, Yarmouth.	

Ch; 1   Glendon William, II.
           M-Bernadette MacKenzie.
           Antigonish.

   1-1   Glendon William. III.

   1-2   Cindy
           M-Bill Maclean. Antigonish.
           Loie, Angus.

   1-3   Gregory

   1-4   Christopher

   1-5   Jeffrey

   1-6   Michelle

Ch; 2   Gail
           M-Jimmy Webster. Florida U.S.A
           Rodney, Loie, Michael

Ch; 3   Karen
           M -Russell Livermore, North
           Carolina, U.S.A.
           Kimberley, Shelli, Genefer, Maura

Ch; 4   Robert
           M-Carol Gibson, Bridgewater
           Nicole, Kara, Rachelle

Ch; 5   Maureen
           M-John Nolasco, Ontario
           Sarah deceased, Adam, Robyn

Ch; 6   Ronald
           M-Barbara Hawkins, St.
           Andrews, N.B.
           Laura, Aimee

Ch; 7   Deidre
           M-Gordon Wilson. Digby
           Nicholas, Cortney, Kyle

       (B)   Clarence   B. 1888
               Unmarried

       (C)   Anna Jane
               (Jenny)   B. 1893
               M. Capt. William L., son of
                 Thomas Ross, Sr.

  Ch:
C-1 Burnley B. 1918
  M. Phyllis, daughter of
   Colby Brannen
  Jean, Joan, William

C-2 George B. 1920
  M. Jean Isobel, daughter of
   Jack MacDonald
  Anna, Jack, Shirley, John

C-3 Allison B. 1924
  M. Mary, daughter of
   VanDeHurk (Holland)
  Mary Ann, Walter, Donna

C-4 Joseph Randall B. 1925
  M. Susan (Peggy), daughter of
   Charles Baltzer
  George

C-5 Alva Jean B. 1930
  M. Gordon, son of
   John Jones
  Kevin, Seldon

(D) Alberta B. 1897
  M. Robert, son of
   Horatio Brannen

  Ch:
D-1 Ann Marie B. 1928
  M. Kenneth, son of
   Paul Errol Littlefield
  Brenda, Allan

(E) James B. 1900
  Married in Florida
  No Issue

  2. Anna Jane
   (Jenny) B. 1860
   Unmarried, died 1877

  3. Charles B. 1863
   M. Alice Oliver
  Moved to U.S.A.

-8 Richard B. 1822
  M. Elizabeth Ellis
  Richard, Elizabeth

-9 Batheshba B. 1824
  M. Henry, son of
   Zephaniah Swaine

-10		Ruth	B. 1826
		M. George Lyle	
		Andrew Chetwyn	
		Ch:	
	(A)	Bertha (Sis)	B. 1864
		M. Thomas, son of	
		Thomas Ross, Sr.	
		2. Samuel, son of	
		William Patterson	

Ch:
Delbert
  M. Annie Symonds, C.S.I.

Ch:
Floyd
  M. Isobel Brown

	(B)	George	B. 1867
		M. Edith	
		Donald	
-11		Lydia	B. 1829
		Unmarried	
4-3-3		Susanna	B. 1788
		M. Silas, son of	
		Samuel Perry	
		Ch:	
		1. Abraham	B. 1816
		2. Susan	B. 1819
		M. Job Towner	
		3. Deborah	
		M. Thomas Crowell	
		4. Nancy	
		Unmarried	
		5. Letitia	
		M. Samuel Crowell	
4-3-4		Abram	B. 1795
		M. Elizabeth, daughter of	
		Jonathan Smith	
		Ch:	
		Sophia	
		Unmarried	
4-3-5		Batheshba	B. 1801
		M. Josiah, son of	
		Benjamin Snow	

	Ch:
	Batheshba
	   M. Josiah Nickerson
	   No issue
		B. 1826

-4-3-6	Letitia
	   M. Tristram, son of
	     Samuel Reynolds
		B. 1803

	Ch:	
-1	Euphemia	B. 1821
-2	Minnie	B. 1823
-3	Lois	B. 1825
-4	Lydia	B. 1826
-5	Knowles	B. 1828
-6	Harriett	B. 1829
-7	Tristram	B. 1834
-8	Batheshba	B. 1837
-9	Letitia	B. 1838
-10	Abram	B. 1840
-11	Samuel	B. 1842
-1	Euphemia M. Agustus Bower	B. 1821

-2	Minnie
	   M. Everard Allen
	Ch:
	  1. Arnold "
	  2. Mabel "
	  3. Morton "
	  4. Elsie "
	  5. Evelyn "
	  6. Laura "
	  7. Lillian "
	  8. Ivy "
	  9. Henriett "
		B. **1823**

-3	Lois M. Edgar Harris	B. 1825
-4	Lydia M. Charles Bower	B. 1826

-5	Knowles
	   M. Elizabeth, daughter of
	     John Reynolds
		B. 1828

-6	Harriett
	   M. Harvey, son of
	     Elkanah Nickerson
		B. 1829

-7		Tristram Unmarried Lost at sea.	B. 1834
-8		Batheshba M. Jonathan, son of Jonathan Crowell	B. 1837

		Ch:
		1. Annie
		    M. Seth, son of
		      James Crowell	

	(A)	Ch:
		Kenneth
		  M. Veda, daughter of
		    James Snow
		Aneta, Earl, Irma	

-9		Letitia Unmarried	B. 1838
-10		Abram Unmarried	B. 1840

-11		Samuel
		M. Dorcas, daughter of
		    Benjamin Newell
		  2. Clementine Snow
			B. 1842

		Ch: 1. Rose 2. Elizabeth 3. Maud 4. Bernard 5. John 6. Ernest 7. Oran	
4-4		Jane M. Samuel Perry of Black Point	B.
		Ch:	
-1		Joseph	B. 1785
-2		Joab	B. 1786
-3		Jonathan	B. 1789
-4		Thankful	B. 1790
-5		Silas	B. 1793
-6		**Deborah**	**born 1799**
-7		Rufus	B. 1801
-8		Abram	B. 1806

-5	Silas
	  M. Susanna, daughter of
	    Abram Smith
	Silas and Susanna were cousins
	refer to page 197, reference
	4-3-3 Susanna for full
	family record.
		B. 1793

4-5	Abagail Unmarried	
4-6	Abijah M. Sarah Ring Moved to Sambro.	
4-7	Elijah Unmarried Died in hospital, W. Indies.	

4-8	Phebe
	  M. Zephaniah, son of
	    Chapman Swaine
	Ch:	

-1	Paul	B. 1780
-2	Lydia	B. 1782
-3	Charity	B. 1790
-4	Peter	B. 1792
-5	Ann	B. 1794
-6	Zephaniah	B. 1796

-1	Paul
	  M. Francis, daughter of
	    John Reynolds
	Ch:
		B. 1780

	1. Margaret
	    M. Joel, son of
	      Joel Worthen
		B. 1806

	2. John B.	B. 1808
	3. Jane ⁄	B. 1810

	4 Rhoda
	    M. William, son of
	      Thomas Bethel
	William
		B. 1814

	5. Charles	B. 1815
	6. Charity	B. 1818
	7. Mary	B. 1820

-2   Lydia   B. 1782
            M. Samuel, son of
              John Reynolds
            Ch:
      2- 1. Tristram   B. 1803
              M. Letitia, daughter of
                Abram Smith
                Tristram and Letitia were cousins.
                Refer to Page 198, 4-3-6
                Letitia for full family record.

      2- 2. Lydia   B. 1805
              M. Charles Bower

      2- 3. Knowles Reynolds   B. 1808
              M. Elizabeth, daughter of
                John Reynolds

            Ch:
(A)   Alfred   B. 1861

(B)   Oscar   B. 1865

(C)   Matilda   B. 1867
        M. Ethron, son of
          Jonathan Crowell

      Ch:
C-1   Edward Crowell   B. 1900
        M. Dorothy, daughter of
          Walter Christie
      Ruth

C-2   Gladys   B. 1896

C-3   Francis   B. 1803

(D)   Eliza   B. 1861

(E)   Robert   B. 1863

(F)   Arthur   B. 1866
        M. Sarah Thomas
          Flora Wilbur
          Edith Lyle

      Ch:

F-1   Lyda
        M. Walter, son of
          Stewart Swaine
      Virginia - U.S.A.

F-2   Charles

F-3   Reginald

F-4   Lyndon

F-5   Ernest

F-6 Harry

F-7 Mary
    M. Hedley, son of
      Windslow J. Swaine
   Jean, Phyllis

2- 4. Harriett   B. 1810
    M. Harvey, son of
      Elkanah Nickerson

2- 5. Tristram   B. 1811
    Lost at sea.

2- 6. Batheshba
    M. Jonathan, son of
      Jonathan Crowell

    Ch:
(A) Annie Ida
    M. Seth, son of
      James Crowell
    Refer to page **199**, -8,
    no. 1 - Annie, for full
    family record.

2- 7. Letitia
    Unmarried

2- 8. Abram
    Unmarried

2- 9. Samuel Reynolds   B. 1842

Refer to page **199**, -11 Samuel
for full family record.

2- 10. Joshua

2- 11. Sarah Ann

2- 12. Samuel

2- 13. Elizabeth
    M. James, son of
      John Swaine

2- 14. Lydia
    M. Aaron, son of
      Elias Banks

   Ch:
   1. Sarah Ann   **B. 1889**
      M. Robert, son of
        John Reynolds

(A)	Ch: Hedley
(B)	Louisa

(C)	John Howard
	   M. Belle, daughter of
	     Smith Wilson

C-1 Ruby
   M. Maynard, son of
     David Flemming
     Jasper Madden
Madora, Alice, Edgar,
Douglas Peggy

C-2 Lamont
   M. Leona, daughter of
     William Lovitt

Ch:
- (A) Nancy   B. 1939
   M. Aubrey Nickerson
Ricky, Stephen, Peter

- (B) Donna
   M. Roy Roberts
Nancy, Mark Tracey

C-3 Freeland
   M. Sylvia, daughter of
     Wilfred Atwood
Freeland

C-4 Alden

C-5 Brenton   B. 1919
   M. Annie, daughter of
     David Stoddard
Brian, Susan, Bruce

2- 3- (G) Ellen Maude   B. 1867
                      M. John R. Snow

Ch:
G-1 Hedley Snow
   M. Cecilia, daughter of
     Josiah Brown

Marie
   M. Hersey Thomas
Hedley
Myra
Richard

G-2 Roy Snow
    M. Katherine, daughter of
        James Swaine
  Thelma
    M. John Christie
  Allen, Carman

G-3 Veda Snow
  Refer to page **199**, A-Kenneth.
  Full family record.

G-4 Earl
    M. Katherine Ketchum

(H) Oran   B. 1866

(I). Levi   B. 1869
    M. Georgina Wasson
      Eliza Donaldson
    Ch:

I-1 Myrtle

I-2 Jenny

I-3 Wasson
    M. Muriel, daughter of
      David K. Smith

I-4 William

I-5 Norman
    M. Rosemond, daughter of
      James Smith
  Vernon, Paul, Terrance,
  Kevin, Carol

I-6 Henry
  B. M. Elizabeth, daughter of
  1889 Gilbert Nickerson
      Annie Goodick, daughter of
        Godfrey MacKay
  Joyce, Helen

1-7 Robert
    M. Aleda, daughter of
      Toorenburg, (Holland)
  Yvonne, John, Robert

1-8 Pauline

1-9 Sadie
    M. Kenneth, son of
      Percy Nickerson
  Betty, David

	1-10	Douglas	
		M. Freda, daughter of Leslie Smith	
		Clara	
4-8-3		**Charity**	**born 1790**
		M. Frederick, son of Christopher Sholds	
		Ch:	
	(A)	Samuel Sholds	B. 1809
		M. Margaret, daughter of Smith Nickerson	
	B	Ann	B. 1812
	(C)	Zephaniah	B. 1815
	D.	Peter	B. 1817
	(E)	Charity	B. 1818
-4		Peter	B. 1792
		M. Matilda, daughter of Smith Nickerson	
		Ch:	
	(A)	Sarah	B. 1841
		M. James, son of Nathan Snow	
		John, James, Phebe	
	(B)	John Leonard	B. 1845
		M. Clemintina Potter	
	(C)	Georgina	B. 1846
		M. Archelius, son of Simon Smith	
		Robert, Cora, Frank, Annie, Bessie, Margaret, Hugh	
	(D)	Margaret	B. 1846
	(E)	Susan	
		M. Peter, son of Peter Sutherland	
		Sarah, Howard, Freeman, Austin, Elizabeth, Rosalie	
-5		Ann	B. 1794
		M. Joshua, son of Caleb Nickerson	
-6		Zephaniah	B. 1796
		M. Patients, daughter of Smith Nickerson	

		Ch:	
	(A)	Smith	
		M. Marcy, daughter of Elijah Nickerson	
	(B)	Reuben	
		M. Louisa, daughter of Elijah Nickerson	
	C.	Henry	
		M. Batheshba, daughter of Richard Smith	
		Miriam, daughter of Theodore Harding	
-7		Jesse	B. 1793
		M. Mercy, daughter of Howes Snow	
		Howes, Sarah, Lydia, Matilda	
-8		Benjamin	B. 1803
		M. Sarah, daughter of Nathan Snow	

Walter & Ida Myrick

SWAINE

Chapman Swaine, Sr. came from Nantucket, his grant of land was at Port La Tour and included Pages Island with his house on cleared land near the old fort. His son, Chapman, Jr. married Susan Nickerson and moved to Blanche. His son, Joseph, married Rachael Snow and moved to Cape Negro.

Swain   Chapman   B. 1708
    M. Sarah Meador

Ch:
1. Joseph
2. John
3. Zephaniah
4. Ephraim
5. Chapman
6. Daniel
7. Sarah
8. Patience
9. Judith
10. Deborah
11. Ruth

Swain CS-1   Joseph
    M. Rachael Snow

Ch:
1-1   Joseph
1-2   Reuben
1-3   John
1-4   David

Swain 1-1   Joseph   B. 1775
    M. Temperance, daughter of
      John Reynolds
    For full family record refer to
    Temperance Reynolds, Page 217

1-2   Reuben   B.
    M. Rebecca Greenwood
    No issue

1-3   John
    M. Ann, daughter of
      Theodore Smith

Ch:
(A)   Ruth   B. 1807
(B)   Reuben   B. 1809
(C)   James   B. 1810
    M. Elizabeth Reynolds

(D)   Dorcas   B. 1813
         M. Ebenezer Smith of
           Barrington Head

1-4   David
         M. Deborah Perry

Ch:

(A)   David
        M. Rebecca, daughter of
          William Greenwood
       Leander, David, ARthur,
       Charles, John, Maria

(B)   John B.
        M. Rachael, daughter of
          Joseph Swaine
       Refer to page 218 for
       family record.

(C)   William
        M. Elizabeth Bell
          Rebecca King
       Ephrain, William, Lydia

(D)   Thomas
        M. Lydia King
       George

(E)   Henry   B. 1813
        M. Mary Perry of
          Black Point

       Ch:
       1. Mary, M. Harvey Smith
       2. William, M. Laura Slate
       3. Stewart, M. Sarah Swaine
       Refer to page 220 for full
       family record.
       4. Sarah, M. Wm. Smith of
          Blanche

(F)   Deborah, M. George Stoddard

(G)   Sarah Ann

(H)   Margaret, M. Josiah Smith
       Refer to page 189 for full
       family record.

(I)   Eleazar, M. Maria Mahaney

(J)   Samuel

CS-2   John
        M. Jerusha Snow
       Rebecca

CS-3	Zephaniah	B. 1753
	M. Phebe, daughter of Jonathan Smith	
	Refer to page 200 for full family record.	
CS-4	Ephraim	B. 1755
	M. Cecilia Carr	

Ch:
a. Chapman M. Susanna, daughter of John Reynolds
Refer to page 223 for full family record.

b. William
　　M. Rebecca Stevens
　Alfred, Richard

c. Mary
　　M. Wm. Greenwood, (Clyde)

CS-5	Chapman	
	M. Susan, daughter of Nathan Nickerson	
CS-5-1	Josiah	B. 1801
	M. Deborah, daughter of John Snow	

Ch:
a. Chapman
b. Andrew
c. Josiah
d. Maria
　　M. Smith Newell

	e. William	B. 1840
	M. Jane, daughter of Stephen Van Nordon	

	Ch:	
e-1	Eva	B. 1874
	M. Robert Taylor Kenneth Backman	
e-2	Ailleen	B. 1882
	M. Collin, son of Ebenezer Smith	
e-2	Ursula	B. 1910
	M. Warren, son of Adelbert Perry	
e-3	William	B. 1883
	M. Matilda Kushy	
e-4	Claude	B. 1884

e-5　Leona Deborah　　　　　B. 1889
　　　M. Guilford Irvin, son of
　　　　James Smith

　　　Ch:
　　　Gerald　　　　　　　　B. 1920
　　　　M. Kathleen Hayes

　　　Howard G.　　　　　　B. 1922
　　　　M. Reta Sullivan

　　　Claire　　　　　　　　B. 1929
　　　　M. Donald, son of
　　　　　Ray & Jessie Snow

　　f.　Driscilla　　　　　　B. 1838
　　　　M. Edwin Griswold
　　　　　Chapman, Edwin

　　g.　Sophia　　　　　　　B. 1847
　　　　M. James, son of
　　　　　John Bethel
　　　　Stanley, Clarence, Gordon,
　　　　Mabel

　　h.　Cynthia　　　　　　　B. 1844
　　　　M. John, son of
　　　　　Thomas Taylor
　　　　Maude, Clara, Frank

　　i.　Emeline　　　　　　　B. 1847
　　　　M. John Rodgers, Yarmouth

CS-5-2　Samuel
　　　　M. Esther, daughter of
　　　　　Joseph Reynolds

CS-5-3　Deborah　　　　　　　B. 1792
　　　　M. Stephen, son of
　　　　　Caleb Nickerson

CS-5-4　Catherine　　　　　　B. 1797
　　　　M. Elkanah, son of
　　　　　Caleb Nickerson

　　　　Ch:

(A)　　James
　　　　M. Margaret, daughter of
　　　　　John Lyle

A-1　　John, M. Estella,
　　　　　daughter of Andrew Snow

A-2　　Josiah

A-3　　George, M. Rebecca Robertson

(B)　　Harvey, M. Harriett Reynolds
　　　　　Margaret Watt
　　　　Eva May

(C) Matthew B. 1830
    M. Martha, daughter of
      James Perry

(D) Sophia B. 1829
    M. James, son of
      Benjamin Snow

Ch:
a. Clarabelle
    M. Gilbert, son of
      Thomas Ross, Sr.
  (Gilbert was drowned,
    Clarabelle moved to U.S.A.)
Albert

b. Wilber Arthur B. 1862
    M. Ida, daughter of
      George Nickerson

c. Georgia B. 1868
    M. Peter Gerrior

d. Ernest B. 1876

(E) Sophronia, M. Isaac VanAmberg

(F) Josiah

(G) Rebecca
CS-5-5 Cynthia
    M. Reuben, son of
      Jonathan Smith, (Page 187)

a. Alexander B. 1830
    M. Susan, daughter of
      William Perry
    Aldenard Austen, M. Emma,
      daughter of Vincent Atwood

b. James P. B. 1843
    M. Elizabeth Parsons,
      daughter of Knowles & Lydia
      (McKenna) Swain

c. Phebe
    M. David Thomas
Refer to page 188 for full
family history

CS-5-6 Susanna
    M. David, son of
      David Thomas

Ch:
a. John, M. Edith Stevens
b. Emma, M. Alex Greenwood
c. Harriett, M. James Heustis
d. Elizabeth Maria

             e. Mary Ann, M. James Thomas
                  Ch: Oscar, Leonard
            d. Maria, Unmarried

CS-6   Daniel
          M. Anna Taylor

         Ch:

6-1   Elizabeth
          M. Knowles, son of
            John Nickerson

         Ch:
         a. Cyrus   B. 1842
            M. Martha, daughter of
              Zephaniah Newell

         b. William   B. 1835
            M. Eliza Jane Duncan,
              Theresa Malone

         c. John   B. 1834
            M. Jemima, daughter of
              Eleazor Crowell

         d. Jane
            M. Anthony MacKay

         e. Eliza

         f. Dorothy

         g. Mary

         h. Sarah Ann

6-2   Rosanna   B. 1839
          M. Alfred, son of
            Benjamin Newell

CS-7   Sarah
          M. Lemuel Horton

CS-8   Patience   B. 1742
          M. Nathaniel, Jr., son of
            Nathaniel Smith, Sr.

         Ch:

8-1   Abagail   B. 1766
          M. James, son of
            Benjamin Barss
         Patience, 1796; Benjamin, 1798

8-2   Mary   B. 1769
          M. James Rice

8-3   Martha   B. 1769

8-4 Sarah B. 1772
    M. Benjamin, son of
        Nathan Snow

   a. Josiah B. 1799
        M. Bathsheba, daughter of
            Abram Smith
        Refer to page 197.

   b. Benjamin, M. Mary Swaine

   c. Temperance B. 1796

D. William B. 1802
    M. Abagail Ryer
        Abagail Swaine, daughter of
            Joseph Swaine

    Refer to page 218

   e. Mary

8-5 Mercy
    M. Nathan, Jr., son of
        Nathan Snow

    Ch:
   a. Samuel, Drowned

   b. William
        M. Betsy, daughter of
            Stephen Smith, Sambro

   c. Mary, M. Thomas Bethel

   d. James
        M. Sarah, daughter of
            Peter Swaine

   e. Sarah
        M. Benjamin, son of
            Zephaniah Swaine

   f. Susan
        M. David K., son of
            Theodore Smith

   g. Elsie, M. Elisha Smith

   h. Catherine, M. Jonathan Greenwood

   i. Rosanna, M. George Greenwood

   j. Freeman

CS-8-6   John. born 1774.
          M. Anna daughter of
              Prince Nickerson
          Hannah daughter of
              Theodore Smith
    Ch:
    6-1 Nancy born 1804
          M. Samuel son of Samuel Smith
    6-2 Anna born 1819
          M. William. Son of William Snow.
    6-3 John born 1820
          M. Eleanor daughter of Howes Snow
    6-4 Theodore born 1821
          M. Rebecca daughter of
              William Worthen
    6-5 Patience born 1824
          M. William Sherard son of
              Isaac Kenney.
    6-6 Hannah
          M. William son of Barry Crowell
    6-7 David Kirby born 1831
          M. Mercy daughter of
              Nathaniel Smith

CS-8-7   Elizabeth born 1776
          M. Stephen son of Nathan Snow
          Ch:
              a. Stephen
                  M. Sarah daughter of
                      Samuel Wood
              b. Anna
              c. Elizabeth

CS-8-8   Hannah born 1778
          M. John son of Nathan Snow
          Ch:
              a. Rebecca born 1795
                  M. James Nelson,
                      Clyde River
              b. Nathan born 1797
                  M. Mary Barss, Sambro
              c. John
                  M. Martha daughter of
                      Benjamin Smith
              d. Deborah born 1801
                  M. Josiah son of
                      Chapman Swaine
                  Refer of page 80.
              e. Abagail born 1802
                  M. Phillip son of
                      Charles Bower
              f. Elizabeth born 1804
                  M. James Covell son of
                      Zebulon Gardner
              g. Letitia
                  M. David Horton
              h. Sophia
                  M. Samuel son of
                      Josiah Snow

  i. Winthrop
   M. Penina daughter of
   Benjamin Smith
  j. David born 1815
   M. Phobe Ann daughter of
   James Snow
  k. William born 1815
   M. Annie daughter of
   Benjamin Smith
  l. James born 1820
   M. Mercy daughter of
   Daniel Crowell

Rebecca born 1780
 M. Seth son of Nathan Snow
Ch:
  a. Hannah born 1794
  b. Thomas born 1796
   M. Mary MacLean
  c. Olivia
  d. Isaac
   M. Louisa daughter of
   Josiah Snow
  e. George
  f. Stephen
   M. Letitia daughter of
   Josiah Snow
  g. Seth

CS-8-10 Nathaniel born 1782
  M. Susannah daughter of
  John Spinney
Ch:
  a. Nathaniel born 1808
   M. Sophia daughter of
   John Spinney
  b. David born 1810
   M. Sarah daughter of
    William Atwood
   Oliva daughter of
    William Crowell
  c. Benjamin born 1812
   M. Nancy daughter of
   Howes Snow
  d. Mary born 1816
   M. Daniel son of
   Barry Crowell
  e. William born 1820
   M. Lydia Ann daughter of
   Thomas Worthen
  f. Susannah born 1823
   M. Archibald son of
   Barry Crowell

CS-8-11 Benjamin born 1784
  M. Eunice daughter of
  Solomon Smith

Ch:
    a. Mary born 1806
    b. Sarah born 1808
        M. Samuel son of
          Thomas King
    c. Martha
        M. John son of John Snow
    d. John
    e. Elizabeth born 1812
        M. Abram son of Abram Smith
        Refer to page 197
    f. Peninsh born 1816
        M. Winthrop son of
          John Snow
    g. Annie born 1819
        M. William son of John Snow
    h. Wealthy
        M. Stephen Van Nordon
    i. Rebecca
        M. Jesse Dexter
    j. Benjamin born 1827
    k. William Alexander

CS-9   Judith
        M. William Stevens. Briar Is.

CS-10   Deborah
        M. Elisha Dexter, Roseway

CS-11   Ruth
        M. Samuel son of
          Jonathan Smith Sr.
        Refer to page 185 for full family file

JOHN REYNOLDS

John Reynolds, a son of John and Thankful Reynolds, came to Barrington when he was 18 years of age from Londonderry by way of Boston, Mass. His mother, Thankful, was a widow and married David Smith of Sherose Island. John Reynolds lived on the Walker lot No. 10 while in Barrington but in 1793 he moved to Cape Negro on the Eel Bay, which became later the village of Reynoldscroft.

JR		John Reynolds M. Temperance, daughter of Joshua Atwood	
		Ch:	
	-1	Temperance	B. 1776
	-2	John	B. 1779
	-3	Francis	B. 1780
	-4	Samuel	B. 1781
	-5	Joshua	B. 1783
	-6	Joseph	B. 1785
	-7	Thankful	B. 1791
	-8	Susanna	B. 1793
	-9	Knowles	B. 1796
	-10	Mary	B. 1799
JR-1		Temperance M. Joseph, son of Joseph Swaine	B. 1776
		Ch:	
	-1	Rebecca	B. 1798
	-2	Joseph	B. 1800
	-3	Rachael	B. 1803
	-4	Temperance	B. 1804
	-5	Abagail	B. 1805
	-6	Samuel	B. 1812
	-7	James Freeman	B. 1813
	-8	Mary	B. 1814
	-9	Hannah	B. 1816
	-10	Deborah	B. 1820
	-11	Nancy	B. 1822
JR-1		Temperance M. Joseph, son of Joseph Swaine	B. 1776

Ch:
- -1 Rebecca — B. 1798
  M. Martin Slate
- -2 Joseph — B. 1800
  Unmarried
- -3 Rachael — B. 1803
  M. John B., son of
  David Swaine

  Ch:
  - (A) Temperance
    M. Daniel Matherson

    Ch:
    - a. John E. — B. 1880
      M. Anna, daughter of
      Rodney MacKinnon

      Ch:
      - a-1 John — B. 1910
        M. Verna, daughter of
        Jesse Obed
        No issue
    - b. Wilford — B. 1882
    - c. Everett — B. 1884
    - d. William — B. 1887
  - (B) Heman
    M. Mary, daughter of
    Howes Smith
  - (C) Joseph
  - (D) Eleazer
    M. Catherine, daughter of
    James Atwood
  - (E) Clifford
- -4 Temperance — B. 1803
  M. Heman, son of
  Nathaniel Horton
- -5 Abagail — B. 1805
  M. William, son of
  Benjamin Snow

  Ch:
  - 5-1 Andrew
    M. Sarah, daughter of
    James Perry
    Reuben, Estelle, Bert

	5-2	Joshiah	
		M. Martha MacGuire	
		No issue	
	5-3	Samuel Snow	
		Unmarried	
-6		Samuel Swaine	B. 1812
		M. Esther, daughter of	
		Prince Nickerson	
		No issue	
-7		James Freeman	B. 1813
		M. Mary, daughter of	
		William Patterson	

Ch:

	7-1	Joseph Freeman	B. 1848
		M. Carrie Hills (Lockeport)	

Ch:

	7-1-1	Florence	B. 1875
		M. Winslow Swaine	

Ch:

(A)   Myra
     M. Frank Hutchins, Roland Wood
  No issue

(B)   Hedley
     M. Mary, daughter of
        Arthur Reynolds
  Jean, Phyllis

(C)   Albert
     M. Ellen
  Geraldine, Albert, Marjory,
  Francis

(D)   Ralph
     M. Mary Reid
  Nancy, Richard

	7-1-2	Mysie	
		M. Douglas Gardner	
		Douglas	
	7-1-3	Gertrude Hills	B. 1877
		Unmarried	
	7-1-4	Stanley	
		M. Maude, daughter of	
		Richard Kline	
		No issue	
	7-2	Mary Ellen	B. 1844
		M. Nathaniel, son of	
		William Smith	

	Ch:	
7-2-1	Minnie	B. 1870
	M. Mitchell, son of Crowell Smith Lena, Deborah, Harold, Earl, Irwin, Frank	
7-2-2	Viola	B. 1872
	Unmarried	
7-2-3	Ardella	B. 1874
7-2-4	Foster	B. 1878
	M. Margaret Holland Daisy	
7-2-5	Collin	B. 1878
	M. Maude, daughter of James MacKay James	
7-3	Marshall	B. 1854
	M. Deborah, daughter of Seth Snow Bessie MacIntosh No issue	
7-4	Sarah	B. 1856
	M. Stewart, son of Henry Swaine	
	Ch:	
7-4-1	Samuel	B. 1880
	M. Leah, daughter of Capt. Wm. L. Ross Ch:	
(A)	Lottie	
	M. Emerson, son of James Thomas Llewellyn	
-8	Mary	B. 1814
	M. Martin, son of Elam Thomas	
	Ch:	
8-1	Elam	
	M. Mary Ellen Perry	
	1. Orville 2. James 3. Stephen 4. Mabel 5. Elvah, M. Capt. Chas. Kenny 6. Ethel 7. Wilfred	

8-2   Joseph
    M. Mary
    1. Joseph, M. Mildred Nickerson
    2. Nettie, M. Ennis Newell
    3. Hira
    4. Lebert
        M. Winnifred, daughter of
          Hiram Newell
        Wanda, M. Alex Atkinson
        Nettie, M. Murray Robinson
        Avis, M. James Dexter
        Clayton, M. Edith Hopkins
        Hilbert, M. Daisy Adams
        Hersey, M. Marie Snow
        Ruby

8-3   John James

7-4-2   Eva   B. 1884
    M. Addo L. Smith
    Ivy, Cecil, Lewis, Harold,
    Ernest

7-4-3   James   B. 1886

7-4-4   Clinton   B. 1887

7-4-5   Bessie   B. 1890
    M. Percy, son of
        Walter Thomas
    Eleanor, George

7-4-6   Everett   B. 1891

7-4-7   Walter   B. 1893
    M. Lyda, daughter of
        Arthur Reynolds
    Virginia

7-4-8   Sarah   B. 1894

7-5   Harriett
    M. Wilson MacLellan

7-6   James
    M. Agnes Kenny

7-7   Jane
    Unmarried

JR-2   John   B. 1779
    M. Margaret Ryer
    Ch:

2-1   Margaret   B. 1832
    M. Cornelius, son of
        William Snow

(A)	Ch:
	Howard
	  M. Jane, daughter of
	    John Worthen
	Clarence, Oscar, Albert,
	Ruby
		B. 1864

(B)	Homer
	  M. Maria, daughter of
	    John Worthen
	Lloyd, Margarete, Dorothy
		B. 1866

(C)	Jessie
	  M. Robert, son of
	    Samuel Smith
		B. 1869

	Ch: Elizabeth	B. 1901
	Jennie	B. 1903
	Reba	B. 1905
	Nellie M. George Rollins	B. 1910
	Gordon	B. 1913

(D)	Mary
	  M. Charles, son of
	    Francis MacGuire
	Mabel, Margaret, John
		B. 1878

2-2	Elizabeth
	  M. Knowles, son of
	    Samuel Reynolds
	
	For a fully family record
	refer to Page 201, no. -2-3
	Knowles Reynolds.
		B 1839

2-3	John Samuel M. Olivia Sholds	

2-4	Robert
	  M. Sarah Ann, daughter of
	    Aaron Banks
	For a fully family record
	refer to Page 202, no. -14-1
	Sarah Ann Banks.	

JR-3	Francis
	  M. Paul, son of
	    Zephaniah Swaine
	For a fully family record
	refer to Page 200, no. -1
	Paul Swaine
		B. 1780

JR-4		Samuel M. Lydia, daughter of Zephaniah Swaine For a full family record refer to Page 201, no. -2 Lydia Swaine	B. 1781

JR-5		Joshua
		  Unmarried
		  Lost at sea.
			B. 1783

JR-6		Joseph M. Rhoda, daughter of Benjamin Snow Ch:	B. 1785
	6-1	Joseph M. Catherine Worthing	B. 1808
	6-2	Rhoda M. Freeman, son of Jonathan Crowell Ch:	B. 1811
	(A)	Grace M. John Sholds Oscar, Eliza	
	(B)	Ernest M. Freda, daughter of Tristram Bower Ralph, Clissie, Harvey, Shirley, Allan	
JR-7		Thankful M. Richard, son of Abram Smith For full family record refer to Page 194, no. 4-3-2 Thankful Smith.	B. 1791
JR-8		Susanna M. Chapman, son of Josiah Swaine Ch:	B. 1793
	8-1	Catherine	
	8-2	Nathan, M. Mary King	
	8-3	Chapman	
	8-4	Paul	
	8-5	Joseph, M. Eleanor Nickerson	
	8-6	John, M. Rebecca Nickerson	

	8-7	Knowles, M. Lydia MacKenna	
		Ch:	
		Elizabeth, M. James Smith	
		Catherine, M. Johnson Perry	
		Lydia, M. Arthur Thomas	
		Cynthia, M. Arthur Thomas	
	8-8	Cynthia, M. Charles Perry	
	8-9	Elizabeth, M. William Perry	
	8-10	Susan, M. Jonathan Perry	
	8-11	Naomi, M. William MacKenna	
JR-9		Knowles	B. 1796
		M. Mary, daughter of Jonathan Smith	
		Ch:	
	9-1	Josiah	B. 1821
		M. Mary Ellen Orman	
		Ch:	
	(A)	Leander	B. 1851
		M. Adelaide, daughter of Samuel Smith	
		Tressell, Kenneth, Herman	
	(B)	Tristram	B. 1854
	(C)	Emma	B. 1857
		M. Edward, son of John Bethel	
	(D)	Oliver	B. 1865
	(E)	Stanley	B. 1868
	9-2	Susannah	B. 1824
	9-3	William	B. 1830
		M. Hannah, daughter of Aaron Banks	
JR-10		Mary	B. 1799
		M. Benjamin, son of Benjamin Snow	
		Ch:	
	10-1	James	B. 1835
		M. Sophia, daughter of Elkanah Nickerson	
		Clara, Wilbert, Georgia	
	10-2	Agnes	B. 1838
		Unmarried	

10-3 Levi B. 1841
   M. Abagail, daughter of
      Nathan Snow

   Ch:
(A) Cordelia
      M. Josiah, son of
         Solomon Spinney
      Amy, Constance, Mabel

(B) Gilbert Snow,
      M.

   Ch:
   1. Donald
   2. Ralph
   3. Rosa
   4. Alvin
   5. Mary

(C) Anna
      Unmarried

(D) Winslow Snow
      M. Julia Spinney
      Iva, Nellie, Everett,
      Wilma, Morton

10-4 Mercy
      M. Samuel Thomas

10-5 Francis
      Unmarried

ISAAC KING

Isaac King and his wife, Lydia, daughter of Joseph Sparrow, came to Barrington with the New Englanders. His grant of land was near Sherose Island. He and his family returned to New England in 1776, his son, Isaac remained.

King   Isaac
            M. Lydia, daughter of
               Samuel Smith and
               Granddaughter of Jonathan Smith

         Ch:
         1. Thomas   B. 1775
         2. Enoch   B. 1777
         3. Isaac   B. 1779
         4. John   B. 1782
         5. Lydia   B. 1791
         6. Hannah   B. 1804
         7. Richard   B. 1814

226

8. Benjamin B.

-1   Thomas   B. 1775
M. Elizabeth, daughter of
John MacKillop

Ch:
1-1 William
M. Martha Perry, Blanche

Ch:
Archibald
Benjamin
Alexander, M. Debra Lewis
James
Jane, M. Frank, son, Paul Swaine
Margaret
Elizabeth
M. Alexander Perry

Ch:
Elsie, Leighton, Minnie

1-2 Samuel
M. Sarah, daughter of
Benjamin Smith

Ch:
Elizabeth, M. Orlando Taylor,
Letitia, M. William Snow,
Jane

1-3 John
M. Rebecca Whitney

Ch:
Bethia, M. Henry Lavers
James H.

1-4 Thomas
Unmarried

1-5 Letitia
Unmarried

1-6 Catherine

1-7 Alexander
M. Hannah Perry

Ch:
Harriett, M. David Thomas
Hannah, M. Dan Manthorn
Isabel, M. James Nichol
Robert, M. Louise Chatwynd
Alexander, M. Martha Perry
William
Edward
John

	1-8	Richard	
		M. Margaret ?	
	1-9	Benjamin	
		M. Mary Ann Noble	
		Ch: Albert	
-2		Enoch	
-3		Isaac	
		M. Martha Ketch	

Ch:
Sarah, M. DeMings
Sophia, M. James Perry
Mary, M. Whitney
Lydia, M. Samuel Whitney
Sylvia, M. Enoch King
Margaret, M. John Aitkens
John, Unmarried
Hannah, M. Capt. John Pierce
Benjamin, M. Margaret ?
   Ch: Colin, George, Abagain

-4   John
      M. Letitia Rice

Ch:

Lydia Matilda	B. 1811
Isaac	B. 1814
Mary E.	B. 1816
Hannah	B. 1819
Ann MacKillop	B. 1821

-5   Lydia   B. 1791
      M. Thomas
         No issue

-6   Hannah
      M. Benjamin Perry, N.E. Harbour

Ch:
Benjamin
Elson
Isaac
Thomas

-7   Richard
      M. Lydia Stevens

Ch:
a. Eliza, M. John J. Thomas
b. Enoch, M. Sylvia,
   daughter of Isaac King
c. Isaac, M. Elizabeth Hagar
d. Sarah, M. William Goodwin

  e. Rebecca, M. Abram Van Norden
  f. James Rice, M. Clarissa Perry
   Ch:
   -1 Emily Jane, M.E. Salibury
   -2 Emeline, M. Chandley Smith
   -3 Elmira, M. Joshia Adams
   -4 Rebecca, M. William Swaine,
    James Telford
   -5 Isaac, M. Emeline Nelson
   -6 Elson, M. Lilian Thomas,
    Janet, McRae, Ada Cameron
   -7 Samuel
   -8 William
  g. Richard
   M. Dorothy, daughter of
   Rev. Edward Reynolds
  h. Almira
   M. Amos H. Pitman, Yarmouth

-8 Benjamin
   M. Lydia ?
  Ch:
   Benjamin

JOHN LYLE

John Lyle was a son of Thomas Alexander Lyle, a tanner of Glasgow, Scotland. John was an officer in the 4th Dragoons. He was in the battle of Bunker Hill. John was given a grant of 200 acres of land in Shelburne. John and his brother, Gavin, bought the house and land of Elkanah Smith at Indian Brook and settled there. John later moved to Smoke House Point. John's sons, Seth and Alexander moved to Blanche.

Lyle John
   M. Sarah Huskins

  Ch:
  1. Sarah

  2. John

  3. Susanna

  4. Seth
   M. Sophia, daughter of
   Howes Snow

  5. Alexander
   M. Eunice Blades

  6. Thomas
   M. Deborah, daughter of
   John Spinney

  7. Margaret

-4   Seth
         M. Sophia, daughter of
            Howes Snow

     Ch:
- 4-1 Charlie
- 4-2 Fred
- 4-3 William
  - M. Margaret
  - No issue
- 4-4 Alexander
  - M. Annie Goodick

     Ch:
- a. Idella
  - Not married
- b. Stella
  - M. Clifford Perry

     Ch:
- b-1 Mervin
  - M. Lillian, daughter of Thomas Scott

-5   Alexander
         M. Eunice Blades

     Ch:
- 5-1 George
  - M. Ruth, daughter of Richard Smith

     Ch:
- a. Bertha
  - 1st M. Thomas, son of Thomas Ross
  - 2nd Samuel, son of William Patterson
  - Delbert
- b. George
  - M. Edith
  - Donald
- c. Elizabeth
  - M. Lemuel Adams
  - Clyde, Carl, Daisy, Viola, Fay
- d. Iza
  - Unmarried
- 5-2 Isaac
  - M. Maggie Messenger

5-2 Isaac
M. Margaret Messenger

Ch:
a. Edgar

b. Gladys

c. Mary

d. Agnes

e. George
M. moved to Shelburne

f. Sadie
M. Greenwood
Moved to U.S.A.

g. Winnie
M. Locke Larkin
Ariel, Margaret,
Leroy, Malcolm

h. Arthur
Unmarried

JAMES OBED

James Obed was on a vessel coming from Sweden when he was ship wrecked on Cape Sable Island, about 1820. He first settled on the South Side of Cape Sable Island and married Elizabeth, a daughter of Robert Barry Crowell. They moved to West Side Blanche. James Obed, Sr. was drowned in 1883.

Obed James, Sr.
M. Elizabeth, daughter of
Robert Barry Crowell

Ch:
1. Archalaus
Mary Ann, daughter of
Steven Smith

Ch:
a. Archalaus
M. Genevieve, daughter of
Silas Towner

a-1 Wilma
M. Louise, daughter of
Fendwick Perry

a-2 Dorothy
M. Coleman, son of
George Ross

231

b. Steven
       M. Lucy, daughter of
       Henry Swaine

   c. Cordelia

2. James
       M. Elizabeth, daughter of
       Steven Smith

Ch:
   a. Guilford
       M. Jessie, daughter of
       Joseph Thomas

       Ch:
       Ida, Irma

   b. Jesse
       M. Odessa, daughter of
       Henry Swaine

       Ch:
       Verna

   c. Reine
       M. Walter Myrick, U.S.A.

       Ch:
       Evelyn, Thomas, Amos, Ada,
       Ina, Bessie, Walter, Lena, Mildred.
       Sadie, Frank

Joseph R. Ross, B.Sc., F.R.S.H.

The Author, born at Cape Negro in 1925, son of Captain William L. and Anna Jane Ross. Attended the Cape Negro School until his parents' death and then moved to Halifax, Montreal, Toronto and Saskatoon where he completed his education. He spent more than 20 years as a medical worker with the Indians of Northern Manitoba and the Eskimos of the Arctic. He was responsible for establishing and organizing the health services in many areas of the Arctic. He speaks two Indian dialects and Eskimo and is passable in French and

English. In 1961 he was awarded the Federal Government Public Health Award, for writing health literature and was awarded the Medical Crest for life. After attending the University of Saskatchewan, he was hospital administrator for 18 years of various federal hospitals. He has written several curriculums and established training schools for medical workers, the last being at Pugwash, the School for Personal Care Workers. In 1976 he was elected to a Fellowship in the Royal Society of Health, London, England. He is now retired spending the winter months in England and the summers at Blanche, Nova Scotia, which he calls home.

Acknowledgements and Sources of Research

Denys French History, France.

Archives du Service Hydrographique de la Marine, Paris.

Public Archives of Canada, Ottawa.

Public Archives of Nova Scotia, Halifax.

Archives, Summerset House, England.

Public Records and Archives, Norwich, England.

History of Barrington Township.

Burdett Perry, Lottie Thomas, Marion Thomas, Hazel MacKay, Ruby Perry, Allan Swaine, Hilbert Thomas, Herbin Pierce, Herbert Thomas, Josie Ross.

Special acknowledgement to Barbara Raisbeck who obtained photo copies of French documents from the University Library in U.S.A. that were not available to me otherwise.

INDEX to HISTORY OF CAPE NEGRO & BLANCHE by Joseph R. Ross

AGAL	SAMUEL		5
ALEXANDER	SIR	WILLIAM	5
APPLEBY	JABEZ	REV.	101
AREY	ABBIE		174
AREY	ABIGAIL		112
AREY	ARTHUR		26
AREY	CHARLES	HENRY	113
AREY	ERNEST		26
AREY	EVERETT		26
AREY	FIDELIA		18, 25
AREY	GORDON		26
AREY	HENRY		25
AREY	JOSEPH	HENRY	114
AREY	JOSEPH		18, 25, 26, 47, 81, 104, 172
AREY	MARY		26
AREY	NICHOLAS		25
AREY	STELLA		26
AREY	WALTER		26, 47, 104, 141, 145
ATTWOOD	HARRY		31, 38, 117
ATTWOOD	HILDA		31, 38
ATTWOOD	MARY		24, 76, 166
ATWOOD	LILLA		32
ATWOOD	VINCENT		32
BACZEWAKI	EDRIS		29
BACZEWAKI	JOHN		29
BAGNELL	HARRY	REV.	101
BALTZER	SUSAN	JANE	37
BANKS	ELIAS		39
BANKS	SOPHIA		39
BANKS	THOMAS		39
BARASS	BENJAMIN		102
BARASS	JAMES		102
BARNES	SACCO		11
BARSS	BENJAMIN		11
BARSS	MARY		11
BAXTER	AGNES		161
BENNET?	PATIENCE		107
BERRY	ABBIE		108
BERRY	JAMES		104, 108, 110
BETHEL	JOHN	ELTON	113
BETHEL	JOHN		42, 104, 157
BIENCOURT			5
BLADES	EUNICE		23
BLAKEMORE	BRUCE		19
BOOTMAN	ELIZABETH		11, 17
BOOTMAN	SAMUEL		11, 17
BORDEN	J.	R. REV.	100
BOWER	(RUFUS) ?		32
BOYD	W.	REV.	101
BRANNEN	ALBERTA		34
BRANNEN	PHYLLIS		37
BRANNEN	ROBERT		34
BRANNEN?	MARIE		34
BROWN	ABBIE		26
BROWN	HENRY	REV.	101
BROWN	ISOBEL		41
BROWN	IZOLA		16, 38
BROWN	JAMES		24
BROWN	LEWIS		69
BRUCE	MR.		166
BRUCE	STANLEY		162
BRYANT	?		29
BRYANT	TIMOTHY		11
BUNCH	GLENDON		21
BURGESS	NELLIE		28
CAMERON	MILDRED		70
CHAMPLAIN			4, 7

NOTE:- check for spelling variations on names, also names may be mentioned more than once on a page.

INDEX to HISTORY OF CAPE NEGRO & BLANCHE by Joseph R. Ross

Surname	Given Name	Other	Page
CHATWIN	ANDREW		109
CHATWIN	RUTH		110
CHATWYND	ANDREW		23
CHATWYND	ASA		82
CHATWYND	CHILD		109
CHATWYND	DURKEE		104
CHATWYND	HILBERT		107
CHATWYND	RANSOME		23
CHATWYND	RANSON		104
CHATWYND	RUTH		23
CHETWYND	THOMAS		13
CHIVERS	VIRGINIA		76
CHRISTIE	ALLIE	SLATE	31
CHRISTIE	ALLIE		32
CHRISTIE	CHARLOTTE	ALSOLDA?	115
CHRISTIE	JESSE		76
CHRISTIE	JOHN	A.	80, 81
CHRISTIE	JOHN		32, 90, 145
CHRISTIE	SARAH		25
CHRISTIE	SYDNEY		32, 99, 129
CLARKE	A.	J. REV.	101
COFFIN	ELIZABETH		17
COFFIN	JOHN	JR.	12, 17
COFFIN	PELEG		11
COLLINS	WILLIAM	REV.	101
CONK	PETER		12, 23
CONNOUGHT	DUKE	OF	37
CONSTABLE	THOMAS	REV.	101
COREY	AGNES		40
COVEY?	AGNES		108
CRAIG	MASTER		120
CROMWELL	JAMES	OLIVER, REV.	98, 100
CROOKS			35
CROWE	WILLIAM		8
CROWELL	EDWARD		135
CROWELL	ELIZABETH		12, 24
CROWELL	ROBERT	BARRY	12, 24
DANIELS	A.	REV.	101
DASH	FLORA		34
DAVIS	HIRAM	REV.	101
de la TOUR	CHARLES		5, 6, 8
de la TOUR	CLAUDE		5, 6
DEMONTS			4, 5
DEMPSEY	RONALD	REV.	101
DENSMORE	DR.		57
DENYS			7, 8, 27
DOANE	DAVE		133
DOANE	SAMUEL		127
DOMVILLE	W.	J. REV.	101
DOWLING	MERCY		28
DOWLING	WILLIAM		28
DREW	CAROLINE		16, 20
DREW	ELIZABETH		20, 72, 114
DREW	FRANCES		20
DREW	FRANCIS		34
DREW	GEORGE		20, 72, 104, 114
DREW	JACK		117
DREW	JOHN		16, 20, 34, 134,
DREW	JUDY		16, 20, 34
ENNIS	BEATRICE		155
ENNIS	GORDON		155
ENZOR	?		16
FARMER	CHILD		114
FARMER	JAMES		41
FARMER	JIMMIE		159
FARMER	RUSSEL		41, 154
FARMER	RUSSELL		117

NOTE:- check for spelling variations on names, also names may be mentioned more than once on a page.

INDEX to HISTORY OF CAPE NEGRO & BLANCHE by Joseph R. Ross

Surname	Given	Other	Title	Pages
FARMER	VIOLET			41
FIDLER			REV.	98, 100
FITZGERALD	EMALINE			37
FLEMMING	DAVID			104
FLEMMING	DORA			108
FLEMMINGS	DAVID		SR.	21
FLEMMINGS	DAVID			25
FLEMMINGS	FRED			31
FLEMMINGS	KATHERINE			21
FLEMMINGS	MERCY			25
FORSYTHE	W.		H. REV.	101
FREEMAN	JOSEPH		CAPT.	122
GAGNONG	WILLIAM		F.	7
GARDINER	MYSIE			116
GARDNER	MYSIE		MRS.	161
GARDNER	MYSIE			28, 120, 175
GARDNER	REBECCA			39
GARDNER	STANLEY	DOUGLAS		112
GARDNER	SYLVIA			76
GARRETSON	FREEBORN		REV.	98, 100
GLOUCESTER	WILLIAM		M.	112
GOODICK	ANNIE			16
GOODWIN	ADA			37
GOULDING	DEAN			161
GRASBILL	JANET			25
GRASBILL	SYDNEY			25
GRAY	MARY		S.	111
GRAY	MARY			40
GREENWOOD	SADIE			40
GREENWOOD	STAN			104
GREENWOOD	STANLEY			21
HARRIS	EMMA			39
HART	J. A.		T. REV.	101
HENSLER	BASIL			19
HERBERT	BARBARA	JANE		115
HERBERT	CHARLES	WM.		113
HERBERT	CLINT			117
HERBERT	MARDRIA			114
HERSEY	EVERETT			134
HILL	BERT			117
HILL	BERTRAM			28, 29
HILL	EDRIS			29
HILL	LILY			28, 29
HILLS	CARRIE			28
HINES	HAZEL			175
HOCKIN	A.		REV	100
HOGG	HENRY			17, 117
HOGG	INA			17, 164
HOPKINS	MARY	ELIZA		109
HOPKINS	MATILDA			36
HORTON	ELIZA			108
HORTON	HEMAN			31
HORTON	MRS.			107
HORTON	NATHANIEL			104
HORTON	SARAH			31
HOUGAN	MR.			134
HURBERT	CHARLES	WILLIE		41, 103, 154
HURBERT	CLINT			41
HURBERT	FLORENCE			41
HURBERT	IVY			41
HURBERT	MANNY			41
HURBERT	MAUDE			41, 159
HURBERT	PETER			41, 117
HURBERT	WILLIAM		CAPT.	104
HURBERT	WILLIAM			159
HUSKINS	ADDISON			159
HUSKINS	TERRANCE			175

NOTE:- check for spelling variations on names, also names may be mentioned more than once on a page.

INDEX to HISTORY OF CAPE NEGRO & BLANCHE by Joseph R. Ross

HUTCHINS	FRANK		38
HUTCHINS	MYRA		38, 169
ISLEY	BELLE		37
JACQUES	MARIE	PETA	115
JARDINE	JANET		25
JEFFERIES	DR.		35
JEFFERIES	LINDA		35
JESSOP		REV.	98, 100
JONES	ALVA	JEAN	37
JONES	BRUCE		19
JONES	GORDON		37
JONES	HUGH		19, 20
KEELING	LOVIE		104
KEILING	LLOYD		108
KELLY	DIANNA		108
KENNEY	LIZZIE	MRS.	109
KENNY	C.	B. CAPT.	100
KENNY	ELVA		100
KING	ALEXANDER		21
KING	ARCHIBALD		21
KING	BENJAMIN		21
KING	BESSIE		17
KING	ELIZABETH		21
king	genealogy		225 - 228
KING	ISAAC	JR.	13
KING	ISAAC		13, 21
KING	JAMES		21
KING	JANE		21
KING	JOHN		128
KING	MARGARET		21
KING	MARTHA		21
KING	MILFORD		17, 117
KING	SAMUEL		128
KING	SOPHIA		13
KING	THOMAS		21, 128
KING	WILLIAM		21, 128
KIRK	?		5
KNOWLES	SAMUEL		11
LALLOUE	ARMAND		8
LALLOUE	ELIZABETH		8
LAMROCK	HATTIE		39
LARKIN	ANNIE		25
LARKIN	ARIEL		40
LARKIN	LEROY		40
LARKIN	LOCKE		40
LARKIN	MALCOLM		40
LARKIN	MARGARET		40
LARKIN	WINNIE		40
LAWRENCE	GOVERNOR		9
LEBLANC	DAVID	REV.	101
LONGHURST	CAPT.		11
LOWE	ANNE		42
LOWE	ANNIE		110
LOWE	BRADFORD		35, 36, 41, 42, 104, 116
LOWE	EFFIE	E.	111
LOWE	EFFIE		41
LOWE	FERNWOOD		35, 42
LOWE	GRANT		42, 117, 121
LOWE	HAZEL		35
LOWE	KENNETH		42
LOWE	LORNE		42
LOWE	MARGARETTE		42
LOWE	MILDRED		42, 121
LOWE	SEATTLE		35
LOWE	THOMAS		35, 42
LUIS	LAZARO		3
LYDIA	KING		13

NOTE:- check for spelling variations on names, also names may be mentioned more than once on a page.

INDEX to HISTORY OF CAPE NEGRO & BLANCHE by Joseph R. Ross

LYLE	AGNES		40
LYLE	ALEC		136
LYLE	ALEX	S.	88, 94
LYLE	ALEX		81, 82, 89, 91, 92, 93, 131, 134
LYLE	ALEXANDER	STILLMAN	115
LYLE	ALEXANDER		15, 16, 23, 104, 108
LYLE	ANNIE		15
LYLE	ARTHUR		40, 117
LYLE	BERTHA		41
LYLE	CHARLES		110
LYLE	CHARLIE		16, 92
LYLE	DONALD		42
LYLE	EDGAR	R.	108
LYLE	EDGAR		39
LYLE	EUNICE		23
LYLE	EVELYN		118, 162
LYLE	FRED		16
LYLE	GAVIN		127
lyle	genealogy		228 - 230
LYLE	GEORGE		23, 40, 41
LYLE	GLADES	V.	108
LYLE	GLADYS		39
LYLE	IDELLA		16
LYLE	ISAAC		14, 23, 39, 40, 104, 112
LYLE	JAMES		23
LYLE	JOHN	JR.	127
LYLE	MARGARET	A.	114
LYLE	MARGARET	JEANETTA	115
LYLE	MARGARET		14, 20, 23, 39, 40
LYLE	MARY		40
LYLE	RUTH		23
LYLE	SADIE		40
LYLE	SARAH	E.	112
LYLE	SARAH		16, 20
LYLE	SETH		16, 20, 23
LYLE	STELLA		16, 155
LYLE	W.	E.	83, 85, 87
LYLE	WILL		104, 143, 178
LYLE	WILLIAM	E.	80, 81, 113
LYLE	WILLIAM		16, 20, 94, 131, 156
LYLE	WINNIE		40
MACARTHUR	ROBERT	REV.	100
MACBETH	GORDON	REV.	101
MACDONALD	JEAN	ISOBEL	37
MACDONALD	JESSE		36
MACDONALD	ROSS	REV.	101
MACDOUGAL	DONALD	REV.	101
MACK	BARRY	REV.	100
MACKAY	ALICE		38
MACKAY	ANNIE		118
MACKAY	ELSIE		21, 42
MACKAY	GEODFREY		42
MACKAY	GODFREY		21, 121
MACKAY	GRACE		25, 172
MACKAY	GRANT		35, 117
MACKAY	HAZEL	V.	160
MACKAY	HAZEL		118, 233
MACKAY	HILDA		31
MACKAY	IDA		76
MACKAY	JAMES		31, 104
MACKAY	LEVINIA		31
MACKAY	MARY		82
MACKAY	MAUDE		31
MACKAY	MILDRED		1, 42, 118, 121, 162
MACKAY	WILLIAM		25, 38, 39
MACKILLOP	ELIZABETH		21
MACKILLOP	JOHN		11, 21, 127

NOTE:- check for spelling variations on names, also names may be mentioned more than once on a page.

INDEX to HISTORY OF CAPE NEGRO & BLANCHE by Joseph R. Ross

Surname	Given	Initial/Title	Pages
MACKINLEY	HELEN		33
MACKINNON	ANNA		27
MACLAREN	FRED		153
MACLAREN	MR.		158
MACLELLAN	MAY		30
MACNEIL	H.	H. REV.	101
MACQUEEN	DONALD	REV.	101
MAILMAN	GERALD		37
MANN	JAMES	REV.	98, 100
MATHERS	GEORGE		104
MATHERSON	?		11
MATHERSON	ANNA		27
MATHERSON	DANIEL		11, 26, 27, 69, 104, 114, 120
MATHERSON	JOHN	D.	116
MATHERSON	JOHN	E.	116
MATHERSON	JOHN	JR.	18, 27, 29, 32, 66, 70, 145, 159
MATHERSON	JOHN	SR.	27, 60, 66, 70
MATHERSON	JOHN		133, 144
MATHERSON	MARION		118, 162
MATHERSON	ROY	MRS.	1, 120
MATHERSON	SR.		141
MATHERSON	TEMPERANCE		27, 113, 120
MATHERSON	VERNA	E.	116
MATHERSON	VERNA		27, 29, 32, 169
MATHERSON	WILL		134
MATHERSON	WILLIAM		27
MATHERSON	WILLIE		58
MATHEWS	SERETHA		112
MAULE	BESSIE		31
MAULE	WILLIAM		31
MCCLARK	D.	REV.	101
MCKAY	LEVINIA		112
MELLISH	J.	M. REV.	101
MESSENGER	BERTHA		21
MESSENGER	DOUGLAS		21
MESSENGER	ETHEL		21
MESSENGER	FRANCIS		21
MESSENGER	KATHERINE		21
MESSENGER	LEE		21, 118
MESSENGER	LEONA		21
MESSENGER	LORENZO		21
MESSENGER	MARGARET		23, 40
MILLAR	ROBERT		107
MILLER	CLARA		34
MILLS	RACHEL		110
MOLIN	LAURENT		8
MONK	WILLIAM		38, 117
MOOR	ARTHUR		117
MOORS	ARTHUR		16, 20, 134
MOORS	NELL		16
MORRISON	CHARLES		127
MYRICK	ADA		17
MYRICK	AMOS		17, 134
MYRICK	BESSIE		17
MYRICK	EVELYN		17, 144, 168
MYRICK	FRANK		17, 18, 28
MYRICK	IDA	(PERRY)	116
MYRICK	IDA		17
MYRICK	INA		17, 164, 165
MYRICK	JENNY		17, 28
MYRICK	LENA		17
MYRICK	LORENA		163, 164
MYRICK	MAYNARD		32, 112
MYRICK	MILDRED		17
MYRICK	ORETERIA	M.	112
MYRICK	RANDALL		134
MYRICK	REINE		17, 18

NOTE:- check for spelling variations on names, also names may be mentioned more than once on a page.

INDEX to HISTORY OF CAPE NEGRO & BLANCHE by Joseph R. Ross

MYRICK	SADIE		17, 168
MYRICK	THOMAS		17
MYRICK	WALTER	JR.	19, 134, 165
MYRICK	WALTER	SR.	17, 18, 83, 104, 131, 134
MYRICK	WALTER		17, 85, 117, 134, 163, 164
MYRICK	WATER		134
NELSON	JAMES		127
NELSON	NORMAN		57
NEWELL	EARL		111
NEWELL	ELLEN		111
NEWELL	ERIC		28
NICHOLSON	CAPT.		30
NICKERSON	ALLIE		162
NICKERSON	ARTHUR		162
NICKERSON	CHARLES	E. JR.	112
NICKERSON	DEBORAH		113
NICKERSON	ELDRED	L.	111
NICKERSON	ELRED		104
NICKERSON	EVERETT		133, 134
NICKERSON	F.	G.	82
NICKERSON	FLORENCE		35, 81, 82
NICKERSON	FLOSSIE		162
NICKERSON	GEO.		108
NICKERSON	GERTRUDE		19
NICKERSON	IVAN		162
NICKERSON	JAMES	A.	99
NICKERSON	JOHN	CAPT.	159
NICKERSON	JOHN		35, 39, 104, 151, 153,
NICKERSON	JOSEPH	CAPT.	159
NICKERSON	JOSHUA		34
NICKERSON	MADONNA		34
NICKERSON	MARGARET	J.	113
NICKERSON	MARTHA		108
NICKERSON	MARY		26, 34, 162
NICKERSON	MATTHEW	R.	108
NICKERSON	MATTHEW		104
NICKERSON	MERTON		162
NICKERSON	MORTON		134
NICKERSON	NATHAN		12, 15
NICKERSON	R.	HANNAH	110
NICKERSON	SADIE		175
NICKERSON	SEATTLE		35
NICKERSON	SETH		74, 78, 104, 110
NICKERSON	SMITH		26
NICKERSON	SOPHIA		39
NICKERSON	STANFORD		18
NICKERSON	SUSAN		12, 15
NICKERSON	WILL		175
NICKERSON	WILLARD	CAPT.	159
NICKERSON	WILLIAM	H.	109
NICKERSON	ZEPHANIAH	CAPT.	22, 25, 152, 157, 173, 179
NICKERSON	ZEPHANIAH	MRS.	179
NICKERSON	ZEPHANIAH		35, 153
NIGHTENGALE	W.	REV.	101
NUGENT	HELEN	JEAN	19
NUGENT	PAUL		19
NURSEY?	SARAH	M.	109
O'CONNELL	GEORGE		41
O'CONNELL	LOLA		19
O'CONNELL	VIOLET		32
O'CONNELL	WHITFORD		19
OBED	ADELINA	ODESSA	116
OBED	ARCH	MRS.	82
OBED	ARCH		104
OBED	ARCHELAUS		12
OBED	ARCHELIUS	JR.	25
OBED	ARCHELIUS		24, 39

NOTE:- check for spelling variations on names, also names may be mentioned more than once on a page.

INDEX to HISTORY OF CAPE NEGRO & BLANCHE by Joseph R. Ross

OBED	ARCHELUS	C.	109
OBED	ARCHILUS	JR.	24
OBED	ARCHILUS	SR.	24
OBED	CORDELIA		24
OBED	DOROTHY		25
OBED	EITHEL		29
OBED	ELIZABETH	S.	109
OBED	ELIZABETH		18, 24, 79, 80, 81
OBED	EMILY		24
OBED	G.	A.	84
obed	genealogy		230 - 231
OBED	GENEVA	AUGUSTA	114
OBED	GENEVIEVE		24, 39
OBED	GILFORD		104, 179
OBED	GUILFORD		18, 19, 114
OBED	IDA		18, 19
OBED	IRMA		18, 19
OBED	JAMES	JR.	17, 18, 19, 24
OBED	JAMES		12, 79, 80, 81, 88, 90
			104, 111, 131, 143, 164, 168
OBED	JESSE	CLAYTON	114
OBED	JESSE		18, 27, 29, 32, 72, 76, 104, 166
OBED	JESSIE	EXELENA	115
OBED	JESSIE		19
OBED	KENNETH		29
OBED	LORENA		164
OBED	LOUISE		24, 25
OBED	LUCY	FRANCES	113
OBED	LUCY		24, 28, 29
OBED	MARY	ANN	110
OBED	MAXINE		24
OBED	ODESSA	MRS.	161
OBED	ODESSA		29, 31, 32, 33, 72, 76
			120, 144, 166, 169, 179
OBED	REINE		17, 18
OBED	ROBERT	ARCHILAUS	114
OBED	SLATE		104
OBED	STEPHEN	JAMES	114
OBED	STEVEN		24, 28, 29, 104
OBED	VERNA		27, 29, 32, 58, 72, 118, 144, 179
OBED	WILMA		24, 25, 117
OLIVER	ALICE		34
PAGE	MAMIE		144
PAGE	MARY		29, 31
PALMER	W.	H. REV.	101
PARKER	M.	REV.	101
PARSONS	ELIZABETH		104
PARSONS	LIBBY		31
PATERSON	WM.	A.	99 ✓
PATTERSON	BERTHA		41
PATTERSON	EFFIE		41
PATTERSON	ELLEN		107
PATTERSON	H.	P. REV.	101
PATTERSON	MARY		27
PATTERSON	SAMUEL	CAPT.	41
PATTERSON	SAMUEL	SMITH	114
PATTERSON	WILLIAM		27, 41, 126, 127, 128, 153, 154
PERRY	ABRAM		13
PERRY	ALEXANDER		21
PERRY	ANNA		39
PERRY	ANTHONY	D.	110
PERRY	ANTHONY		20, 104
PERRY	BENJAMIN		127, 128
PERRY	BETTY		21, 119, 169
PERRY	BRAD		96, 175
PERRY	BRADFORD		20, 104, 145
PERRY	BURDETT		21, 28, 119, 122, 169, 233

NOTE:- check for spelling variations on names, also names may be mentioned more than once on a page.

INDEX to HISTORY OF CAPE NEGRO & BLANCHE by Joseph R. Ross

Surname	Given Name		Pages
PERRY	CARL		20
PERRY	CECIL		24, 25, 117, 119, 169,
PERRY	CLAUDE	HUGH	113
PERRY	CLAUDE		20, 104
PERRY	CLIFFORD		16, 117, 143
PERRY	EDNA		25, 32
PERRY	ELITA		19
PERRY	ELIZABETH		21
PERRY	ELLA		18, 19
PERRY	ELSIE		21
PERRY	ERNEST		17, 18, 19, 20, 104, 114
PERRY	FENDWICK		24, 25, 32, 117
PERRY	FRANK		19
PERRY	FRANKLIN		17, 19
PERRY	FRED		21, 119, 169
PERRY	FREELAND		134
PERRY	GERTRUDE		19
PERRY	GRACE		24, 25, 32, 169
PERRY	HARRY		35, 118, 134, 174
PERRY	HELEN	MRS.	117
PERRY	HELEN		20
PERRY	IDA	MRS.	178
PERRY	IDA		17, 18, 19, 20,
PERRY	ISAAC		21
PERRY	JAMES		13
PERRY	JOHN		21
PERRY	LEIGHTON		13, 21, 117, 134, 137
PERRY	LETA		21, 119
PERRY	LLETA		178
PERRY	LLOYD		19, 117
PERRY	LORRETTA		24, 25
PERRY	LOUISE		24, 25
PERRY	MARION		35
PERRY	MARTHA		21
PERRY	MERVIN		16, 77
PERRY	MINNIE	MARIE	21, 22
PERRY	OLSON		16, 25, 71, 117, 144
PERRY	PERCY	EARL	112
PERRY	RALPH	L.	109
PERRY	ROSS		39
PERRY	RUBY	SMITH	170
PERRY	RUBY		25, 233
PERRY	SAMUEL		13
PERRY	SILAS		13
PERRY	STELLA		16
PERRY	STEPHEN		127, 128
PERRY	SUSAN		21
PERRY	SUSANNA		13
PERRY	TONE		133, 157
PERRY	VIOLET		21, 169
PERRY	WALTER		35
PERRY	WILLIAM	JR.	127
PERRY	WILLIAM		21, 128
PHALEN	J.	REV.	101
PIERCE	DAVID	REV.	101
PIERCE	ESTER		110
PIERCE	ESTHER		33, 38
PIERCE	HANNA	KING	38
PIERCE	HERBIN		27, 33, 144, 152, 169, 233
PIERCE	JOHN	CAPT.	38
PIERCE	JOHN	HOWES	38
PIERCE	JOSHUA		11, 21, 31, 38, 109
PIERCE	MARY		38
PIERCE	ROWENA		27, 144, 169
PIERCE	VIOLET		32
PIERCE?	HERBIN		32, 33
PIERCE?	ROWENA		32

NOTE:- check for spelling variations on names, also names may be mentioned more than once on a page.

INDEX to HISTORY OF CAPE NEGRO & BLANCHE by Joseph R. Ross

Surname	Given Name	Other	Pages
PIERCE?	VIOLET		33
PORTER	CARRIE	B.	108
POUTRINCOURT			5
POWER	REUBEN	CAPT.	134
PREBBLE	JEDDIDIAH		9
PRICE	CLAIRE		20
PRICE	CLARENCE		117
PRICE	NAN		20
PURDY	STELLA		26
RAISBECK	BARBARA		233
RAISBRECK	BARBARA		31
RAISBRECK	TONY		31
REID	MARY		38
REYNOLD	ARTHUR		30
REYNOLD	JOHN		12
REYNOLD	LYDA		30
REYNOLDS	A.	J. REV.	101
REYNOLDS	ARTHUR		38, 42
REYNOLDS	EDWARD		120
REYNOLDS	ELIZABETH		110
REYNOLDS	FRANCIS		161, 175
reynolds	genealogy		217 - 225
REYNOLDS	HANNAH		107
REYNOLDS	JOHN	H. MRS.	107
REYNOLDS	JOHN	HOWARD	42
REYNOLDS	JOHN		15, 24, 34, 42, 104
REYNOLDS	KNOWLES		127
REYNOLDS	LEVI		42, 153
REYNOLDS	MARY		38, 42
REYNOLDS	NORMAN		42, 153
REYNOLDS	PETER		24
REYNOLDS	ROBERT		42
REYNOLDS	ROSEMAN		153
REYNOLDS	THANKFUL		34
REYNOLDS	WILLIAM		104, 113
ROBERTSON	CYRIL		142, 144
ROBERTSON	ELEANOR		24
RODGERSON	LILLIAN		36
ROSS	ALBERT		16, 19
ROSS	ALLISON		34, 37
ROSS	ALVA	JEAN	34, 37
ROSS	ALVA		119
ROSS	ANNA	JANE	37, 114, 232
ROSS	ANNA	JANE SMITH	1
ROSS	ANNIE	GERTRUDE	114
ROSS	ANNIE		41
ROSS	BARRETT	TYLER	34
ROSS	BERTHA		41
ROSS	BURLEY		34
ROSS	BURNLEY		37, 103
ROSS	CARRY		170
ROSS	COLEMAN		25
ROSS	DELBERT		41
ROSS	DORA		36, 37, 110, 170
ROSS	DOROTHY		16
ROSS	DOUGLAS		24, 26
ROSS	FLORA		34
ROSS	FLOYD		41, 134
ROSS	GEORGE		28, 34, 35, 37, 117
ROSS	GILBERT		19
ROSS	ISOBEL		41
ROSS	JAMES		104
ROSS	JASON		34
ROSS	JEAN	ISOBEL	37
ROSS	JENNY		152, 153
ROSS	JIM		170
ROSS	JOHN		104, 107

NOTE:- check for spelling variations on names, also names may be mentioned more than once on a page.

INDEX to HISTORY OF CAPE NEGRO & BLANCHE by Joseph R. Ross

Surname	Given Name	Middle	Suffix/Title	Pages
ROSS	JOSEPH	R.		232
ROSS	JOSEPH	RANDALL		34, 37
ROSS	JOSEPH			17, 19, 119
ROSS	JOSIE	SWAINE		76
ROSS	JOSIE			26, 233
ROSS	JUDY			34
ROSS	KATHERINE			19
ROSS	KENNETH			34
ROSS	LAWRENCE			16
ROSS	LEAH			16, 26, 30
ROSS	LIZA			19
ROSS	MADONNA			34
ROSS	MARIE			37
ROSS	MILFORD			107
ROSS	MITCHELL			19
ROSS	NANCY			110, 170
ROSS	PHYLLIS			37
ROSS	SUSAN	JANE		37
ROSS	SUSAN			17
ROSS	TAMMY			34
ROSS	THOMAS		JR.	41, 110
ROSS	THOMAS		SR.	36, 41, 111
ROSS	THOMAS			104, 170
ROSS	WALTER			34
ROSS	WILLIAM	L.	CAPT	16, 26, 30, 34, 36, 37, 39, 42, 104, 152, 232
ROSS	WILLIAM	LEWIS		114
RYER	CHRIS			38
RYER	MARY			38
SAINT	J.	R.	REV.	101
SCHRAGE	ANNE			22
SCOTT	LILLIAN			16
SCOTT	THOMAS			16
SEAMON	JOHN			53, 159
SEARS	SADIE			17
SEELIG	JOSHUA			111
SELIG	EVERETT			18
SELIG	JENNY			17
SELIG	JOSH			92, 94
SELIG	JOSHUA			17, 18, 104
SELIG	PHOEBE			18
SELVAGE	MERILLA	S.		113
SHEDIAC	JOHN			28
SHELLY	DEREK		REV.	101
SHOLDS	ANN			26
SHOLDS	CHARITY			26
SHOLDS	FREDERICK			26
SHOLDS	GEORGE			26, 104, 111
SHOLDS	HANNAH			108
SHOLDS	MARY			26
SHOLDS	MILDRED			1, 119, 169
SHOLDS	PETER			26
SHOLDS	SAMUEL			26
SHOLDS	ZEPHANIAH			26
SIMMONS	ALBERT			19
SLATE	ABBIE			26
SLATE	ALICE			173
SLATE	ALLIE			24, 25, 30, 32, 70
SLATE	ANNIE	PATRICIA		114
SLATE	ANNIE			25, 173
SLATE	ANNIS			25
SLATE	BARBARA			12
SLATE	BENJAMIN			25, 82, 104, 111, 145
SLATE	BESSIE			25, 173
SLATE	CATHERINE			12
SLATE	DAVID			25, 162, 173, 174
SLATE	DEBRA			25

NOTE:- check for spelling variations on names, also names may be mentioned more than once on a page.

INDEX to HISTORY OF CAPE NEGRO & BLANCHE by Joseph R. Ross

Surname	Given Name	Middle	Pages
SLATE	DORIS		25, 173
SLATE	ELMA		25
SLATE	EVA		25
SLATE	FREDERICK		12, 23, 172
SLATE	GEORGE	L.	107
SLATE	GEORGE		25, 104, 108
SLATE	GRACE		25, 172
SLATE	HARVEY		74, 78, 82, 104, 109
SLATE	HERBERT		25
SLATE	IDA		25, 118, 173
SLATE	IRA		25
SLATE	LAMONT		25
SLATE	LAURA		29
SLATE	LENARD		25
SLATE	LESTER		25, 162, 171, 172
SLATE	LILLIAN		25, 162, 171, 173
SLATE	MARION		25, 171
SLATE	MARTHA		25, 112
SLATE	MARTIN		12
SLATE	MARY		26
SLATE	MERCY		25
SLATE	MILLIE		25, 70, 162
SLATE	MINNIE		24
SLATE	MONTE		70
SLATE	NEIMA		24, 25, 29, 32
SLATE	OSTENA	MAE	109
SLATE	PERCY		25
SLATE	REBECCA		107
SLATE	SANDFORD		24, 25, 30, 112
SLATE	SARAH	ELIZABETH	109
SLATE	SARAH		25, 112, 145
SLATE	STANFORD		32, 70, 173
SLATE	WILBERT		25
SLATE	WINNIE		25
SMITH	ABRAM		13, 34
SMITH	ADA		76
SMITH	ALBERT		21
SMITH	ALBERTA		34, 119
SMITH	ALDO		25, 29, 30, 172
SMITH	ALEXANDER	CAPT.	21, 104, 109, 157
SMITH	ALICE		34, 38, 121, 169
SMITH	ANNA	JANE	34, 37
SMITH	ANNA		111
SMITH	ANNE		22
SMITH	ARCHELAUS		135
SMITH	BARBARA		12, 16, 107
SMITH	BATHSHEBA		34
SMITH	BENJAMIN		29, 39
SMITH	BERT	S. S.	107
SMITH	BERT		22
SMITH	BESSIE		31
SMITH	BIGELOW		30, 39
SMITH	BILL		14, 177
SMITH	CECIL		25, 29, 162
SMITH	CLARA		34
SMITH	CLARENCE	A.	112
SMITH	CLARENCE		34
SMITH	COLLIN		31
SMITH	CROWELL		39
SMITH	CYNTHIA		21
SMITH	DAVID		11
SMITH	DONALD		36
SMITH	DOROTHY		35
SMITH	ED		82
SMITH	EDWARD		29, 32, 34, 82, 109, 145
SMITH	EDWIN		21, 22, 58, 117
SMITH	EFFIE		16

NOTE:- check for spelling variations on names, also names may be mentioned more than once on a page.

INDEX to HISTORY OF CAPE NEGRO & BLANCHE by Joseph R. Ross

SMITH	ELEANOR		24
SMITH	ELIZABETH		16, 18, 24
SMITH	ELLA		21, 35
SMITH	EMMA		39
SMITH	ENOCH		30, 39
SMITH	ERNEST		25, 29, 118, 162
SMITH	ESTHER		33, 38
SMITH	ETHEL		35
SMITH	EVA		25, 29, 30
SMITH	FLORENCE		38, 170
SMITH	FRANCES		16, 20
SMITH	FRANCIS		36, 177
SMITH	FRANK		34
smith	genealogy		181 - 206
SMITH	GEORGE		35
SMITH	GLENDON		34
SMITH	HAROLD		25, 29, 162
SMITH	HATTIE		34, 37, 110
SMITH	HENRY		16
SMITH	HOWES		33, 38
SMITH	INFANT		108
SMITH	IVY		25, 29
SMITH	IZOLA		38, 169, 170
SMITH	JAMES	H.	37, 104, 115, 154
SMITH	JAMES	HARVEY	34, 35, 114
SMITH	JAMES	P.	104
SMITH	JAMES		24, 119, 145
SMITH	JAMIE		31, 162
SMITH	JANE		39
SMITH	JEROME		35, 36
SMITH	JESSE		36
SMITH	JOHN	B.	134
SMITH	JOHN	CAPT.	11, 21, 22, 104, 109, 120, 152, 157, 161
SMITH	JOHN	W.	117
SMITH	JOHN		16, 29, 38, 39, 66, 93, 96, 104
SMITH	JONATHAN	SR.	13
SMITH	JONATHAN		11, 22, 35, 36, 104, 109, 126, 127, 152
SMITH	JOSIAH		36, 99
SMITH	LAURIE		38, 117
SMITH	LEAH	E.	116
SMITH	LEAH	MRS.	139
SMITH	LEAH		16, 34, 144, 170, 177
SMITH	LESTER	ALTON	115
SMITH	LESTER		30, 31, 104, 153
SMITH	LEWIS		25, 29
SMITH	LORRETTA		24, 25
SMITH	LOUIS		162
SMITH	LOUISA		39
SMITH	LYDIA		13
SMITH	MARTHA		16
SMITH	MARY	ANN	16
SMITH	MARY		16, 33, 34
SMITH	MATILDA	J.	110
SMITH	MATILDA		35, 36
SMITH	MAUDE		31
SMITH	MINA		21
SMITH	MINNIE	MARIE	21, 22
SMITH	MURIEL		34
SMITH	MURRAY		29, 32, 141
SMITH	NAN		30
SMITH	NANCY		22
SMITH	NATHANIEL	SR.	29
SMITH	NEIMA		29, 32, 35
SMITH	PRINER?		108
SMITH	R.	A.	87
SMITH	R.		128
SMITH	REBECCA		39

NOTE:- check for spelling variations on names, also names may be mentioned more than once on a page.

INDEX to HISTORY OF CAPE NEGRO & BLANCHE by Joseph R. Ross

Surname	Given Name	Suffix/Mid	Pages
SMITH	REUBEN	A.	83, 85, 89, 90, 91, 94, 104, 116, 133
SMITH	REUBEN		16, 21, 34, 46, 65, 71, 72, 89, 92, 93, 130, 131, 139, 142, 143, 144, 177
SMITH	RICHARD		23, 34, 35, 39
SMITH	ROBERT	H.	110
SMITH	RONALD		34
SMITH	ROSEMAN		153
SMITH	RUBY		16, 64, 123, 139, 177
SMITH	RUTH		22, 23
SMITH	SAMUEL	CAPT.	159
SMITH	SAMUEL	S.	113
SMITH	SAMUEL		11, 13, 22, 31, 34, 35, 99, 145
SMITH	SARAH	A.	109
SMITH	SARAH	ANN	14, 16, 29, 30, 38, 113, 177
SMITH	SARAH	JANE	29
SMITH	SARAH		16, 31, 112, 145
SMITH	SOLOMON		12, 127
SMITH	SOPHIA		39
SMITH	STEPHEN		104
SMITH	STEVEN		12, 16, 18, 24
SMITH	SUSAN	S.	111
SMITH	SUSAN		21
SMITH	SUSANNA		13
SMITH	THANKFUL		34, 39
SMITH	THEODORE		12
SMITH	VIOLET		30, 31, 116, 153, 169
SMITH	W.	A. B.	86, 87, 90, 91
SMITH	WILLIAM	ARTHUR	113
SMITH	WILLIAM	B.	83
SMITH	WILLIAM	E.	104
SMITH	WILLIAM	EDWARD	115
SMITH	WILLIAM		16, 29, 30, 36, 38, 131, 133, 145
SMITH	?		11
SMITH?	CHARLES		34
SMITH?	JAMES		34
SNOW	ABIGAIL		107
SNOW	BASHEBA		31
SNOW	DEBRAH		28
SNOW	ETHEL		19, 76, 166
SNOW	GEORGE		28
SNOW	HANNA	KING	38
SNOW	HOWES		39
SNOW	JAMES		30, 127
SNOW	JANE		39
SNOW	JOSIAH		104, 112
SNOW	KATE		28
SNOW	MAHALA		28
SNOW	MARTHA		109
SNOW	MERCY		28, 121
SNOW	OLIVIA		28
SNOW	ROY		28
SNOW	SAMUEL	J.	110
SNOW	SAMUEL		104
SNOW	SETH		28
SNOW	VERA	ETHEL	76
SNOW	VIOLET		30
SPINNEY	ARRON		39
SPINNEY	LOUISA		39
STAKER	JOHN	JR.	126
STOCKER	JOHN		127
STOCKER		REV.	98, 100
STODDARD	JIMMY	MRS.	169
SURETTE	?		17
SUTHERLAND	CHARLES		104
SWADEN	F.	W. REV.	101
SWAIN	ALFRED		107
SWAIN	ANN		111

NOTE:- check for spelling variations on names, also names may be mentioned more than once on a page.

INDEX to HISTORY OF CAPE NEGRO & BLANCHE by Joseph R. Ross

SWAIN	CLIFFORD	D. S.	107
SWAIN	ELIZABETH		107
SWAIN	ESTHER		107
SWAIN	EZRA		108
SWAIN	FLORENCE	D.	113
SWAIN	HENRY		107, 108
SWAIN	HOWIE		108
SWAIN	JAMES	C.	94, 116
SWAIN	JAMES	H.	113
SWAIN	JOE	HENRY	111
SWAIN	JOHN	B.	107
SWAIN	JOSEPH	CAPT.	109
SWAIN	JOSEPH		11
SWAIN	JOSEPHINE		111
SWAIN	LAURA	A.	112
SWAIN	LAWRENCE		108
SWAIN	MARGARET		111
SWAIN	MARY	R.	111
SWAIN	MARY		107
SWAIN	PAUL		107
SWAIN	RACHEL		108
SWAIN	STEWART		95
SWAINE	ALBERT		38, 119, 162
SWAINE	ALDRED		32, 81
SWAINE	ALICE		23, 38, 39
SWAINE	ALLAN		35, 36, 71, 119, 121, 143, 169, 173, 233
SWAINE	ANN		20
SWAINE	ARTHUR	V.	110
SWAINE	ARTHUR		23, 38, 39
SWAINE	AUSTIN		88
SWAINE	BENJAMIN	E.	109
SWAINE	BESSIE		30, 144
SWAINE	BLANCHE		18, 19
SWAINE	BRADDOCK		104
SWAINE	CAROLINE	HILLS	144
SWAINE	CARRIE		28, 161
SWAINE	CARROL		19, 117
SWAINE	CARRY		38
SWAINE	CASSIE		32
SWAINE	CHAPMAN	JR.	12, 15, 18
SWAINE	CHAPMAN	SR.	15, 27
SWAINE	CHAPMAN		20, 22, 104
SWAINE	CHARITY		26
SWAINE	CLIFFORD		33
SWAINE	CLINTON		30
SWAINE	CYNTHIA		21
SWAINE	DARRELL		35, 36
SWAINE	DAVID	JR.	99
SWAINE	DAVID		126, 127
SWAINE	DOROTHY		35, 118
SWAINE	EDGAR		16, 18, 19, 20, 23, 37
SWAINE	EDITH		18
SWAINE	EDWIN		29
SWAINE	EITHEL		29
SWAINE	ELIZABETH		77
SWAINE	ELLEN		32, 38
SWAINE	ETHEL		19, 76, 157, 166
SWAINE	ETTA		18, 19
SWAINE	EVA		25, 29, 30
SWAINE	EVERETT		30
SWAINE	EZRA	CAPT.	31
SWAINE	EZRA		30, 104, 159, 161
SWAINE	FLORENCE	ELENOR	114
SWAINE	FLORENCE		23, 24, 28, 35, 38, 39, 71, 120, 152, 169
SWAINE	FLOSSIE		169, 173
SWAINE	FOSTER		28, 29, 144
SWAINE	FRANCIS		20, 21, 38

NOTE:- check for spelling variations on names, also names may be mentioned more than once on a page.

INDEX to HISTORY OF CAPE NEGRO & BLANCHE by Joseph R. Ross

SWAINE	FRANK		20
swaine	genealogy		207-216
SWAINE	GEORGE		20
SWAINE	GERALDINE		119
SWAINE	GERTRUDE	H.	116
SWAINE	GERTRUDE		28, 161
SWAINE	HAROLD		18
SWAINE	HATTIE		34
SWAINE	HAZEL		35, 58, 118, 161, 162
SWAINE	HEAMAN	CAPT.	110
SWAINE	HEDLEY		38, 119, 162
SWAINE	HELEN		32, 162
SWAINE	HELEN?		118
SWAINE	HEMAN	CAPT.	33, 152, 174
SWAINE	HEMAN	MRS.	161
SWAINE	HEMAN		33, 102, 104, 120
SWAINE	HENRY		29, 30, 33
SWAINE	HERMAN		30, 119
SWAINE	HOWIE		28
SWAINE	IDA		19, 20
SWAINE	J.	S. B.	104
SWAINE	JAMES	C.	83, 85, 91, 104
SWAINE	JAMES	FREEMAN	27, 30
SWAINE	JAMES	H.	38, 104
SWAINE	JAMES	H.?	110
SWAINE	JAMES	HOWE	104
SWAINE	JAMES	JR.	31
SWAINE	JAMES	S.	79, 80, 81, 87, 88, 89, 90, 91, 104
SWAINE	JAMES	STEWART	113
SWAINE	JAMES		18, 19, 20, 23, 24, 26, 28, 34, 99, 100, 104, 131, 134, 160, 175
SWAINE	JANE		21, 35
SWAINE	JOHN	B.	27, 99, 120
SWAINE	JOSEPH	CAPT.	161
SWAINE	JOSEPH	FREEMAN	11, 28, 104
SWAINE	JOSEPH	FREEMAN, CAPT.	30, 38, 59, 104, 144
SWAINE	JOSEPH	MRS.	161
SWAINE	JOSEPH		27, 29, 30, 32, 33
SWAINE	JOSEPHINE	MRS.	161
SWAINE	JOSEPHINE		30
SWAINE	JOSIE		24
SWAINE	KATE		28, 158
SWAINE	KATHERINE		19
SWAINE	KNOWLES		23, 24, 31, 39, 74, 76, 78, 117, 166
SWAINE	LAURA		29
SWAINE	LAWRENCE		28
SWAINE	LEAH		26, 30, 33, 177
SWAINE	LEVINIA		31
SWAINE	LIBBY		31
SWAINE	LILLA		32
SWAINE	LILLIAN		36
SWAINE	LILY		28
SWAINE	LINDA		35
SWAINE	LIZA		19
SWAINE	LLOYD	RICHARD	35, 36
SWAINE	LLOYD		32, 35, 58, 59, 71, 104, 117, 129, 143, 145, 154, 161, 175
SWAINE	LOTTIE		16, 26, 33, 177
SWAINE	LUCY		29
SWAINE	LYDA		30
SWAINE	LYDIA		31
SWAINE	MARGARET	S.	18
SWAINE	MARGARET		19, 20, 23
SWAINE	MARION		35, 36
SWAINE	MARTHA	S.C.	109
SWAINE	MARY	ANN	23
SWAINE	MARY	ATTWOOD	77

NOTE:- check for spelling variations on names, also names may be mentioned more than once on a page.

INDEX to HISTORY OF CAPE NEGRO & BLANCHE by Joseph R. Ross

SWAINE	MARY		24, 27, 29, 30, 31, 33
			38, 42, 76, 118, 162, 166
SWAINE	MATTHEW	CAPT.	11, 29, 32, 33, 35, 37, 154
SWAINE	MATTHEW		104, 113
SWAINE	MAUD		116
SWAINE	MAURICE		19, 76, 166
SWAINE	MAY		30, 32
SWAINE	MERLE		26, 28, 157, 158
SWAINE	MILDRED		17
SWAINE	MYRA		38, 119
SWAINE	MYSIE		28
SWAINE	NANCY		71, 169
SWAINE	NELLIE	MRS.	158
SWAINE	NELLIE		26, 28, 104, 157, 169
SWAINE	NELLY		18
SWAINE	ODESSA		18, 29, 31, 32, 76, 166
SWAINE	PAUL	JR.	19, 20, 21
SWAINE	PAUL	SR.	20, 21
SWAINE	PAUL		17, 19, 82
SWAINE	RALPH		38, 118, 162
SWAINE	RAYMOND		17
SWAINE	REBECCA		74, 76
SWAINE	RICHARD		38
SWAINE	RUTH		22
SWAINE	SADIE		30, 116
SWAINE	SAMUEL	L.	109
SWAINE	SAMUEL		16, 26, 30, 33, 104, 177
SWAINE	SARAH	ANN	29, 30
SWAINE	SARAH	JANE	29
SWAINE	SARAH		14, 145
SWAINE	SOPHIE		17
SWAINE	STANLEY		28, 116
SWAINE	STEWART		14, 16, 25, 26, 29, 30, 145
SWAINE	SUSAN		15
SWAINE	SYDNEY		32
SWAINE	TEMPERANCE		27, 120
SWAINE	THELMA		118, 162
SWAINE	VIRGINIA		42
SWAINE	W.	HERBERT	109
SWAINE	WALTER		30
SWAINE	WILBERT		18
SWAINE	WILETTA		110
SWAINE	WILLIAM	A. B.	104
SWAINE	WILLIAM	H.	104, 110
SWAINE	WILLIAM	HENRY	29, 30, 31, 32
SWAINE	WILLIAM	SR.	74, 76
SWAINE	WILLIAM		162
SWAINE	WINSLOW	J.	38, 42, 104
SWAINE	WINSLOW	JOHNSON	115
SWAINE	WINSLOW		21, 33, 71, 152
SWAINE	ZEPHANIAH		26
SWALLOW	ALBERT		30, 37, 117
SWALLOW	NAN		30
SYMMONDS	ANNIE		41
TEMPLE	THOMAS		8
THIBEAULT	AMY		22, 159
THIBEAULT	RAY		22
THOMAS	?	FRANCIS	115
THOMAS	'ALVIN		155
THOMAS	ADDIE		82
THOMAS	ALBERT		18, 108
THOMAS	ALLEN	W.	112
THOMAS	ALLIE		24, 25
THOMAS	ANGIE	(MRS.)	134
THOMAS	ARMOUND		35
THOMAS	ARTHUR	O.	24, 25, 104, 111
THOMAS	AUSTIN		19, 79, 80, 81, 82, 90, 104, 111

NOTE:- check for spelling variations on names, also names may be mentioned more than once on a page.

INDEX to HISTORY OF CAPE NEGRO & BLANCHE by Joseph R. Ross

THOMAS	BARBARA		12, 16
THOMAS	BESSIE		30
THOMAS	BEVERLEY		32
THOMAS	BLANCHE		18, 19, 20, 117
THOMAS	CHARLES		26, 28, 32, 35, 117, 134, 137, 141, 145
THOMAS	CLAYTON		117
THOMAS	CLIFFORD		18, 19, 77, 104, 117
THOMAS	CYNTHIA		24, 82
THOMAS	CYNTHIE		113
THOMAS	DAVID		18, 19, 104
THOMAS	DEBORAH		19, 109
THOMAS	DERELL		33
THOMAS	EDNA		25, 32
THOMAS	ELAM	JR.	16
THOMAS	ELAM		12, 16, 17, 104
THOMAS	ELGIN		32
THOMAS	ELINA		35
THOMAS	ELITA		19
THOMAS	ELLA		18, 19
THOMAS	ELROY		104, 134
THOMAS	EMERSON		16, 32, 33, 69, 104, 117 145, 152, 153, 178, 179, 180
THOMAS	ETHEL	M.	108
THOMAS	ETTA		19, 23
THOMAS	F.	HOWE	111
THOMAS	FANNY		111
THOMAS	FIDELIA	L?	114
THOMAS	FIDELIA		25, 81
THOMAS	FIEDEL		70
THOMAS	GEORGE	W.	112
THOMAS	GEORGE		104
THOMAS	HELEN		20, 33
THOMAS	HERBERT		25, 26, 32, 33, 65, 102, 117, 233
THOMAS	HILBERT		117, 142, 233
THOMAS	HILDA		16
THOMAS	HOWARD		16, 17, 18, 89, 92
THOMAS	HOWE		104
THOMAS	IDA		19, 77
THOMAS	ILETA		112
THOMAS	IRMA		18, 19
THOMAS	IZA		39
THOMAS	J.	MARSDEN	111
THOMAS	JAMES		16, 33
THOMAS	JANE		81, 82
THOMAS	JENNY		16, 17, 18
THOMAS	JESSIE		18, 19
THOMAS	JOE		111
THOMAS	JOHN	J.	82, 113
THOMAS	JOHN		12, 17, 19, 25, 39, 82, 117
THOMAS	JOSEPH	ARTHUR	116
THOMAS	JOSEPH		104
THOMAS	JOSIAH		81, 104, 112
THOMAS	JOYCE		18, 19
THOMAS	KATHALEN	G.	115
THOMAS	KATHLEEN		16
THOMAS	KENNETH		26, 28, 35, 66, 117
THOMAS	KNOWLES		81, 104, 111
THOMAS	LABERT		104
THOMAS	LEANDER		117
THOMAS	LEBERT	FORRESTER	115
THOMAS	LENA		111
THOMAS	LERMAN		19, 70
THOMAS	LERMOND		18
THOMAS	LEROY		18, 19, 20
THOMAS	LEVI		82
THOMAS	LILLIAN		82
THOMAS	LINNEY		28

NOTE:- check for spelling variations on names, also names may be mentioned more than once on a page.

INDEX to HISTORY OF CAPE NEGRO & BLANCHE by Joseph R. Ross

THOMAS	LLEWELLYN		33, 119, 169
THOMAS	LOLA		19
THOMAS	LOTTIE	SWAINE	177
THOMAS	LOTTIE		32, 33, 58, 153, 169, 180, 233
THOMAS	LYDIA	LORRIANE	114
THOMAS	M.		85, 87
THOMAS	MABLE		115
THOMAS	MARIA		108
THOMAS	MARIE		18, 19, 169
THOMAS	MARION	SLATE	172
THOMAS	MARION		233
THOMAS	MARSDEN		18, 19, 25, 79, 80, 81, 82, 83 88, 89, 90, 91, 93, 94, 104
THOMAS	MARTHA	N.	113
THOMAS	MARTHA		25
THOMAS	MARTIN		74, 104
THOMAS	MARY	ANN	110
THOMAS	MARY	E.	111
THOMAS	MATILDA		110
THOMAS	MATTIE		107
THOMAS	MAUDE		31
THOMAS	MAVIS		32
THOMAS	MELISSA	JANE	115
THOMAS	MELISSA		16
THOMAS	MERCY		82, 112
THOMAS	MERLE		26, 28, 32, 35, 169
THOMAS	MERVIN		78
THOMAS	MYRTLE		16
THOMAS	OLIVER		104, 111
THOMAS	OSCAR		24
THOMAS	OWEN		35
THOMAS	PERCY		30
THOMAS	RUBY		111
THOMAS	SOPHIA	M.	110
THOMAS	SOPHIE		17
THOMAS	STEPHEN	CAPT.	109
THOMAS	THOMAS	O.G.	74, 78
THOMAS	THOMAS		17
THOMAS	TRUEMAN		16, 18, 19, 133, 134
THOMAS	WALTER		31
THOMAS?	GEORGE		134
THOMAS?	VERNA		18
THOMSON	ROBERT		126, 127, 128
THORPE	ALFRED	REV.	101
TOBEY	ARTHUR	REV.	101
TOBIN	JENNY		113
TOMSON	ROBERT		120
TOWNER	ALICE		23, 38, 39
TOWNER	ANNA		39
TOWNER	BERNARD		39, 117
TOWNER	FLORENCE		23, 24, 39
TOWNER	FOSTER		39
TOWNER	GENEVIEVE		24, 39
TOWNER	GRACE		25
TOWNER	HATTIE		39, 116
TOWNER	INFANT		107
TOWNER	IZA		39
TOWNER	JAMES		107
TOWNER	JANE		39
TOWNER	JOB		39
TOWNER	MARGARET		39, 112
TOWNER	RUSSELL	HALLETT	39
TOWNER	SILAS	P.	112
TOWNER	SILAS		24, 38, 39, 104,
TOWNER	STAN		141
TOWNER	STANDFORD		39, 143,
TOWNER	STANFORD		116

NOTE:- check for spelling variations on names, also names may be mentioned more than once on a page.

INDEX to HISTORY OF CAPE NEGRO & BLANCHE by Joseph R. Ross

TWEEDY	JAMES		REV.	100
UNKNOWN	PERSON			110
VAN ZOOST	W.		D. REV.	101
VANDE HURK	MARIE			37
WEBB	GEO.		MRS.	107
WEBB	GEORGE			104, 157
WEBB	?			108
WEEKS	JANE			35
WESTHAVER	C.		G. REV.	101
WHITE	MR.			88
WILLIAM	ELINA			35
WILLIAM	R.		REV.	101
WILLIAMS	MERLIN			39
WILLIAMS	PHOEBE			18
WILLIAMS	R.		REV.	101
WILLIAMS	SARAH	ANN		108
WOOD	LENA			155
WOOD	MYRA			38
WOOD	ROLAND			38
WRAY	JAMES		REV.	98, 100
YOUNG	ANNA			39
YOUNG	CARL			39
YOUNG	OBDEN?		D.	109
YOUNG	SCOTT		B. REV.	101
YOUNG	WALTER		MRS.	68
	INFANT			111

NOTE:- check for spelling variations on names, also names may be mentioned more than once on a page.

www.ingramcontent.com/pod-product-compliance
Lightning Source LLC
Chambersburg PA
CBHW070730160426
43192CB00009B/1389